ART IN A DEMOCRACY

ART IN A DEMOCRACY

Edited by
Doug Blandy and Kristin G. Congdon

Teachers College, Columbia University
New York and London

Published by Teachers College Press, 1234 Amsterdam Avenue,
New York, NY 10027

All photographs by Russ McKnight

Quotation in Chapter 1 from K. P. Etzkorn, "On the sociology of musical practice and
social groups," *International Social Science Journal*, *34*(4), 561–562, is reproduced by permis-
sion of UNESCO.

Library of Congress Cataloging-in-Publication Data

Art in a democracy.

  Bibliography: p.
  Includes index.
  1. Art and society. 2. Art—Political aspects.
3. Freedom and art. I. Blandy, Douglas Emerson,
1951–   . II. Congdon, Kristin G.
N72.S6A744   1987   701'.03   87-18049

ISBN 0-8077-2882-9
ISBN 0-8077-2881-0 (pbk.)

Manufactured in the United States of America

92 91 90 89 88 87   1 2 3 4 5 6

To Candy Ducat, our secretary,
who quietly creates and assertively provides for our creativity

and to our family members,
David C. Congdon and Linda, Brendan, and Lydia Blandy

Contents

Foreword

Most readers of this book will be rigorously challenged to rethink many of their preconceptions of the meaning of *art* and *democracy*. They will be startled even more when these meanings are analyzed in the context of art valued and practiced democratically and democracy influenced by its art. Add to these the meanings of *multicultural art* and *multicultural democracy* and the thrust of this book becomes more evident.

The editors, Doug Blandy and Kristin Congdon, have selected authors and organized their contributions brilliantly so as to focus attention on these interactions. Inquiry, analysis of less obvious relationships, and questioning of priorities and practices permeate this book, with each chapter coming from a somewhat different perspective. The concepts of art and democracy take on new significance through this multifaceted inquiry, within each individual chapter and throughout the book as a whole. The editors lead us adroitly through their perspectives, and, true to their goal of democratic process, conclude by inviting two scholars with quite different perspectives to respond to the contributions.

Throughout the book the meanings of democracy and art in the lives of people are explored. An underlying question the contributors seem to be asking is: If art can be studied, practiced, and taught in a truly democratic context, and democracy humbled through its art, will this not have a humanizing effect in civilizations aspiring to be democratic? This book has great potential for impact because both the social functions and the meanings of democracy and art are analyzed as they relate to one another. The long history of effort in aesthetics to define art and in political theory to define democracy has not produced these same results. Only rarely has art been defined and its functions analyzed within a context of democratic values as these are practiced in the current complexity of culture within nations. Certainly little effort has been made in the past to relate democracy to evolving concepts of culturally diverse art. This book makes a critical effort to do so.

The innovative thrust of many of these chapters is to explore how ideal democratic values affect the selection of art, the motivations for producing art, the artistic processes, and the evaluation of art. The book looks at the implications of these factors in culturally complex societies trying to achieve political democracy. Questions are raised about cultural transmission and education through art: What art is relevant to which people? Where? When? Which qualities of art are universal to everyone? Which are culture specific? What artistic traditions support democratic values? How democratic are the social organizations that sponsor, support, and maintain art? How well do publicly supported art institutions sustain the art traditions of all the people? Are criticism and dialogue in the arts based on hierarchical values or democratic ones? Do they support and encourage freedom of choice? What is the relationship of theory to practice?

While the visual arts are the main focus, this book has implications for all the arts. All have social organizations that promote certain aspects over others. All tend to be affected by hierarchical groupings of people. All vary depending on the cultural group fostering them. The critical evaluation of undemocratic practices in the visual arts contained herein will be useful in assessing similar impact on the other arts. This book should also become part of the literature in the social foundations of education as well as for the arts.

Art in a Democracy throws light on the nature of social organizations, traditions of shared beliefs, and systems of education. This is accomplished through analysis of the process of the democratization of art. One of the themes that occurs in these chapters is that the recognition and acceptance of diversity in democracy may increase the range and extensions available to people for expression and recognition of their artistry. Stereotypes of what is work and what is play, particularly the belief that art is play and not work, are diffused.

These authors illustrate the inadequacy of familiar linear methods of problem solving, the assumption of direct cause-and-effect relationships, and the use of categorical true-false and in-out modes of thought. Systemic, multivariant, interrelated analyses are necessary for dealing with these topics—for defining them, for showing their relationships to their changing contexts, and for describing the processes and responses that may be evoked. Learning opportunities must be provided to children and adults that lead to greater options for individual choice and for thinking beyond one's own learned cultural patterns of thought, while still preserving respect for one's own cultural roots. Thus each student is given the freedom to retain and/or transcend her culture.

This book is written toward the ideal of democracy and is not about any one nation. The strong surge for human rights within nations makes the search for the ideal most crucial. Sociocultural, ethnic, and racially and sexually defined groups and individuals are searching for their identities and rights as fully functioning human beings. This search produces the forces for change. The contributors to this anthology take the position that ideal democracy provides the best vehicle for achieving freedom of thought and expression.

Some of the areas of change that are analyzed in relation to the arts and democracy are (1) traditional and emerging sexually defined roles and opportunities; (2) the present social stratification of human institutions and values and hopes for increasing equality of opportunity; (3) educational ideals of a melting pot or of a rich stew of peoples, both culturally and individually; and (4) the power and popularity of new technology and its emerging effects on the human scale of things. All these areas require us to analyze critically our traditions, social structures, modes of thought, and our belief systems as a more humane society is sought.

Before reading any part of this book in detail, I encourage readers to scan the whole book first and read the editors' introductory chapter and the beginnings of each part. The breadth and depth of the inquiry, as a whole, affects each individual section and paper. Each author stimulates rigorous dialogue, and each contribution differs from the others; together, they all contribute to this challenging thrust of ideas.

While almost all authors are art educators, each has specialized in varied aspects of the topic and drawn on different social, historical, psychological, aesthetic, educational, and philosophical foundations. Not since the Penn State Seminar in 1965 has such a compilation of groundbreaking papers been made.[1] However, in 1965 it was necessary to couple papers by art educators with those of specialists in fields such as psychology and sociology. Art educators are now well grounded in these areas. This reflects the growth in interdisciplinary doctoral and post-doctoral study in art education during the last 20 years. The contributors to this anthology also relate additional fields to art education, such as folk art, philosophy of science, women's studies, therapy, museology, and ecology. The author of Chapter 10 is a leading specialist in folk art whose contribution to this anthology gives perspective to the whole.

The book concludes with two quite different art educators responding to the book. Their interpretations vary because of their backgrounds, philosophical assumptions, and areas of specialization. The editors are to be commended highly for including these commentaries because they

---

1. In 1965 a group of art educators met to analyze and redefine the field of art education. This meeting was noteworthy because it set the research agenda for the following two decades.

encourage individual readers to compare the two perspectives and search for their own summaries and critical assessments. This final touch better prepares readers to meet the demands for more humane, multicultural, art-sensitive democracies.

JUNE KING MCFEE
San Luis Obispo, California
January 1987

Acknowledgments

We would like to thank Carol Rehmus and Carol Roth for their help with final editing, and the secretarial staff in the Bowling Green School of Art for their help with correspondence, typing, and copying and for their words of encouragement. We are especially indebted to Candy Ducat, who did the majority of secretarial work and enabled us to meet every deadline. She is a professional who excuses our mistakes, maintains a sense of humor, and makes our scholarly life easier. We also thank the past director of the Bowling Green School of Art, Maurice Sevigny, and its present interim director, Tom Hilty, who have supported our work; and we thank the students in the Division of Art Education/Art Therapy, who have listened to our ideas and offered feedback. We are grateful to our other division members, especially Paulette Fleming, who have helped to guide our thinking. We would like to express our gratitude to Ken Marantz and Vincent Lanier, who taught us to be strong in stating our opinions and to feel comfortable with debate and conflicting dialogue. We offer sincerest thanks to Russ McKnight for providing the photographs that enhance this book. To June King McFee, who has set the stage for much of our work, we will always be indebted. We offer tribute to our families, who have taken great joy in this publication and its ideas. And last, but certainly not least, we thank the staff of Teachers College Press, especially Audrey Kingstrom, who encouraged our prospectus from the very beginning, and Peter Sieger and Susan Keniston, who worked with us to bring this project to completion.

Introduction

In the fall of 1984 we found ourselves working together in the Division of Art Education/Art Therapy at Bowling Green State University, Bowling Green, Ohio. One of us had extensive experience working with art and disabled populations. The other had been working with other cultural groups in a variety of settings. Between us we had experience in public schools, rehabilitation treatment centers, correctional facilities, alternative schools, museum settings, community centers, recreational facilities, and a small press.

Within the art education field, one of us is categorized as a special educator, the other as a specialist in multicultural art education. These distinctions are somewhat misleading, because in fact we speak the same language and feel that our studies, goals, and directions are similar. Indeed, we both recognize and talk about the same issues: freedom of expression, empowering those who have been left out of "the system," social role valorization, cultural pluralism, feminism, multiple levels of intelligence, the recognition and acceptance of variety in visual creation and verbal expression, and the acceptance and expansion of different organizational structures. This book expands our dialogue to include others who are concerned with art education theory and practice and the impact of their ideas on the individual, society, culture, and environment. This is, therefore, not a book limited to special and multicultural educational concerns. It is more encompassing than that. It is about democratic principles and art education.

This anthology addresses the questions of art education theory and practice that should be raised in a democratic society. In doing this it does not assume that "art education" is synonymous with the services offered by university-trained or professionally sanctioned art specialists. The contributors to this volume acknowledge that art educators can be artists, craftspersons, museum curators or educators, art bureaucrats, and people teaching about art informally in the home or workplace. The contributors to this book do not define democracy in terms of any historical or contemporary political state that claims, or has claimed, a democratic form of government. For the purposes of this volume, *democracy* is defined by a set of principles that have come to be commonly associated with a conceptual and philosophical view. These principles include popular self-government, free speech, the importance of a mature citizenry prepared for self-determination through active involvement in a community, and democracy as a modifier in the relationship between individuals and their community.

Though this volume is conceptually based, it is both grounded in and critical of current art education theory and practice. We believe that the contributors' recognition of the incongruencies between a conceptual view of democracy and its flawed practice give this book its purpose and power. In these pages the reader will also note the strong desire to recognize the artistic process and aesthetic response as integral to our lives, not only to be preserved in museums but to be practiced in our day-to-day experiences in the educational process.

There is a strong tendency to draw boundaries around what it is art educators know and do. This is a problem because approaches that confine tend to limit exploration and encourage a belief that cause-and-effect studies (otherwise known as linear thinking) can provide the best answers to art education questions. This process of focusing on isolated questions in a circumscribed world makes it simple for bureaucrats to control educational systems. For this reason an exclusively linear approach to problem solving and program development is dangerous in any society, educational system, or art context, for it overinstitutionalizes and works against creativity.

An alternative is a systemic (or ecological) approach to problem solving, which assumes that one change creates many others and encourages a multifaceted view of a situation by including interrelationships, total contexts, radical alternatives, and long-range ramifications. Systemic approaches do not disregard but rather insure input from the economically poor, people of color, those having different abilities, and those institutionally isolated. Consequently, a systemic approach to art education must, by definition, be democratic. It celebrates the educational quilting process passed on from mother to daughter in the rural South, the aesthetic experiences of the person with visual impairment, and the Hmong immigrant who brings her needlework to Toledo, Ohio, to share with her new neighbors.

Art history, viewed systematically, becomes more than just a chronicle of the Western European world view. It embraces the African perspective and the Oriental path. It includes art and artistic processes from those people who are politically oppressed as well as those in a position of power. It will include a written record as well as the oral history of those who cannot and could not write. Works of art will not just be sanctioned by the New York critic and the academically blessed. The expert in neon sign making, the Oregon chainsaw carver, and the Swedish-American lacemaker will have the right to express their value judgments and have their artistic creativity acknowledged.

Art criticism will include critical processes developed and utilized by the Iowa farm family, the Harlem native, and the Mississippi beautician. New words and phrases for describing art may become recognized and appreciated as poetry. The way we talk about art becomes mind broadening as we discover new possibilities for problem solving, valuing, and living. A reaffirmation of old ideas seen through the eyes of those who are culturally similar may bring about a renewed sensitivity to one's potential for aesthetic response.

When approached systemically, art in the public school classroom, the folk art group, arts organizations, an art museum, a community art center, and other formal and informal artistic groups will involve organizational structures encompassing more than the white male social organization or those directions proposed by the academic elite.

We have divided the chapters in this anthology into five parts:

1. Individual Differences, Cultural Pluralism, and "Social Role Valorization"
2. Public Dialogue on Art
3. The Citizens' Responsibility to Individual and Group Processes
4. Freedom of Aesthetic Choice in Work and Play
5. Responses to *Art in a Democracy*

The first four are general topic areas; however, they cannot be seen as distinct when viewed from a systems approach. The boundaries among the areas are fluid, and there is information in each topic area that interrelates with the others. These groupings function merely to assist authors and readers in focusing on specific issues that will make democratic theory work more effectively in practice. The chapter authors respond to myriad topics, including the relationship of art to culture, conceptions of masculinity and feminity in art and democracy, museum education, art and politics, history, aesthetics, technology, economics, and ecology.

We are aware that there are dangers in the systemic approach to research and study. In a systemic approach the definition of one's field of study widens. A broadened collective purpose might cause a loss of identity and direction in art. However, we ask that the reader be patient with the authors as they approach the topic of art and art education in a democracy, bearing in mind that their definitions may not be comfortable or compatible. Relating areas of impact with which we are not very familiar (such as economics and political science) to our field does make us wary, but we cannot ignore areas of knowledge just because they are new to us. It is our hope that this volume will raise more questions than it will answer. Inherent to this book is the dialogue among the authors that will evolve as their chapters reinforce and contradict one another. As editors we encouraged disagreement and controversy for the purpose of engaging the reader in the debate that is integral to this book's subject.

We sincerely hope that this effort on our part will provide the reader with the impetus for personal direction and action. Democracy is a process. Artistic creation and appreciation are processes. So, too, is education. Without taking the risk of studying, from varying perspectives, art education's history, art criticism structures, or economic power in art organizations, there is the danger of excluding the majority of people from all that the established worlds of art can offer. In turn, the formal bureaucratic art organizations and classrooms lose tremendously by excluding the participation of such a large portion of our world's population.

ART IN A DEMOCRACY

PART I

Individual Differences,
Cultural Pluralism,
and "Social Role Valorization"

DEMOCRACY ASSUMES THE PRESENCE OF CITIZENS who respect, revere, and celebrate individual differences and cultural diversity. All people are perceived as cultivating myriad forms of aesthetic experience. Consequently, artistry will be recognized in the unself-conscious work of the production papermaker, in the whittling of a retired carpenter who concentrates his carving on seagulls and terriers, in the self-expression of a Soho neo-expressionist painter, and in the traditional basketry of a mother and son of the Ojibwa tribe.

Art educators teaching in a democratic community prepare people of all ages to clarify their aesthetic attitudes and values as they simultaneously seek a noncompetitive relationship with, and understanding of, the aesthetic viewpoints of other individuals and cultural groups. This is not an easy task for teacher or student. Aesthetic attitudes and values are subject to an ever-fluctuating array of ethnic, racial, religious, occupational, sexual, generational, recreational, political, and philosophical influences.

We do not know of any contemporary political state that claims a democratic government in which individual differences and cultural pluralism have not been oppressed to some extent. De Tocqueville's warnings on tyranny by the majority or the wealthy have proven correct in many spheres. This imposition of values is accomplished through organizational structure and the curriculum of educational institutions which dictate what may be appreciated aesthetically. Exploitation and banishment of individuals and cultures because of their cultural identification is well documented in the present day: The "apartheid-like" conditions in which many disabled people live and the attempt to extinguish Native American culture are two examples in the United States and Canada.

Special educator and philosopher Wolf Wolfensberger (1972; see Selected Bibliography) has developed the principle of "social role valorization" for use in guiding program development and personal interaction with persons who are disabled. This principle promotes the recognition and use of cultural norms on personal, local, and large institutional levels. We believe this principle should be applied by art educators in their work with people of all ages. No person should be encouraged to conform to alien cultural norms. A democratic community should be made up of people with diverse social roles and cultural values who can respect the roles and values of their neighbors.

The chapters in this section of the anthology will confront the reader with three points of view on the issues of individual differences, cultural pluralism, social role valorization, and art education in a democracy. These issues will be discussed in terms of gender bias, cross-cultural consciousness, culturally based approaches to art (as opposed to a universal approach), and the ways in which cultural institutions support or conflict with foundational democratic premises. All of the authors represented here are committed to democratic principles and make recommendations for their implementation in the presentation and appreciation of art in today's society.

Chapter 1

Culturally Based Versus Universally Based Understanding of Art

__F. Graeme Chalmers

For some time I have argued that it is not particularly useful for art educators to pay too much attention to entrenched ideas in philosophical aesthetics and to some other typically Western "high art" approaches to art "appreciation" (Chalmers, 1971, 1981). Connoisseurs in aesthetic education have exerted a particular influence on art education. I have posited that such approaches, which may claim to be universal, are, in fact, elitist and culture bound. Those who argue that approaches to connoisseurship taught and promoted in some museums, galleries, and schools are *not* ethnocentric fail to see that appreciating *form* is not the same as understanding *art*. In terms of seeing art as an important part of *everyone's* life, what is the use of teaching a person to make art, to study its history, or even to talk about it, if that person does not see that art may relate to the social order in a causal and functional manner?

Art still edifies people. It can maintain and improve their collective existence. Art, directly and indirectly, may bolster the morale of groups working to *create* unity and social solidarity. As used by dissident groups, art may create awareness of social issues. In this context it provides a rallying cry for action and for social change. To be sure, art can be used for decoration and enhancement; but, to fulfill its total function, art has to achieve communication with its audience. If art has no communicative role, then it cannot maintain or change cultures or even be said to be

4

enhancing. If we, as art educators, are to produce artists or art consumers who can see art's function in society, then we need to consider the cultural foundations of art and broaden our definitions of art to include the cultural artifacts of all cultures and subcultures.

Some advocates of so-called "discipline-based" art education may indeed approach art education from a broad perspective. For example, Clark and Zimmerman (1981) see the "disciplines" that influence art education as including "education, psychology, sociology, anthropology, history, philosophy/language arts, and the fine arts" (p. 53); and McFee (1981) sees art education as related to 15 other fields. In reality, however, most current conceptions of discipline-based art education, such as that proposed by the Getty Center for Education in the Arts, smack of four narrow specialisms: art criticism, art history, art production, and aesthetics. Within these specialisms there is even more narrowness. To give two examples, "aesthetics" seems to equal "philosophical aesthetics," and "art history" seems to equal the study of "Western" monuments—hardly universal! It is posited in this chapter that a corrective that helps us to see and to understand art as a democratic activity is to be found by adding the disciplines and perspectives of the social sciences, particularly anthropology and sociology.

In the West, interest in the sociology of the visual arts might be traced back to Vasari in 1542 (Vasari, 1946); despite courses in universities and an increasing number of publications, the study of the cultural and social foundations of art still needs to win wide recognition. This is particularly the case in North American art education. Bird (1979) maintains that in Europe sociology *has* become a way of looking at the world and has "infected" the neighboring arts-based disciplines. For example, Bird shows that within art history there is more work being done on patronage and economic support for artists, and there are increasing attempts to analyze the ideological components of works of art. In art criticism, she states, there has been an extension from literary criticism, textual analysis, and semiology, to an analysis of the image. Cultural and film studies have also had an impact on the ways in which images are studied, as well as on what images are studied.

In 1971 I completed a doctoral dissertation (Chalmers, 1971) that included reviews of more than 500 studies on art and culture. The work of two social scientists seemed to me to be particularly important, namely, the Dutch anthropologist Adrian Gerbrands and the German sociologist Alphons Silbermann. In order to establish a definition of the sociology of art, Silbermann (1968) reviewed the work of European scholars in a number of related disciplines, beginning with the work of Madame de Staël (1800/1959) in literature, Amiot (1799/1973) and Kieswetter (1842/

1968) in music, and Vasari (1542/1946) in the visual arts. Silbermann (1968) does not get very far into his historical review before he feels able to make claims such as the following:

> Since objective creations of the mind can never be opposed to what happens in society, but only seen in a functional relation with it in particular cultural spheres of influence (Konig, 1967, p. 160), no modern thinking social scientist . . . can overlook the fact that the arts, like economics, law, religion, the state, etc., are ultimately expressions of culture and society, as is already clear from the fact that they can be viewed from such different angles as symbolic representation, communication processes or, in the last analysis, social processes. All thinking and research on the sociology of art . . . inevitably leads to the spheres of influence of art and must embrace them all. (p. 573)

Silbermann argues that with art or the arts we are dealing with a social phenomenon that manifests itself as a social process, as a social activity, and consequently needs two partners, a giver and a receiver. Putting it in sociological terms, he stresses that this process needs both a producing group and a consuming group within the "art society." Whether through group contact, group conflict, group dynamics, group transformation, or other group processes, these groups must touch each other in relationships of interdependence, interrelation, and interaction. The ramifications of these relationships, insofar as the producer groups (i.e., the artists) are concerned, reveal new aspects of producing and consuming. They also accord the consumer groups the importance due to them *as recipients and influencers and as validators of artistic creation,* something that has been largely ignored in art education.

In a later paper, Silbermann (1982) suggests that the sociology of music has three tasks. The first is to illustrate the dynamic character of the social phenomenon called "music" in its various forms. The second is to establish a methodology for studying "the something" that is intended to be perceived and understood in various kinds of music. An accessible, convincing, and valid approach will, Silbermann posits, show things as they are as well as show changes that have taken and are taking place. The third task is to predict. He states that the area of musico-sociological investigation aims at shedding light on individual and collective behavior in the consumption of music, including motivations and behavior patterns in the choice of music and in the manner of listening to it. Musical fashion and taste are studied, as are the politics and economics of music, the sociocultural control and change, and the various functions of music.

I suggest that visual arts educators engage students in similar investigations. The Getty Center for Education in the Arts concept of discipline-based art education is too narrow and is insufficient for understanding art in its full complexity. Perhaps because of ethnomusicology and the more "visible" presence of many types of music, music educators have been more democratic and embracing than visual arts educators. I will return to this notion later in this chapter.

In his study of the art of Black Africa, Gerbrands (1957) documents the function and role of art in society. He finds that art is used to perpetuate and maintain cultural values, that sometimes it can urge and promote change in cultural values, and that it is used to decorate and enhance the environment. Intertwined with these three general "uses" is art's role in perpetuating and making comprehensible a society's religious beliefs, its role in conferring social status, its political function as an identity and ideal giver (a symbolic asset) to particular groups, its economic function, its role in leisure and play activities, its relationship to available technologies, and its more "aesthetic" role. Karbusicky (1968) would call this a communication model of art, with what he calls gnoseological ("functioning to give a knowledge of the spiritual"), hedonistic, and recreational components. When viewing a communication model of art, it is certainly important to keep in mind the caution, advanced by Karbusicky, that the sociology of art may isolate for analysis certain phenomena from an autonomous series of interrelations. He suggests that we often forget to reintegrate the isolated element afterward. This is liable, he says, to give rise to "pan-sociological theories" that explain the whole process too simply. For example, he suggests that sociologists often disregard psychology and aesthetics and promote the view that sociology solves everything. In our desire to be democratic, we must not short-circuit the relationship between society and the work of art. However, neither Gerbrands (1957) nor more contemporary anthropologists such as Maquet (1979) or sociologists of art such as Wolff (1981, 1983) deny this complexity. They cautiously admit that not all aesthetic judgments are easily reducible to the sociological or ideological.

I accept such ideas, but, inasmuch as I am particularly concerned that art education broaden its definition of art to include the democratically popular, folk, and vernacular arts, I will use the remainder of the chapter to look particularly at art as a system of signification. Only in its historical context—and then only in the work of a few art educators—has art as a repository of social meaning been sufficiently considered in art educaton. We have not focused on the role of the audience and "reader" in the various worlds of art. In her important book *The Social Production of Art*, Wolff (1981) argues that "film, literature, painting, and rock music can all, in some sense, be seen as repositories of cultural meaning, or, as it is sometimes put, systems of signification" (p. 4). Artistic creativity, she states, is not different in any relevant way from other forms of creative action. Wolff posits that an individual artist "plays much less of a part in the production of the work than our . . . view of the artist as a genius, working with divine inspiration, leads us to believe" (p. 25). She argues that many people are involved in producing the work, that sociological and ideological factors determine or affect the artist's work, and that audiences and "readers" are active participants in *creating* the finished product (cultural artifact). This is particularly true if we consider many art worlds and not just "the artworld." But even within "the artworld," Vasquez (1973) has written that to deny that the artist is subject to the tastes, preferences, ideas, and aesthetic notions of those who influence the market is absolute twaddle! We have to help our students see that art encodes values and ideologies. As Wolff (1981) says, art criticism is never innocent "of the political and ideological purposes in which that discourse has been constituted" (p. 143). Although this does not mean that aesthetic enjoyment and aesthetic experience do not exist, it does call for more politically and culturally aware concepts of art education.

Jauss (1975) proposes a *Rezeptionasthetik* and emphasizes that a work both depends for its meaning on the expectations with which it is received and poses the questions that it must answer. Jauss calls these expectations *horizons*, which are characterized as the product of the discourse of a culture. As Culler (1981) states, "*Rezeptionasthetik* is not a way of interpreting works but an attempt to understand . . . changing intelligibility by identifying the codes and interpretive assumptions that give them meaning for different audiences at different periods" (p. 13).

Becker, who has done some important work on the nature of an art world (1976, 1982), posits that art involves *all* those people and organizations whose activity is necessary to produce the kinds of events and objects that a particular group defines as *art*. This includes people who might conceive the idea of the work, people who execute it, people who provide necessary equipment and materials, and people who make up the audience for the work. Becker argues that it is sociologically sensible and useful to see art as the joint creation of all these people. For some people not used to considering popular, vernacular, and folk expressions in the visual arts, this is perhaps easier to see in music than in the visual arts.

An issue of the *International Social Science Journal* (UNESCO, 1982) was devoted to the sociology of music. The illustrations point to the many different ways particular groups define *music*. Some of the first illustrations concentrate on setting and show, for example, the ornate ceremonial hall at the University of Vienna, with Beethoven meeting Haydn in 1808. A subsequent illustration shows an experimental space at the Georges Pompidou Center in Paris, where variable acoustical properties are used for recording, research, and performance. Next we see a group of "traditional"

American musicians at an outdoor festival in Virginia, followed by the rock group The Police at a New York recording studio and Vangelis, a self-taught Greek composer who does not read music, surrounded by a grand piano, electric drums, Moog synthesizer, and two digital sequencers. There is a London street musician, a small girl taking a piano lesson, a classical concert, a pop concert, and an accordianist in an Irish pub. All point to different audiences and expectations.

Silbermann, who has published widely on music, presents a boiled-down theory of the relationship of art to society in the following statement:

> On the one hand the work makes a certain impression on certain large or small social groups, whose reaction determines the reputation of the work and its position within the sociocultural situation; while on the other hand this process exerts a certain influence on the musician and to some extent conditions and regulates his activity. . . . In strictly sociological terms and to avoid any misunderstanding, let us say that we regard the overall artistic or musical process, involving the interaction and interdependence of artist, work and public, as constituting the framework of reference for all the different aspects of musico-sociological thought and activity. (1982, p. 572)

These concepts apply equally well to the visual arts. As art educators we could be more democratic if we looked at the way visual art is used to strengthen social bonds and how it is used to reach out to others for mutuality, to say "we belong." While the visual arts should be recognized as universal, they can become barriers to social intercourse, because of group-sanctioned artistic traditions. For example, when groups of young people regard rock videos as the *only* art form worth associating with, or when art educators ally themselves with museum traditions of connoisseurship, they are perhaps less likely to be tolerant of and interested in other art forms. I have pointed out in other places (Chalmers, 1981, 1982) that this need not be the case. Gaining knowledge about the variety, place, and role of the visual arts in social life is important if we wish to increase intercultural understanding, because in its diversity we can see the common functions belonging to art. While we as art educators may have cultural preferences, these should not restrict the universality of our approach.

Consider the situation in music. Echoing the work of some "popular" art educators, Etzkorn (1982) writes about the sociology of musical practice and social groups. He states that there has never been a period in musical history in which the simultaneous presence of traditional and contemporary stylistic expressions, of the simple and the complex, the folk and the urban, the private and the commercial, the acoustic and the electronic, has been as extensive as it is today. If one group or society cherishes the most ear-piercing type of music, another group will abhor such productions. In short, Etzkorn states, "at this very moment somewhere on this globe one can find examples of almost every kind of musical expression in active practice or preference by a social group" (p. 557). Politicians prescribe works by particular composers and artists, ethnic and age groups have particular preferences, the symphony is considered appropriate for the socially active and the economically comfortable.

Consider the comments that Etzkorn (1982) makes about musical audiences and supporters as they apply to the visual arts:

> Musical activities always involve people, either as creators or performers, as listeners or audiences, or as cultural supporters who, while not directly involved in a specific musical activity, positively legitimate its practices. This category of musical supporter assumes an importance, though frequently not specially studied role, for the life of music. Performers and creators of music are embedded in the culture of audiences and diffuse supporters. Without diffuse supporters musical activities would be difficult to sanction; neither audiences nor listeners could offer complementarity. Supporters may be considered as the silent majority, the backdrop against which musical activities take place. They may not take issue with major cultural displacements, such as the relegation of folk music traditions to the exotic arena of ethnomusicologists or the takeover of the radio airwaves by rock'n'roll. Supporters may sanction new practices not for explicit aesthetic or musical, but perhaps for economic reasons; whatever the reason, however, they do not permit creation, sponsor performances, or vindicate the teaching, of musical practices without being directly involved in them. In short, they provide the institutional setting within which music is created, performed and listened to. . . .
>
> Musical acculturation works through social groups. Groups use cultural markers to set their boundaries, and musical practices frequently assume this function. Jazz players, followers of serial compositional theory, rock'n'roll musicians, to name a few, form such distinct groups. In them ethnocentrism can be rampant, intolerance of other styles of music or musicians frequent, and the willingness or ability to perform in other musical styles lacking. The ethos of such groups may be well developed to rule out other musical experiences, not as threatening to their practice, but as unworthy of consideration. Much music teaching at school takes on such a flair, where non-Western music or pop music are often deemed unworthy of serious study. Social groups that define what is proper in music set performance standards and aesthetic norms, and pass on criteria of taste. In this regard they perform functions comparable to other groups in social life. In music, the social bases for such groups have often been aligned with religious and political interests (pp. 561–562).

Although the youth market may predominate in North America, disparate social or "taste" groups are more widely acknowledged in music than they are in the visual arts. The recording industry and radio programming acknowledge various forms of popular and "serious" music—music as ideology, music as entertainment, as well as the musics of various age and ethnic groups. As visual arts educators and researchers, we need to be concerned with what is acknowledged as art by a greater variety of individuals and groups. We need to realize "that what is taken, in any world of art, to be the quintessential artistic act, the act whose performance marks one as an artist, is a matter of consensual definition" (Becker, 1974, p. 749).

In other words, as art educators in a pluralistic society we need to consider the *many* answers to the following questions: What is art? What is it for? What constitutes good art? Who decides these things, and by what standards and for what reasons? This necessitates moving beyond elitist and narrow conceptions of art history, art criticism, philosophical aesthetics, and approved studio practice. There is a need for all work that undergirds art educational theory, particularly that which deals with the nature of art, to be more anthropological in method and more semiotic in intent.

References

Amiot, J. (1973). *Memoire sur la musique des Chinois.* Geneva: Minkoff. (Original work published 1799)

Becker, H. (1974). Art as collective action. *American Sociological Review, 39*(6), 767–776.

Becker, H. (1976). Art worlds and social types. *American Behavioral Scientist, 19*(6), 703–718.

Becker, H. (1982). *Art Worlds.* Berkeley and Los Angeles: University of California Press.

Bird, E. (1979). Aesthetic neutrality and the sociology of art. In M. Barrett, P. Corrigan, A. Kuhn, & J. Wolff (Eds.), *Ideology and cultural production* (pp. 25–48). London: Croom Helm.

Chalmers, G. (1971). *Towards a theory of art and culture as a foundation for art education.* Unpublished Ph.D. dissertation, University of Oregon, Eugene.

Chalmers, G. (1981). Art education as ethnology. *Studies in Art Education, 23*(3), 6–14.

Chalmers, G. (1982). Aesthetic education as a social study. *Canadian Review of Art Education Research, 9,* 4–11.

Clark, G., & Zimmerman, E. (1981). Toward a discipline of art education. *Phi Delta Kappan, 63,* 82–85.

Culler, J. (1981). *The pursuit of signs: Semiotics, literature, deconstruction.* Ithaca, NY: Cornell University Press.

de Staël, Madame. (1959). *De la litterature considerée dans ses rapports avec les institutions sociales.* Geneva: Librairie Droz. (Original work published 1800)

Etzkorn, K. P. (1982). On the sociology of musical practice and social groups. *International Social Science Journal, 34*(4), 555–569.

Gerbrands, A. (1957). *Art as an element of culture, especially in Negro Africa.* Leiden, West Germany: E. J. Brill.

Jauss, H. R. (1975). The idealist embarrassment: Observations on Marxist aesthetics. *New Literary History 7*(1), 191–208.

Karbusicky, V. (1968). The interaction between reality–work of art–society. *International Social Science Journal, 20*(4), 644–655.

Kieswetter, R. (1968). *Die musik der Araber.* Weisbaden, West Germany: M. Sandig. (Original work published 1842)

Konig, R. (Ed.). (1967). *Soziologie.* Frankfurt am Main: Fischer Taschenbuch.

Maquet, J. (1979). *Introduction to aesthetic anthropology.* Malibu, CA: Undena Publications.

McFee, J. K. (1981, April). *Defining art education in the eighties.* Paper presented at the National Art Education Association Conference, Chicago, IL.

Silbermann, A. (1968). A definition of the sociology of art. *International Social Science Journal, 20*(4), 567–588.

Silbermann, A. (1982). What questions does the empirical sociology of music attempt to answer? *International Social Science Journal, 34*(4), 571–581.

UNESCO. (1982). *International Social Science Journal, 34*(4).

Vasari, G. (1946). *Vasari's lives of the artists: Biographies of the most eminent architects, painters, and sculptors of Italy.* (Betty Burroughs, Trans.). New York: Simon and Schuster. (Original work published 1542–1550)

Vasquez, A. (1973). *Art and Society: Essays in Marxist aesthetics.* London: Merlin Press.

Wolff, J. (1981). *The social production of art.* London: Merlin Press.

Wolff, J. (1983). *Aesthetics and the sociology of art.* London: George Allen and Unwin.

Chapter 2

Qualifications and Contradictions of Art Museum Education in a Pluralistic Democracy

___Karen A. Hamblen_____

Increasingly, art educators are questioning whether studio instruction alone adequately prepares students to understand and appreciate art. In addition to the making of art, art educators are calling for instruction that includes the study of aesthetics, art history, and art criticism. As the repository of authentic objects selected on the basis of perceived aesthetic quality and historical significance, art museums are seen as playing a crucial role in this new discipline-based art curriculum.

Concomitant with a new emphasis on the museum's role in art education is the availability of a wealth of visual forms made possible through modern means of visual production, film, videotape, and ongoing anthropological and archaeological studies. To paraphrase Buckminster Fuller's famous metaphor, we now occupy an aesthetic global village. Students of art can have access to essentially all the extant art forms produced since the dawn of human history. In addition, popular, folk, and commercial arts that are an integral part of students' life-worlds have experienced a veritable renaissance. Rapid social change, cultural diversity, and movements supportive of ethnic pride have paralleled a proliferation in the development of diverse aesthetic taste cultures.

Although some of the social and aesthetic diversity in our live museum-without-walls is reflected in art museum exhibitions, many types of art forms have not been incorporated into the official pantheon of the fine-art museum.[1] Art museums tend to collect and display particular types of works that already have established value or, through exhibition, are believed capable of developing a reputation of value. When one looks to the universe of possible aesthetic choices, it is clear that the art museum is not a democratic institution in the sense of allowing for equal representation. The art museum has been described as being "largely exempt from the requirement to give all tastes their due, to treat all claims as legitimate" ("On the Third Realm," 1985, p. 11) in its function of exhibiting the highest achievements of artistic expression for peak aesthetic experiences. How aesthetic acheivement is defined and by whom, and the entire selection process involved in the collection, preservation, and exhibition of art, have a problematic, political dimension that has received scant attention and examination.

The purpose of this chapter is to examine the political nature of art museum education and how that political dimension has come to be obscured and presented in a more-or-less neutral manner. The qualifications and contradictions that have resulted from placing an apolitical patina on the differential distribution of aesthetic knowledge will also be examined. It will be proposed that, by displaying works selected by the dominant culture, the art museum is involved in the reproduction of class stratifications. In this chapter, the following areas will be covered: (1) how art museum education comes to be depoliticized, (2) the origins of art museums and democratic paradoxes, (3) the contradictions and democratic fallacies of art museum education in a society based on class distinctions, and (4) a critical theory of art museum education. It will be proposed that all types of education, including museum education, need to incorporate a reflexive component involving an examination of what is chosen for study, why it is chosen, who makes such choices, and the possible consequences of such choices. Such a critical stance needs to be taken in order to develop a consciousness of other options and of the selective, political nature of educational programs in our society. This chapter should not be construed as being a critique of museum education per se. Rather, it examines the paradoxes and problems endemic to many educational activities occurring in a class-bound society that espouses the ideals of democratic equality. The reader is urged to consider similar contradictions between the rhetoric of educational policies and the realities of practices in many elementary and secondary schools.

---

1. In this chapter, *museum art* refers to historic arts, masterpieces, and avant garde art found in fine-art museums.

The Ostensible Depoliticization of Museum Education

In all societies, individuals learn prescribed modes of behavior. Through formal and informal socialization processes, individuals build up a repertoire of workable knowledge by which they give meaning to their behaviors and responses. Such knowledge often becomes so taken for granted that its historical origins and hence its chosenness is obscured (Bowers, 1974). In Apple's (1979) terminology, such learning becomes embedded in the bottom of our brains; it takes on a correctness, a givenness, a sense of "that's the way things are." It becomes a tradition.

In a pluralistic society, there is a variety of repertoires of knowledge, traditions, and shapes of consciousness. All socialization processes, however, do not carry equal weight in a society in which there are class distinctions. According to Gouldner (1979), knowledge and skills are forms of cultural capital that provide access to income and, more significantly, to a particular type of consciousness. Problems and contradictions begin to develop when only certain shapes of consciousness are given institutional credence. When particular patterns of socialization are given more value than others, official institutions, such as schools and museums, often become involved in the differential transmission of the dominant culture. Other traditions do continue to exist, but they are not given institutional status. Certain selected traditions become represented as correct, and these must be learned if one is to participate in the dominant culture.

Museum educators are acutely aware of their educational responsibilities and of the complexities that develop in any setting in which educational activities occur (P. B. Williams, 1985; Zeller, 1985). Much discussion has been devoted to whether museum programs should be primarily adjuncts to school curricula, how lengthy identifying labels should be and where they should be placed, whether classroom teachers should conduct tours, how to increase viewer participation, and so on. These and administrative concerns regarding delivery systems and numbers of viewers are certainly not inconsequential topics of discussion. Such matters can easily detract from more fundamental issues involving the role museums play in the distribution of aesthetic knowledge and, more importantly, in the distribution of particular, selected types of knowledge that are often not representative of the broad base of aesthetic preferences in our pluralistic society.

A large part of the museum's depoliticized stance seems to be due to the belief that the aesthetic rises above the exigencies of time and place and is, therefore, apolitical. "In this decade museums are not to be criticized on political grounds, but on their ability to address educational concerns, including the development of aesthetic sensitivity and standards of taste" (*Summary of Toledo Meeting*, 1985, p. 2). There appears to be a certain acceptance that aesthetic standards are agreed upon and that they exist outside political concerns. Admonishments are found in the literature against "substituting ideological criteria for aesthetic ones or for falling victim to a political process" (Lilla, 1985, p. 86). Such statements are made in the face of numerous examples whereby the reputation of an artist or even a single work of art has risen and fallen with changing cultural values and commensurate changing aesthetic criteria. This is merely one of many contradictions that develops when it is believed that it is possible to rise above choice and above the relativity of history. The political nature of museum education is embedded within the presentation of selected traditions that are regarded as representing the standards of aesthetic excellence.

The trick to having individuals accept the correctness of a selected tradition is to have it *appear* depoliticized; it must appear neutral. Part of this is accomplished by the mere fact that official institutions often present only the tradition of the dominant culture and, if one is to venture outside one's immediate subcultural sphere, that dominant tradition must be learned to some extent. However, the depoliticization of a selected tradition is more subtly accomplished by its being presented as ahistorical and as being beneficial. Socialization into the dominant culture is not a matter of coercion or the result of a conspiracy to oppress. Rather, such learning provides opportunities and participation in areas given widespread social credence. Successful entrance into the dominant culture can eliminate disturbing questions of variable value and meaning. For example, school children do not enter a museum to question whether certain aesthetic choices should have been made but rather to learn to appreciate what has already been socially sanctioned as being worthy of study. There is a self-fulfilling, tautological promise of success and assurance of correctness involved in much dominant culture socialization.

When choices are made by official institutions, they have the power to shape the consciousness of those who would participate in the dominant culture. Herein begin some of the more disturbing qualifications and contradictions of museum education. Within a pluralistic democracy, diversity of expression, unpopular viewpoints, and minority rights are supposedly protected and given credence. Educational access for all is, in many instances, legally decreed. Yet access often means being educated, not in the diversity a democratic pluralism would seem to indicate, but rather toward a selected tradition which is presented as being the correct and only valid tradition, supposedly exempt from selective interpretations and conflicting options. For many individuals, this results in a severe disjuncture between the formal socialization patterns required by official institutions and the informal life-world of their subculture.

It is not a matter of mere serendipity that the development of museums, democratic forms of government, and modern education has had more-or-less coinciding historical and cultural origins. At the basis of each is the assumption that some traditions are of more value than others and that equality means having access to those selected traditions, not the equal representation of all traditions.

Origins of Contradictions and Paradoxes

Santayana (1953) suggested that history be studied to avoid repetition of the past; Apple (1979) suggests that it be studied to reveal the historicity and selection processes involved in the development of traditions that, over a period of time, acquire a sense of givenness. The rise of museums, democratic governments, and modern education, as well as the politics of differential aesthetic knowledge distribution and the contradictions of the democratic ethic, have their sources in the Enlightenment of eighteenth-century Europe. Museums and democracies emerged from the optimistic acultural belief "that we are all part of one [human-made] civilization" (Osborne, 1985, p. 29). Pansocial, universalistic human ideals, beliefs, and rights were presupposed. What emerged was an ethnocentric, manifest destiny of political, aesthetic, and cultural ideals based on predefined Western standards of excellence. The original and persisting contradiction has been that "correct" standards are supposedly readily recognizable and that they should be made available to all citizens. This occurs at the expense of other traditions that are often ignored, denigrated, misinterpreted, or co-opted.

> Always selectivity is the point; the way in which from a whole possible area of past and present, certain meanings and practices are chosen for emphasis, certain other meanings and practices are neglected and excluded. Even more crucially, some of these meanings are reinterpreted, diluted or put into forms which support or at least do not contradict other elements within the effective dominant culture. (R. Williams, 1976, p. 205)

This latter point certainly applies to how the life-world[2] functions of art objects are co-opted in favor primarily of the aesthetic experience when

---

2. Life-world refers to the ongoing physical, psychological, and cultural milieus in which individuals learn and create meaning and significance. Life-world is used in contradistinction to formalized systems of thought and singular, selected interpretations that are given to individuals rather than directly experienced by them.

they enter the museum environment. In a society based on class distinctions, standards of excellence have been determined by those who are in power to define them as such, that is, those who are part of and in control of the cultural standards being promulgated. This is much like asking the cat to watch the mouse.

Related to the growth of the middle class and philanthropic impulses in the nineteenth century, art museums flourished within the confines of a civic humanism designed to bring a particular type of aesthetic enlightenment to a diverse immigrant population.

> Museums, the philanthropists believed, would provide the moral uplift needed to raise the common man (read: urban worker and immigrant) to a level of culture at which he could be expected to act like a citizen. (Lilla, 1985, p. 89)

Providing access to a predefined, culture-specific standard of excellence at the expense of broad, diverse representation remains the hallmark of political democracies in societies based on class distinctions. It is also the source of numerous inconsistencies and contradictions. As noted earlier, it can separate individuals from their life-worlds of informal socialization patterns, and it can severely limit participation in the democratic process it was actually designed to serve. For example, art museums offer for public viewing certain works of art that might otherwise be held in private ownership, in a sense providing access to all citizens. Yet, the art of museums is often not easily understood by those not schooled in the aesthetic values of the dominant culture. Thus, what is offered is exclusionary, and the value of other aesthetic traditions is negated through omission. Nonetheless, the erroneous view is often held that

> the museum is an "empowering" institution meant to incorporate all who would become part of *our shared* cultural experience. All citizens have the opportunity to walk into a museum and appreciate the highest achievements of *their* culture. (Lilla, 1985, p. 90, emphasis added)

In a study of art museum education, Eisner and Dobbs (1984) state, "We agree with one museum director who said 'the role of the museum is to expand the elite' " (p. 16). The assumption that there is an agreed-upon, superior aesthetic and that certain members of society are the arbiters of its parameters supplies grist for a critique that far exceeds the art museum per se. Such an assumption touches on the discriminatory base of socialization processes in our pluralistic democracy. A paradox of democratic processes in a class-bound society is that equality is dependent on achieving a standard predefined by a group whose power is maintained as long as the standard is exclusionary. "Knowledge must be available to all citizens, yet accessibility must be limited or knowledge will lose its power" (Hamblen, 1984, p. 30).

> On the one side, [the dominant culture] presses to undermine all societal distinctions and, on the other, believing its own culture best it wishes to advantage those who most fulfill and embody it. Its own culture, then, contains . . . the "seeds of its own destruction" (Gouldner, 1979, p. 86)

Gouldner puts the name to the lie; the altruistic, seemingly democratic goal of educating the general population to understand and appreciate the best is actually exclusionary.

In art this contradiction has surfaced numerous times when an art form or style loses status as it gains in popularity. Sontag (1966) specifically faulted Op-Art for being too understandable to the general population and too amenable to use in industrial and commercial design. And, of course, there is the often-cited apocryphal statement that once the general population comes to appreciate a painting it should be burned. It would appear that some museum personnel are alternately pleased and uncomfortable at the high attendance at blockbuster exhibitions, for there is the lurking suspicion that the motives for attendance may be wrong. That the museum may be unduly appealing to popular tastes is a cause of concern. "Over the past twenty-five years, the museum has been told by ideologists that, as a progressive institution, its galleries must be open to ethnic, folk, and political art" (Lilla, 1985, p. 81). "Attracting new audiences, hiring minority staff members, acknowledging folk art and popular tastes, and reaching out to the citizenry through satellite installations and traveling programs . . . overlap to a certain extent with the education function, but not entirely" (Eisner & Dobbs, 1984, p. 93).

Construction of a Consensus Theory of Art

So-called fine art is "fine" partly because it is not readily accessible and is also scarce. It must remain so if it is to retain its designation of desirable, high-status knowledge. Moreover, to maintain scarcity and desirability, the selection process must be exclusive, and selection must be based on criteria that are not readily defined, even among experts themselves. Aesthetic criteria certainly qualify on this latter point.

It needs to be noted that the aesthetic itself is not scarce; aesthetic qualities are found in everyday life activities, the natural environment, and numerous human-made objects, as well as nonmuseum art objects. Even the often-cited criterion that fine art has depth of meaning is not exclusive to fine art. Many art forms that do not reach art museum exhibition status have meaning and significance that require extensive study. That the art of the museum constitutes a selected, problematic tradition is obscured behind an implied consensus of experts. Those who have aesthetic cultural capital and are in charge of institutions that distribute aesthetic knowledge create the aesthetic criteria that are given credence. Over time the fact that a tradition is based on problematic decisions and has been humanly created becomes obscured. Likewise, the class origins of such decisions become neutralized.

> What was often in the past a conscious attempt by the bourgeoisie to *create* a consensus that was not there, has now become the only possible interpretation of social and intellectual possibilities. What was at first an ideology in the form of class interest has now become *the* definition of the situation in most school curricula. (Apple, 1979, p. 82)

Experts are notoriously unable to agree on most issues, but, in all subject areas of education, expert-formulated information is presented to the lay public without note of the problematic decision-making process that produced such information (Apple, 1979). That a pluralistic democracy should be guided by any type of consensus of opinion, expert or other, is in itself a contradiction.

In addition to maintaining an effective dominant culture, selective traditions more subtly limit consciousness of the role individuals play in creating their reality. A consensus theory of art obscures the role people play in creating the very categories that constitute the framework for decision making. Art becomes presented as a ready-made, as a given, rather than as having meaning in relationship to the ongoing choices and interpretations of numerous individuals. Meaning and value appear to exist outside one's self and one's control. This is not to suggest that controversy does not precede art museum selections or that museum personnel do not have ongoing debates on the appropriateness of exhibition decisions, but rather that such conflict is obscured. Museum choices are not considered open to serious question by the lay public.

Neutralizing a Selected Tradition

According to Lilla (1985), "The museum's task is to acquire and display the very best work available to it, that is all. It is an art institution and nothing more" (p. 82). The political nature of the art museum is consistently denied, even when it is stated that the museum's role is to lead aesthetic tastes and to shape society. The art museum provides "the only environment in which a true aesthetic experience is possible," states Levi (1985, p. 29), who considers the museum to be "the major salvation of genuinely *aesthetic* experience" (p. 31). The museum environment sets up expectations for aesthetic experiences as part of the presumed consensus that this is the place for such experiences. Again, it is not that there is no conflict or argument, but rather that there is a claim of impartiality, and conflict is institutionalized within the boundaries of art through such discussions as whether or not a given artist has surpassed her previous accomplishments, whether the paint is on the surface of the canvas or is part of the canvas, and so on. Debate centers on the art itself, not the process by which it was selected.

Relegating aesthetic experiences to a neutral environment not only may separate art from much of society but also may tend to flatten out strong pro and con feelings. A certain leveling occurs. Haskell (1985) marvels that the masses, whose ancestors were exploited by those who commissioned much museum art, have not destroyed museums. He attributes the lack of destruction of masterpieces to the fact that museums are open to the public. An alternative explanation might be that museums, in the outward display of neutrality and consensus, have made themselves inconsequential to those interested in drastic social changes. It is not that art does not elicit strong emotional responses and commitments, but, possibly, that museum art is seen as outside the purview of action and input. One comes to a museum to appreciate, not to question. This is not the case with other types of art. Public statuary is a favorite target of revolutionaries and, in the United States, art commissioned for public environments often raises a loud hue and cry among those who are directly affected.

Just as education in the schools is often perceived as being unrelated to students' life-world experiences, art museum experiences, designed specifically to be different from other aesthetic encounters, obligate museum visitors to accept many of the assumptions formulated by the dominant culture. Efland (1976) and Wilson and Wilson (1977) have noted that the art produced and studied in schools differs drastically from the informal, nondirected graphic expressions of children outside those institutions. The more obvious consequences of this disjuncture are the abrogation of self from having input in educational situations and alienation from institutional learning. Without further education, wherein the individual becomes part of the dominant culture, it is highly unlikely that museum activities result in life-long attitudinal and behavioral changes. This appears to be borne out by the fact that museum attendance primarily consists of those who are college educated (Eisner & Dobbs, 1984).

Recommendations for an Aesthetic Pluralism

Perhaps the ultimate irony of education in a pluralistic democracy built on a class-bound structure is that the selected, dominant tradition is presented as the best, as what is good for us, as that which will provide enlightenment. One feels like a bit of a nay-sayer even to suggest that fine art, which often provides such exquisite visual delights, might be involved in something as crass as the reproduction of social and economic inequities. That the museum has the right to be the leader in aesthetic taste has become part of our accepted knowledge. As part of the dominant, institutionalized pattern of socialization, such an assumption is as difficult to resist as it is to debunk. In fact, the more one becomes educated in the arts as traditionally defined, the less one has the ability to see other possibilities and to examine current assumptions. To gain some perspective, it is necessary to look beyond one's immediate socialization patterns.

Art museums are a very recent phenomenon, and, despite there being a variety of fine-art museums, they still present a fairly narrow range of artistic expression. According to Gowans (1971), art throughout time and space has had the four functions of beautification, persuasion, illustration, and substitute imagery. He suggests that the popular arts best exemplify these four functions, inasmuch as fine art of this century has abrogated much of the meaning it had historically in the lives of people. In a somewhat similar vein, Gans (1974) places artistic functions and preferences firmly within the framework of socioeconomic class. A pluralistic society encompasses a number of aesthetic taste cultures that are as valid as the belief systems of the people that produce them.

I certainly am not suggesting that fine art not be studied nor that it is an invalid cultural expression. Much to the contrary, fine art needs to be studied for its aesthetic value and specifically as a cultural expression, but as only one expression among many. For example, much modern fine art is difficult to understand specifically because it is very much about the complexities of modern life (Hamblen, 1983, 1986b). In a pluralistic democracy, the artistic production of all groups needs to be considered a valid expression of significant needs and beliefs. It is important to note that it is not being suggested that the popular, folk, and commercial arts be studied in order to interest students and to pique their attention for the implicit goal of moving them on to the fine arts. This would merely compound the contradictions.

Contradictions of Pluralism

While one might like to believe that it is possible to gather all aesthetic traditions under the benevolent umbrella of democratic principles, such is not the case. Instruction in aesthetic pluralism is not without its qualifications and contradictions, either. For example, there is a limit to the number of cultural hats any one person can wear. It is the rare individual who is able truly to live and understand more than one culture beyond a somewhat abstract, scholarly level (McFee, 1970). The study of aesthetic pluralism can develop into an aesthetic smorgasbord of brief samplings, none of which provides much nourishment.

All aesthetic taste cultures represent selected traditions, and it is impossible in the study of any subject to rise above choice. Aesthetic pluralism, by itself, is not an antidote to the tendency to neutralize certain less valued traditions. Both art museum directors and collectors of folk art tend to look askance at paint-by-number art. For all types of study, selections are made on the basis of defined quality. Even if a more encompassing and tolerant view is taken toward aesthetic traditions, care must still be taken that broader selections are also perceived as relative to one's assumptions rather than having universal application. In aesthetics, as in society, while equality often is espoused and even claimed, in truth some people and some art forms are seen as being a bit more worthy than others.

A final qualification and contradiction of instruction in aesthetic pluralism is that one must face the fact that fine art is the institutionalized, aesthetic norm. Just as English is the so-called cash language in the United States, museum art is the cash aesthetic culture. Educating students in ways substantially counter to the dominant culture may curtail their ability to participate in it in a way that affords them mobility and various types of options. It may actually be elitist not to educate students in what is defined as "best" by institutions that have the ability to shape and define social reality.

It is recommended that the study of art encompass a range of aesthetic traditions inclusive of museum and nonmuseum art, and that artworks be studied and appreciated as objects worthy of aesthetic contemplation. In addition, if we are to educate toward an aesthetic and societal respect for diversity, complexity, and conflicting traditions, our framework of study needs to allow for, if not embody, controversy (Hamblen, 1986a). Democratic pluralism in society and aesthetics should allow for elitism and populism, for the good and the not-so-good, for paradox and for nonsolutions. Through debate and contrast, the problematic, value-laden nature of our selections is revealed. There are dangers in education when choices are not available, but merely allowing for diversity is not sufficient without an ongoing critical, reflexive stance toward what is chosen. Care must be taken to see the origins of any approach as being a matter of selection. Selection itself needs to be made meaningful by the knowledge that it is a choice and by the consciousness that what is chosen is politically embedded. Museum education and other forms of education need to be imbued with an ongoing critical theory that provides no lasting answers but rather affords constant vigilance.

Summary

The purposes of museums are often stated as consisting of the collection, preservation, and exhibition of objects for purposes of providing aesthetic experiences and appreciation in the education of the general public. In addition to the obvious educational benefits of studying museum art, I am proposing that museums themselves be studied in terms of their participation in the selection and distribution of aesthetic knowledge. Aesthetic choices are firmly embedded within the political structures of meaning, power, and distribution in society. Contradictions occur when educational issues are not seen as politically grounded and motivated. As currently presented, museum art does not foster serious questions of why certain objects were selected, who made those choices, why they were made, who is best served by such choices, and which objects were *not* selected and why they were not.

Students need to examine the institutions that make educational choices, the assumptions underlying those choices, and how we often come to accept without question choices that are made for us. Access to a range of art forms is but the first step toward aesthetic pluralism; it is necessary also to see one's choices as problematic and as proceeding from particular viewpoints that are themselves embedded in political motivations. Weitz (1962) has described art as a contested concept inasmuch as definitions of art change and no one definitional set applies to all art objects. A spirit of ongoing debate and examination of premises and motives is necessary if the selective nature of our choices, aesthetic or other, is to be understood. As Apple (1979) has noted, it is impossible to rise above choice.

References

Apple, M. (1979). *Ideology and curriculum.* London: Routledge & Kegan Paul.
Bowers, C. (1974). *Cultural literacy for freedom: An existential perspective on teaching, curriculum, and school policy.* Eugene, OR: Elan.

Efland, A. (1976). The school art style: A functional analysis. *Studies in Art Education, 17*(2), 37–44.

Eisner, E. W., & Dobbs, S. M. (1984). *The uncertain profession: Observations on the state of museum education in twenty American art museums.* Los Angeles: The J. Paul Getty Center for Education in the Arts.

Gans, H. J. (1974). *Popular culture and high culture: An analysis and evaluation of taste.* New York: Basic Books.

Gouldner, A. W. (1979). *The future of intellectuals and the rise of the new class.* New York: Seabury.

Gowans, A. (1971). *The unchanging arts: New forms for the traditional functions of art in society.* New York: J. B. Lippincott.

Hamblen, K. (1983). Modern fine art: A vehicle for understanding Western modernity. *The Bulletin of the Caucus on Social Theory and Art Education,* (3), 9–16.

Hamblen, K. (1984). The culture of aesthetic discourse (CAD): Origins, implications, and consequences. *Bulletin of the Caucus on Social Theory and Art Education,* (4), 22–35.

Hamblen, K. (1986a). Exploring contested concepts for aesthetic literacy. *Journal of Aesthetic Education, 29*(2), 67–76.

Hamblen, K. A. (1986b). There you go again, Tom. *Art Education, 39*(3), 52–54.

Haskell, F. (1985). Museums and their enemies. *Journal of Aesthetic Education, 19*(2), 13–22.

Levi, A. W. (1985). The art museum as an agency of culture. *Journal of Aesthetic Education, 19*(2), 23–40.

Lilla, M. (1985). The museum in the city. *Journal of Aesthetic Education, 19*(2), 79–91.

McFee, J. K. (1970). *Preparation for art* (2nd ed.). Belmount, CA: Wadsworth.

On the third realm—Art museums and education. (1985). *Journal of Aesthetic Education, 19*(2), 5–12.

Osborne, H. (1985). The end of the museum? *Journal of Aesthetic Education, 19*(2), 41–51.

Santayana, G. (1953). *The life of reason; or, the phases of human progress* (one-volume edition, revised with Daniel Cory). New York: Scribner's.

Sontag, S. (1966). Non-writing and the art scene. In G. Battcock (Ed.), *The new art: A critical anthology.* New York: E. P. Dutton.

Summary of Toledo meeting discussion on museum education—November, 1985. (1985). Los Angeles: The J. Paul Getty Center for Education in the Arts.

Weitz, M. (1962). The role of theory in aesthetics. In J. Margolis (Ed.), *Philosophy looks at the arts: Contemporary readings in aesthetics.* New York: Scribner's.

Williams, P. B. (1985). Educational excellence in art museums: An agenda for reform. *Journal of Aesthetic Education, 19*(2), 105–123.

Williams, R. (1976). Base and superstructure in Marxist culture theory. In R. Dale (Ed.), *Schooling and capitalism: A sociological reader.* London: Routledge & Kegan Paul.

Wilson, B., & Wilson, M. (1977). An iconoclastic view of the imagery sources in the drawings of young people. *Art Education, 30*(1), 4–12.

Zeller, T. (1985). Museum education and school art: Different ends and different means. *Art Education, 38*(3), 6–10.

Chapter 3

Masculine Bias and the Relationship Between Art and Democracy

___Georgia C. Collins _____

The marginal status of art in the public school curriculum makes it clear to the art teacher and other concerned parties that, in our society, art is not regarded as an essential component of democratic education. On the other hand, the efforts of art teachers to shape art instruction to the needs and interests of democratic citizens are attended by fears that any pedagogical acknowledgment of popular taste or marketplace vulgarity will compromise the integrity of art. While public school art teachers struggle on a daily basis with the seemingly discontinuous value systems associated with traditional concepts of art and democracy, the field of American art education adjusts and readjusts the balance between art and democratic values in its prescriptive theories of art curriculum and instruction. A checks-and-balances approach to the problem has tended to reinforce rather than challenge the general assumption that art and democracy are by their very natures disparate pursuits, at best irrelevant to one another and at worst in conflict with one another.

Improving the relationship between art and democracy will require more than a precarious balancing of art against democratic goals in education. At a minimum, it will require the discovery of some significant common ground between them. It has not escaped my attention as an art educator that there is at least one similarity between art and democracy, namely, that women have historically been excluded from equal participation in the mainstream traditions of both of these spheres of cultural activity. An examination of this otherwise unfortunate similarity between art and democracy might provide us with a deeper level of understanding upon which to build a more mutually beneficial relationship between them.

This chapter explores the possibility that residues of masculine bias in our traditional concepts of art and democracy are closely related to, if not responsible for, the tenuous and problematic relationship between them. In her article "Aesthetic Consciousness: The Ground of Political Experience," Hilde Hein (1976) analyzes various interpretations of art's political utility and theorizes that there is a foundational consciousness underlying politics which is aesthetic in nature. After reviewing more familiar ways of thinking about the relationship between art and democracy, this chapter goes on to examine both Hein's theory and a feminist critique of our society's mainstream traditions of art and democracy, in an effort to identify significant continuities of value and purpose between these traditions. Following a discussion of how such continuities have affected the relationship between art and democracy, the chapter concludes by suggesting possible changes in attitude that will be needed before we can bring about a mutually beneficial relationship between them.

Before proceeding, a few definitions are in order. In this chapter, the terms *mainstream art* and *mainstream tradition of art* refer to the fine arts, as distinct from the folk, commercial, domestic, popular, and applied arts of Western culture. The progress of mainstream art is recorded and defined by Western art history texts and courses, presented and preserved by major European and American museums and galleries, and critically monitored in journals such as *Art News*, *Art in America*, and *Artforum*. The professionals and volunteers who produce, record, criticize, teach about, buy and sell, and otherwise actively involve themselves in mainstream art and its institutions are collectively referred to as the *artworld*.

Similarly, a distinction is made in this chapter between *mainstream democracy* and *nonmainstream democracy*, a distinction that acknowledges the dual meanings attached to the concept of democracy. Herein, the mainstream tradition of democracy refers to formal governmental structures instituted by law and custom in the United States and other nations described loosely as "the free world," as distinct from democratic practices associated with a wide variety of informal, private, communal, experimental, and/or cooperative living and working arrangements freely undertaken by groups of individuals within the larger society. The progress of mainstream democracy is recorded and defined in Western history texts and courses; instituted and preserved by politicians, police, and the military under constitutional law; and critically monitored by elected representatives, the courts, the news media, and the voting public. The professionals and citizens who exercise the franchise; who run for or are appointed to public office; who pass, enforce, judge, and abide by the laws; and who otherwise actively engage in mainstream democracy and its institutions are in this chapter referred to collectively as the *political world* or *political sphere.*

Familiar Ways of Thinking About the Relationship Between Art and Democracy

In his article "Democracy, Education, and Art," Francis T. Villemain (1966) reminds us that in the history of Western thought relatively little attention has been paid to the "interrelationships among democracy, art, and mass education" (p. 407). When attention is given such matters, it typically involves speculation on the usefulness of one realm of activity to another (Hein, 1976). Thus, for those who take art as their primary concern, discussions of the relationship between art and politics focus on the value of politics, democratic or otherwise, for art. For those whose primary concern is politics, these discussions focus on the value of art for politics. How each realm has assessed the utility value of the other is of initial interest for those concerned with understanding the relationship between them.

The Art Value of Democracy

Given the history and values of the Western mainstream art tradition (Collins & Sandell, 1984), assessments of a political system's usefulness to art inevitably include discussion of that system's impact on artistic freedom and patronage.[1] Politics may also provide a motivation and context for art. Political systems are not usually assessed in terms of their ability to inspire art, however, and such inspirations for mainstream art are generally suspect. While many mainstream artists make explicit political statements in and about their art, and while any work of art would seem subject to political interpretation, art historians, critics, and teachers are quick to note that political inspiration can result in propaganda statements of little art value. Some artworld individuals, for example, describe socialist art as "strong on message but often weak as art" (Gablik, 1984, p. 33). This and similar statements serve to remind us that, while we

---

1. Effective support for art in Western culture has involved the brokerage of power, money, protection, favoritism, prestige, and endorsement. The terms that best describe such support and those who provide it are *patronage, patron, patroness,* and *patronizing.* I am not unaware of the linguistic roots and historical associations of these terms and do not wish to perpetuate the sexism and elitism they inevitably must connote. Nevertheless, no other terms are quite as accurate and concise in the meaning they convey.

might find more excitement and meaning in art with political content, art, as such, is judged primarily on aesthetic grounds. Political inspiration in no way guarantees aesthetic merit.

If a political system's ability to inspire art seems irrelevant in assessing that system's value for mainstream art, how political systems differ regarding the provision of artistic freedom and patronage is a major artworld concern. Patronage without control is a rare occurrence, even in a democracy. When discrepancies exist between the tastes of artists and their patrons, this control becomes a source of possible artistic corruption and the more art-worthy choice is to forgo patronage for the sake of free expression. One positive value of democracy lies in its ability to encourage and protect the artist's right to this freedom of expression. In a democracy such as exists in the United States, however, where practical concerns outweigh the aesthetic, securing patronage for art is far more problematic. Popular and commercial forms of art flourish, but artists educated in the mainstream tradition find it difficult to locate and secure the patronage of individuals and institutions whose tastes coincide with their own. Democracy's failure to provide such patronage would seem to limit severely its value for mainstream artists.

Some highly influential democrats, including a founder of our democracy, John Adams (Arts, Education and Americans Panel, 1977), and the American philosopher John Dewey (Villemain, 1966), have been interpreted as suggesting that a major goal of democracy is the extension of the aesthetic franchise, as it were, to all citizens. More recently, Smith (1985, 1986) argues for excellence in art education by explaining how the provision of an equal opportunity for all citizens to enjoy the best in art is compatible with, and perhaps a logical requirement for, the full realization of our liberal democratic ideals. The corollary of these positions would seem to be that the pursuit of democratic goals could be highly useful to art by incidentally encouraging its wider patronage. According to Hein (1976), however, in the context of our otherwise pragmatic and materialistic society, the idealism inherent in these readings of democratic purpose tends to reinforce rather than to counter notions that art is a luxury and, as such, desirable but not necessary. In any case, extending the privilege of art experience to all has been viewed as a long-range goal of democracy and, in our public schools as elsewhere in our society, long-range goals are repeatedly set aside until more immediate goals have been met.

On the whole, then, we might understand that democracy has served art by guaranteeing freedom of choice and expression and by keeping alive the idea that viewing and making art are desirable experiences for all individuals. To date, however, American democracy's inability to provide broad-based patronage and its penchant for postponing desirable but unnecessary experience have severely restricted its utility value for mainstream art.

The Democratic Value of Art

For those who take politics as their primary concern, discussions of the relationship between politics and art focus on the value of art for politics, or, in the case of this inquiry, for democracy. Hein (1976) summarizes general theories of art's political value by dividing them into three basic types: the contrapuntal, the propadeutic, and the propulsive. According to Hein, contrapuntal theories of the political value of art are those that see art as a conservative political force by virtue of its ability to release and channel potentially disruptive energies into politically harmless, therapeutic forms of expression and appreciation. Insofar as art gives innocuous aesthetic form to desires and dissatisfactions, it serves as a release valve for those who might otherwise challenge more directly the existing political order. An authoritarian regime, for example, might find art useful for this purpose (Efland, 1976). In an ideal democracy, where energies born of dissatisfaction are to be channeled into direct participation in the political process, the contrapuntal value of art would be minimal or even negative.

Propadeutic theories of art's political value also see art as a conservative force but a more positive one giving support to the political status quo. These theories suggest that the "arts are the paradigm source of understanding for most people as to what lawfulness and order really are" (Hein, 1976, p. 146). Although Americans might be able to understand the order and discipline inherent in their crafts or in many art works of the past, they are likely to consider examples of contemporary mainstream art as lawless exercises in disorder. This common perception is reinforced by those critics and historians who often analyze contemporary art in terms of its creative breaking of the rules and its risk-taking rejection of old orders. Indeed, it is unlikely that the great majority of democratic citizens can find propadeutic value in America's mainstream art.

Propulsive theories of art's political value view art as a liberating, revolutionary force in its propensity for idealistic opposition to the merely given. Like contrapuntal theories, propulsive theories see art as an expression of dissatisfaction with the existing order of things. However, propulsive theories suggest that art's expression of opposition provides a powerful paradigm for other challenges to existing forms, including the political. Art is seen as capable of sparking the revolutionary spirit in artist and viewer alike. "Neither an apologist for the status quo nor a house jester who provides relief from the pain and tedium of it," the artist is "a critic of the existing system and an architect of the future" (Hein, 1976, p. 148). For obvious reasons, great credence is given this view of art within the mainstream artworld. Aside from the fact that existing market systems have tended to co-opt the idealistic values of art by turning its expressions into commodities, the failure of contemporary art to engage the revolutionary imagination and energy of the greater populace has diminished art's propulsive value. If United States democracy were to perfect the political machinery by which its citizens could bring about better futures, it is not at all clear that such an ideal democracy would need the inspiration of art that breaks with old forms. In that event the greater need might be an art that provides reminders of the spirit that was needed to found a self-perfecting political arrangement.

Unconventional Ways of Thinking About the Relationship Between Art and Democracy

Familiar ways of thinking about the relationship between art and democracy suggest that, even under ideal circumstances, each has only marginal value for the other. Furthermore, discussions of this relationship which assess the value of one sphere in terms of its usefulness to the other produce only partial and distorted accounts of each sphere's nature and purpose (Hein, 1976). Individuals devoted to the sphere undergoing this type of assessment are likely to resist and resent such accountings. The unilateral evaluations of utility which typify our more familiar ways of thinking about the relationship between art and democracy fall far short of providing either the theoretical or practical bases for developing a mutually beneficial relationship between these two cultural spheres of activity. For this reason it might be worthwhile to explore less conventional ways of thinking about art, democracy, and their problematic relationship. Two possibilities suggest themselves in this regard. One is Hein's theory of aesthetic consciousness as the ground of political experience, and the other is the recent feminist critique of art and democracy.

Hilde Hein's Theory of Aesthetic Consciousness

In Hein's (1976) article "Aesthetic Consciousness: The Ground of Political Experience," she acknowledges that ethical and practical considerations will influence a culture's preference for this or that political order. Hein claims, however, that the need for and ability to envision and establish order itself stems from a preliminary or foundational aesthetic consciousness. Thus, theories that judge the value of art in terms of its contribution to the achievement of political goals fail to recognize "that such goals could not have been formed in the first place without a prior aesthetic consciousness" (p. 149). In this article, however, Hein considers only assessments of art's political value, but not the value politics might have for art. Perhaps for this reason she fails to address a major implication of her theory which is of relevance to this inquiry. If there is a foundational consciousness in which the human need for and ability to envision and establish order are initially situated, this same consciousness must underlie our artistic as well as our political traditions. Thus, an extension of Hein's theory invites us to contemplate the possibility of a single consciousness underlying both art and democracy in which we may discover a key to understanding their problematic relationship.

Masculine Bias in Art and Democracy

If art and politics share a foundational aesthetic consciousness, we should be able to discover certain similarities between them which are rooted in this consciousness. As noted earlier, women have been excluded from equal participation in the mainstream traditions of both Western art and democracy. On its face, this condition seems but an accurate reflection of prejudices and customs prevailing in the larger society. A deeper significance attaches to the historical exclusivity of art and democracy when we realize that, from their beginnings, their mainstream traditions have been dominated by and shaped primarily to meet the needs and interests of males. Whether or not one "approves" of the results, these traditions were established and developed by men who rarely questioned the exclusion of women from these spheres of activity. The artistic and political hegemony of males is eroding, but there remains the probability that historical patterns of male dominance have left behind a residue of masculine bias in the generic values and practices of art and democracy. How male dominance results in masculine bias has been the subject of numerous recent inquiries (Gilligan, 1982; Maher & Rathbone, 1986; Martin, 1985; Shakeshaft & Nowell, 1984; Spender, 1981). As a potentially significant similarity between art and democracy, this bias invites further investigation.

MASCULINE BIAS. Before we can examine art and democracy for evidence of residual masculine bias, we need to know what masculine bias is and what it is not. According to Martin (1985), sexism can take at least three forms: the exclusion of women, the stereotyping of women and men, and the devaluation of "characteristics the society considers feminine" (p. 3).

Male bias as distinguished from masculine bias might explain the exclusion of women from participation and recognition, and sexual stereotyping might explain the presumption that women have no contribution to make to mainstream art and democracy. Masculine bias, however, involves the devaluation of feminine-identified characteristics and the preference for that constellation of behaviors and values referred to by the term "masculine." In the absence of male bias and sexual stereotyping, masculine bias would reveal itself as a distinct preference for individuals, *male or female*, who exemplify masculine values. Divested of its association with the male, the term "masculine" would seem somewhat a misnomer for those attitudes and behaviors it purports to describe. Nevertheless, by means of this theoretical divestment we are able to understand the possible effects of masculine bias on the mainstream traditions of Western art and democracy.

According to Simone de Beauvoir in her exhaustive study of women in Western culture, *The Second Sex* (1949/1961), the complementary sets of attitudes, behaviors, and values we call masculine and feminine do not lose their human significance when dissociated from the male and the female. Far from being fanciful collections of unrelated adjectives, our notions of masculinity and femininity derive their basic coherence from two distinct and equally compelling ways we experience ourselves in the world. When we become conscious of ourselves as an "I," separate from yet capable of changing the world to achieve our freely chosen ends, we experience our transcendence. On the other hand, when we become conscious of ourselves as a "me," a small part of a larger world whose safety and value depend on our ability to accommodate interests beyond our own, we experience our immanence. We are more likely to experience transcendence when engaged in self-directed, competitive activities which enhance our sense of autonomy, individuality, and power. We are most likely to experience immanence when we engage in responsive, cooperative activities which enhance our sense of interdependence, similarity, and empathy. Although all human beings are capable of experiencing transcendence as well as immanence, in Western culture the behaviors, attitudes, and values growing out of transcendence have been called "masculine" and those stemming from immanence are called "feminine." From the experience of transcendence we learn the "masculine" values of independence, initiative, assertiveness, and responsibility to one's self (Tolson, 1977). From the experience of immanence, we learn the "feminine" values of connectedness, nurturance, identification, and responsibility to others (Gilligan, 1982). In effect, masculine bias is a preference for the values associated with transcendence and, in cases of extreme bias, a repudiation of the values associated with immanence.

If masculine bias exists in the theory and practice of art and democracy, we should expect to find central values in each that put a premium on the independence and power of individuals who are capable of acting on the world for the purpose of achieving their freely chosen ends and who stand ready to take credit for the results of self-initiated and self-directed activity. And, in fact, such values are central to the mainstream traditions of both democracy and art in the West.

MASCULINE BIAS IN ART. Since the Renaissance, the mainstream tradition of Western art has tended to define itself and measure its achievements in terms of the artist's ability to transcend the givens of this world, including those of art itself (Collins, 1977). Great value is placed on the invention of new forms, the break from established styles, the expression of individuality, and the transformation or redirection of the mainstream tradition itself by means of these inventions, breaks, and expressions. The preferred art media, subject matter, periods, movements, and artist-heroes of the mainstream are those that invite or exemplify the possibility of such transcendent effort and purpose.

In contrast, art traditions biased toward the feminine-identified values of immanence put a premium on the cooperation and skill of those who are capable of recognizing and serving the preestablished or emerging interests of the world, including those of art itself, and who can share a common pride in their small contributions to these essentially responsive and anonymous activities. The popular, commercial, folk, applied, and "hiddenstream" of women's art (Collins & Sandell, 1984) are examples of such traditions. They place great value on the reproduction of useful and decorative forms, the perfection of established styles, the disciplines of craft, and the continuation of their art tradition by means of these reproductions, perfections, and disciplines.

Obviously there are overlaps between mainstream and nonmainstream art. Works in the mainstream will reveal and be appreciated for their excellent crafting; a piece of craftwork, on the other hand, might be admired for its inventiveness. On the whole, however, our schools, museums, art critics, historians, and artists make a distinction between fine and applied art and give us to understand that art based primarily on the pursuit of transcendence has more permanent human value, is more culturally prestigious, is of a higher order, and, in fact, is more worthy of the honorific title "art" than is that based on the alternative values of immanence.

MASCULINE BIAS IN DEMOCRACY. If the mainstream of Western democracy shares a similar bias toward the masculine, we should expect it also to manifest a preference for behaviors, attitudes, and values associated with transcendence. As generally defined, democracy is a theory or form of government in which the people control the state and share equally in the duties and privileges of direct or indirect self-rule. In itself this definition does not suggest an overriding concern with the values of transcendence. When we examine our liberal assumptions about the purposes and value of this form of government, however, we find that experiencing, pursuing, and expressing transcendence is central to democratic purpose and value. For example, the notion that democracy is "a way of safeguarding and reconciling individual and group interests" (Benn, 1967, p. 340) implies that individuals and groups have their own separate interests, that the free pursuit of these interests should be safeguarded, that these interests will inevitably come into conflict from time to time, and that we need a lawful and orderly way of reconciling disparities between them. The image of each individual or group within the larger society pursuing his, her, or its own interests speaks quite clearly to the business of transcendence. Self-determination, freedom to pursue one's freely chosen ends short of impinging upon another's right to do the same (Levine, 1981), and enlightened self-interest are notions associated with democracy that reveal a preoccupation with the values of transcendence. The bias toward the masculine-identified values of transcendence is not found in the principle of equal citizenship, but in the assumption that citizens are "independent, autonomous units" (Okin, 1979, p. 182) and that democracy is a political arrangement between these units which allows for the maximum transcendence of each. According to Parenti (1980, p. 38), "Americans continue to think of themselves as self-reliant individualists. What they seem to be referring to is the privatism and atomization of their social relations and the relative absence of cooperative endeavor."

In contrast to the emphasis on transcendent values in mainstream American democracy are those recurring theories and practices in democratic living which place greater stress on the values and behaviors associated with immanence. Rarely devised for large "faceless" numbers of people, nonmainstream democratic communities such as the Quakers, the Israeli kibbutzim, the New Harmony, Indiana, experiment, as well as the communes and support groups that sprang up during the activist 1960s and 1970s are examples that come to mind. In varying degree, all provide a contrast to mainstream democracy in that they emphasize cooperation, accommodation, sharing, humble service, and dedication to the needs and interests of others and to the larger group.

Obviously there are overlaps between main and nonmainstream democratic traditions. Citizens in either tradition might reveal and be praised for virtues more typically associated with the other. For example, Parenti

(1980) points out that "the lack of community does not prevent Americans from identifying with larger collective entities, such as a school, a town or nation. But," he observes, "even this identification is expressed in terms that are competitive with other schools, towns or nations" (pp. 39–40). Similarly, an individual in a commune might be admired for her initiative, not perhaps for its own sake but rather because it was able to contribute to the welfare of others. On the whole, our schools, civic celebrations, historians, and politicians distinguish between mainstream democracy and "utopian" experiments in democracy and give us to understand that democracy based primarily on the pursuit of transcendence has more permanent human value, is more culturally respectable, is of a more practical order, and, in fact, is more worthy of the honorific title "democracy" than is that based on the alternative values of immanence.

MASCULINE BIAS IN HEIN'S THEORY OF AESTHETIC CONSCIOUSNESS. If a similar bias toward masculine-identified values of transcendence exists in both mainstream art and democracy, Hein's (1976) assertion of a foundational consciousness that they share suggests that this bias is not a superficial one. According to Hein, this consciousness arises from our initial awareness "of self as distinct from and yet as causally interactive with the world outside ourselves" (p. 150). Because it determines and perfects itself through the discovery, creation, and imposition of order in the world and our relationship to it, its concerns are, in the most elemental sense, aesthetic. In tracing out the nature and significance of this consciousness, Hein unhesitatingly casts the self as actor, the world as that which is acted upon, and the interactions between them as optimally involving transformations of the world brought about by chosen interventions. Thus, along with the ability to pose and solve what are essentially aesthetic problems, this consciousness includes and enhances our sense of separateness, agentry, choice, and responsibility. In short, the consciousness described by Hein is clearly one of transcendence.

If an aesthetic consciousness provides a common foundation for mainstream art and democracy, it is in all probability the one Hein describes. We must question, however, the implication that this particular consciousness is the only possible one to be derived from our preliminary awarenesses of self, world, and the interactions between them, for there is an equally valid alternative consciousness: the consciousness of immanence. Although she does not acknowledge its foundational status, in a later article (Hein, 1978) she refers in passing to this alternative consciousness when she addresses ecological concerns. Running counter to the "fundamental doctrine of the domination of [humanity] over nature" she finds an "emerging compensatory consciousness that [humankind] also has obligations . . . to promote and care for the well-being of the non-human world" (p. 170). If an unbridled bias toward transcendence has had a negative impact on the physical environment, what side effects has it had on art and democracy and the relationship between them?

The Impact of Masculine Bias on the Relationship Between Art and Democracy

Art history suggests that, prior to the democratic revolutions and the rise of the middle classes, European mainstream artists placed high artistic value on transcendence. Art nevertheless retained a balance of immanent and transcendent concern by virtue of its service to the utilitarian needs and interests of a succession of powerful patrons—the church, the court, and the upper classes. When political and economic power shifted to the people, however, mainstream art failed, as de Tocqueville (1835/1900) warned, to secure the support of the democratic majority who did not share the cultivated tastes and surplus funds associated with previous mainstream patronage. As it entered the democratic era, then, mainstream art was "freed" for a more exclusive pursuit of transcendence. In his book, *Theories of Modern Art*, Herschel B. Chipp (1968) quotes Mark Rothko as putting it this way:

> The unfriendliness of society to his activity is difficult for the artist to accept. Yet this very hostility can act as a lever for true liberation. Freed from a false sense of security and community, the artist can abandon his plastic bank-book, just as he has abandoned other forms of security. Both the sense of community and of security depend on the familiar. Freed of them, transcendental experiences become possible. (p. 548)

As transcendence became a preoccupation of mainstream art, it became more esoteric (Toynbee, 1970) and detached itself further from the needs and interests of its new, potentially more numerous, if individually less powerful, patrons. Indeed, according to Gablik (1984),

> modernism so embraced notions of freedom and autonomy—and of art needing to answer to its own logic, its own laws, the pure aesthetic without a function—that we now have whole generations of artists who doubt that it was ever meant to be organically integrated with society in the first place." (p. 119)[2]

---

2. It should be noted that, throughout her text, Gablik (1984) uses a concept of transcendence which is at variance with the definition of this term put forth by de Beauvoir (1949/1961) and accepted by the author of this chapter.

While we cannot fully agree with Ortega Y Gasset (1968) that the main-stream tradition of modern art "will always have the masses against it" because it is essentially "antipopular" (p. 5), its increased bias toward transcendence can be understood as a cause as well as a result of its profound unpopularity. It is tempting to conclude that the problem between art and democracy might be resolved if only we could educate the majority of citizens to appreciate mainstream art on its own terms. A similar bias toward the masculine-identified values of transcendence exists in main-stream democracy, however, and before drawing such a conclusion we need to attend to its particular ramifications.

Democracy takes as its central purpose the protection and regulation of separate individuals and groups pursuing their own transcendence in the public realm (Okin, 1979). With regard to the values of immanence, however, mainstream democracy has taken an entirely different stance (Reardon, 1985). Liberal democratic theory and its conservative practice have relegated the needs, interests, and behaviors associated with our human experience of immanence to a separate sphere. If the appropriate arena of transcendence has been the public, political sphere, until recently the province of men, the appropriate arena for immanence has been the private, apolitical sphere, until recently the province of women (Okin, 1979). A major part of our democratic heritage suggests that we are expected to make private arrangements for our immanent concerns (Martin, 1985; Okin, 1979). If we fail to establish these arrangements for fulfilling our immanent needs, only reluctantly are they admitted as public, political concerns in our democracy. While the right to produce or use art in pursuit of one's own transcendence is held to be a legitimate matter of public and political concern in our mainstream democracy, the complementary right to appreciate art for art's own sake is not.

Art appreciation, as opposed to the analysis and evaluation of art that are thought to enhance that appreciation, is essentially a responsive activity. To appreciate a work of art for its own sake or on its own terms, we are required to assume a receptive, empathetic, caring attitude which is more characteristic of immanence than of transcendence. Our concern will be to relate to, rather than dominate over or use, the work of art before us. Although the work itself may be a supreme example of human transcendence and therefore capable of reminding us of our own transcendent desires and abilities, to appreciate it for its own sake we must set aside our transcendent interests. The responsive attitude characteristic of art appreciation involves the experience of immanence and, in our democracy, immanent concerns have been regarded as private rather than public political matters.

Even if we were capable, then, of providing the education necessary to equip the majority of people to appreciate art for its own sake, this same majority, in their capacity as democratic citizens, might not agree that art appreciation and education for it are proper political concerns. Schools supported by public funds are charged first with providing us with the tools we will need for competitive transcendent activity in the public sphere. Perhaps it is for this reason that art educators shy away from the notion of art appreciation, with its implied feminine-identified values of immanence, and have preferred to discuss the education of the nonartist in terms of models of transcendent activity such as those provided by art historians, art critics, and aestheticians (Lanier, 1985). Until the majority of democratic citizens and their representatives are convinced that immanent concerns have both public and political import, educating citizens to appreciate art for its own sake will remain a luxurious, somewhat frivolous goal for democratic education.

An apt illustration of what happens when artists and politicians meet to assert the transcendent interests of mainstream art and democracy appeared recently in a Long Island newspaper, *The East Hampton Star*:

> Art for art's sake is an adage with apparently little currency as far as the Village Board goes. The trustees were mum when William King, a well-known sculptor, turned up for his third Board meeting to plead for a chance to put art on display at Baiting Hollow Road and the Montauk Highway. Mr. King, an officer with the Jimmy Ernst Artists Alliance, suggested . . . that "Gloria," a sculpture made from two elm trees by David Slivka of Springs, be put on view for a six-month trial period, after which another piece would be put up with the Board's okay. . . . He was told by the Mayor that the answer was "no." (Gifford, 1986, p. 4)

As quoted in the same article, the artist's response to this summary refusal was as follows:

> "I'm here to say that we're very unhappy with the decision—such as it was. This is a major work by a major artist. You could consider it an experiment." There was no comment from the Board. "I think it would be to your credit and renown to give this a try. Nobody'll be hurt." There was no comment from the Board. Finally, in frustration, Mr. King cried out, "If you won't tell us why you're against it, will you tell us who's against it so we can replace you in the next election? . . . I think it's part of your job to nourish the part of the community that gets a kick out of sculpture and art." (p. 4)

As elected representatives pledged to protect the lawful public interests of the democratic majority, the Board explained its final denial of the artist's request by raising these questions: Who would be responsible for selecting the work? How could the success of such an experiment be judged after six months? And how would the possible unpopularity of the exhibit be handled? (Gifford, 1986). Had the Board been convinced of the transcendent value of such a project, one assumes it would have given conditional approval to the project and worked out these details later. Not being so convinced, however, these questions suggest the Board's primary concern was with the establishment and maintenance of the public's transcendence over the project with regard to initial and continuing control and that even these "bottom-line" concerns were unsatisfied.

Artists and politicians who view their jobs strictly in terms of transcendent values often find themselves at cross-purposes and their discussions taking the form of such no-win confrontations. Although cast in the role of supplicant, the artist in our example does not suggest that the art to be displayed will serve the community or its citizens in their public struggles for transcendence, but rather than a revolving experimental display will provide the occasion for immanent experience for that part of the community able to get a private "kick out of sculpture and art." Although given the opportunity to support the transcendent values of art, the Board does not ask how such a display may help the artist or serve the immanent needs of the town's citizens; rather, it raises questions related to the transcendent rights of the public with regard to selection, judgment, and the negative mandates of unpopularity.

The bias toward masculine-identified values of transcendence shared by our mainstream traditions of art and democracy is fundamental to the theory and practice of these traditions. Whether or not it has sprung from a foundational consciousness of transcendence as described by Hein (1976), this bias consistently reinforces and is reinforced by our preferences for transcendent over immanent values in art and democracy. As a result, each sphere finds itself in competition with the other as a specialized route to transcendence, and each must reject opportunities to serve or be used by the other in immanent fashion unless such service can be justified as a means for achieving its own transcendent goals. Given this state of affairs, any attempt to improve the relationship between art and democracy must take into consideration their shared bias toward the values of transcendence.

Conclusion

The bias toward masculine-identified values of transcendence in the foundational consciousness, theory, and practice of Western mainstream art and democracy has had many positive effects. It has produced progressive mainstream institutions which encourage individual initiative and accomplishment by providing models of how transcendent energies may be channeled into areas of culturally valued activity. Akin to racism and classism in its negative impact on Western cultural institutions, sexism continues to distort and impoverish the ideals and practices of mainstream art and democracy. Sexism expressed as male bias and sexual stereotyping has diminished women's participation and recognition in these mainstream traditions. As we begin to dissociate the bias toward masculineidentified values of transcendence from their historical ties to the person and prerogative of the male, we might expect an increase in the participation and recognition of women who subscribe to these values in mainstream art and democracy. If, however, we do not challenge the exclusive emphasis on transcendence in mainstream art and democracy, then the most we can hope for with regard to improving their relationship is a more vigorous exploitation of the marginal use-value each would seem to have for the other.

Those willing to settle for the freedom of producing great works of art that will not be appreciated by the majority of people and those content to exercise their democratic freedoms while remaining perplexed by the best art their culture has been able to produce might ignore or even take some perverse pleasure in the gap in appreciation that yawns between mainstream art and democracy. If the gap itself is a measure of how successful art and democracy have each been as transcendent pursuits, it can only be bridged by a new, equal, and unprecedented concern for the values of immanence in each of these spheres. Art educators will demonstrate such concern when they insist that learning to appreciate art for its own sake and learning to produce art in response to the needs and interests of others have as much value as do the use and production of art for transcendent purposes and are equally matters of valid public political concern. In assuming such an undertaking, we might remember that

> freedom and transcendence are the favored terms of the person who wants to be individuated, to stand apart from the crowd. They are heady words, but they need to be completed by others like responsibility and immanence, the language of identification, the discourse of the person who realizes that doing it alone, however grand, is not nearly as grand as doing it with others. (Tong, 1986, p. 3)

References

Arts, Education and Americans Panel. (1977). *Coming to our senses: The significance of the arts for American education.* New York: McGraw-Hill.

Benn, S. I. (1967). Democracy. In P. Edwards (Ed.), *The encyclopedia of philosophy* (Vol. 2, pp. 338–341). New York: Macmillan.

Chipp, H. B. (Ed.). (1968). *Theories of modern art—A source book by artists and critics*. Berkeley: University of California Press.

Collins, G. C. (1977). Considering an androgynous model for art education. *Studies in Art Education, 18*(2), 54–62.

Collins, G. C., & Sandell, R. (1984). *Women, art, and education*. Reston, VA: NAEA.

de Beauvoir, S. (1961). *The second sex* (H. M. Parshley, Ed. and Trans.). New York: Bantam Books. (Original work published 1949)

de Tocqueville, A. (1900). *Democracy in America* (Vol. 2, rev. ed.) (H. Reeve, Trans.). New York: The Colonial Press. (Original work published 1835)

Efland, A. (1976). The school art style: A functional analysis. *Studies in Art Education, 17*(2), 17–43.

Gablik, S. (1984). *Has modernism failed?* New York: Thames & Hudson.

Gifford, M. E. (1986, August 7). Snag in Gardiner project. *The East Hampton Star*, pp. 4, 26.

Gilligan, C. (1982). *In a different voice*. Cambridge, MA: Harvard University Press.

Hein, H. (1976). Aesthetic consciousness: The ground of political experience. *The Journal of Aesthetics and Art Criticism, 35*(2), 143–152.

Hein, H. (1978). Aesthetic rights: Vindication and vilification. *The Journal of Aesthetics and Art Criticism, 37*(2), 169–176.

Lanier, V. (1985). Discipline-based art education: Three issues. *Studies in Art Education, 26*(4), 253–256.

Levine, A. (1981). *Liberal democracy—A critique of its theory*. New York: Columbia University Press.

Maher, F. A., & Rathbone, C. H. (1986, February). Teacher education and feminist theory: Some implications for practice. *American Journal of Education, 94*, 214–235.

Martin, J. R. (1985). *Reclaiming a conversation—The ideal of the educated woman*. New Haven: Yale University Press.

Okin, S. M. (1979). *Women in western political thought*. Princeton, NJ: Princeton University Press.

Ortega Y Gasset, J. (1968). *The dehumanization of art and other essays on art, culture, and literature* (H. Weyl, Trans.). Princeton, NJ: Princeton University Press. (Original work published 1925)

Parenti, M. (1980). *Democracy for the few* (3rd ed.). New York: St. Martin's Press.

Reardon, B. A. (1985). *Sexism and the war system*. New York: Teacher's College Press.

Shakeshaft, C., & Nowell, I. (1984). Research on theories, concepts, and models of organizational behavior: The influence of gender. *Issues in Education, 2*(3), 186–203.

Smith, R. A. (1985). A right to the best: Or, once more, elitism versus populism in art education. *Studies in Art Education, 26*(3), 169–175.

Smith, R. A. (1986). *Excellence in art education—Ideas and initiatives*. Reston, VA: NAEA.

Spender, D. (1981). Education: The patriarchal paradigm and the response to feminism. In D. Spender (Ed.), *Men's studies modified—The impact of feminism on the academic disciplines* (pp. 155–173). New York: Pergamon.

Tolson, A. (1977). *The limits of masculinity.* New York: Harper & Row.

Tong, R. (1986, January). Liberty, equality—community? [Review of *Gender justice*]. *The Women's Review of Books,* pp. 1, 3.

Toynbee, A. J. (1970). Art: communicative or esoteric? In Solomon R. Guggenheim Foundation, *On the future of art* (pp. 3–19). New York: Viking Press.

Villemain, F. T. (1966). Democracy, education, and art. In E. W. Eisner & D. W. Ecker (Eds.), *Readings in art education* (pp. 407–419). Waltham, MA: Blaisdell. (Original work published 1964)

PART II

Public Dialogue on Art

DEMOCRACY IS REALIZED THROUGH the active participation of all citizens in sensitive, reasoned decisions which influence the well-being of the individual and her or his community. Integral to this participation is the act of public dialogue. Because society is comprised of people with varying lifestyles, world views, and values, it is likely that this dialogue will be passionate and intense as multiple arguments for and against a proposal are expressed.

John Stuart Mill (1859/1966; see Selected Bibliography), in the nineteenth century, recognized and affirmed the inherent fallibility of women and men. His response to this ability to err was to emphasize the need for an expressed diversity of public opinion and to warn of the dangers of adopting singularly valued positions. Present-day philosophers like Paul Feyerabend (1982; see Selected Bibliography) reiterate Mill's caution and advocate that all citizens have the opportunity to debate community and personal interests. Many believe that this public debate should take place even if the results of the debate jeopardize the outcome of the final resolution.

We believe that the warnings of Mill, Feyerabend, and others have been largely ignored in the study and appreciation of art, as well as in the economic and political systems that exist in the established bureaucratic artworld. Instead, the ability to err in artistic judgment has been counteracted in the established artworld through the misguided notion that specialists in art can insure infallibility. These art specialists have been granted this authority by their occupational and social positions; through advanced formal education in art criticism, aesthetics, and art history; or because of their political or economic influence within the community. We believe that the consequence of placing public discourse exclusively in the control of specialists is discourse that is rigid, institutional, and undemocratic in its form and content.

The following chapters address this issue of public dialogue on art. Several approaches are advocated and delineated, including the aesthetic-expressive, the historical, and the technological. Each of the authors suggests strategies by which her or his recommendation can be implemented.

Chapter 4

Art, Social Action, and the Preparation of Democratic Citizens

___Doug Blandy_____

Citizens living in a democratic community have the responsibility of making judicious decisions on moral, ethical, artistic, and practical issues that affect the common good. Voting in national or regional elections is only one way in which citizens participate in a democracy. Other participatory activities include holding opinions as members of institutions such as schools, businesses, and cultural centers. Decisions will also be made on a personal level as family members, friends, casual acquaintances, and strangers are encountered. Integral to the decision-making process is public dialogue in the form of discussion, argumentation, and conflict resolution.

The presence or absence of public dialogue will define the success or failure of a democracy. John Stuart Mill (1859/1966) underlined the importance of public dialogue to a democracy when he recognized that women and men are not infallible; "that their truths, for the most part, are only half-truths; that unity of opinion, unless resulting from the fullest and freest comparison of opposite opinions, is not desirable, and diversity not an evil, but a good, until [humankind] are much more capable than at present of recognizing all sides of the truth" (p. 73). Philosopher Paul Feyerabend (1978) supports Mill's perceptions of humankind in the present day when he argues for the necessity of public debate and the participation of all people in decision making. I concur with Feyeraband's

47

opinion that the need for this public debate is so great that it should occur even if it jeopardizes the ultimate success of the final decision.

Several approaches to public discourse are possible. Habermas (1983) identifies three interactive approaches that characterize discourse on the common good. These approaches are the cognitive, the moral-practical, and the aesthetic-expressive. The cognitive approach is exemplified in the empirical methods of science, the moral-practical in ethical theory. The aesthetic-expressive approach is primarily evidenced in the creations of artists who participate in public discourse through their art. The Art Workers' Coalition (AWC), Artists for Nuclear Disarmament (AND), the Political Art Documentation/Distribution group (PADD), and the Bread and Puppet Theatre are four visual artists' collectives that exemplify this approach in the fine-arts context. The 1985 Peace Ribbon Project was a grassroots example of aesthetic-expressive discourse independent of a specific art world. Organized by Justine Merritt, the Peace Ribbon Project involved thousands of women, children, and men in the successful effort of crafting a 13-mile pictorial ribbon exhibited in the streets of Washington, D.C., for the purpose of commemorating the fortieth anniversary of the nuclear attacks on Hiroshima and Nagasaki.

In Habermas's view (1983), the aesthetic-expressive, moral-practical, and cognitive approaches to public discourse are of equal value. It is his opinion that, in those situations where one approach continually takes precedence over the other two, the result is terrorism. Aestheticized politics, moral rigorism, or doctrinaire politics result from the imbalance.

A democratic community is nurtured by a mature and experienced citizenry prepared through active democratic participation to govern themselves. Democracy will continue in a community only as long as the mature members act personally and through social and cultural institutions to prepare children and youth to be competent members of the community. The ability of children and youth to participate in public dialogue and democratic decision making will require an experiential education in which cognitive approaches can interact with the moral-practical and the aesthetic-expressive. This will insure the continuation of the tradition. According to Habermas (McCarthy, 1981), experience with these approaches is at the heart of identification with the community and contributes to that aspect of ego development that encourages social action and moral consciousness.

There is a substantial body of research that attests to the political awareness of children and youth. A significant recent contribution to this record is *The Political Life of Children* (Coles, 1986), in which Coles chronicles his political conversations with children and youth over the past decade. This cross-cultural investigation clearly indicates that children and youth, worldwide, are astute in their understanding of the larger and smaller issues affecting their lives, the lives of other family members, their community, nation, and the world. Consequently it might seem reasonable to assume that American school teachers, along with parents and significant others, are participating in the experiential education of young people that prepares them to participate democratically. If this were true, teachers would be acting as responsive members of their community who are teaching others to be the same. Unfortunately this is not the current situation. Students are indicating that their teachers are failing in this task and not properly preparing them, for example, to participate in a modern world dominated by the complexities of nuclear politics (Macy, 1983).

There are exceptions. It is one of these exceptions that will spur our discussion in this chapter. This exceptional case exemplifies the contribution that aesthetic-expressive discourse can make to a democracy and one context of many in which such discourse can be effective. The type of environment that can nurture such discourse and some of the forces currently working against public debate and decision making are considered.

A Lima, Ohio, Demonstration

Lima is a small city of approximately 46,000 residents located in northwestern Ohio. A booming city in the early twentieth century, it now suffers the malaise of unemployment and economic hardship typical of many midwestern industrial communities. Lima residents have almost deserted the original business district and adjacent residential areas in favor of the surrounding suburbs. However, in recent years there has been a concentrated effort by the city government to revitalize the inner city through the building of a convention center and the refurbishment of existing buildings. The Lima Art Association, a publicly funded arts organization, assists in this effort by operating an art gallery in the mezzanine of a mid-city auditorium.

In 1985 the Lima Art Association sponsored a sculpture competition for the town square. A committee of leading Lima citizens and Art Association bureaucrats awarded $25,000 to Cincinnati, Ohio, sculptor Stuart Fink for the design and installation of a 12-foot high, fluted-columned, double-arched, cast concrete fantasy mounted on a two-tiered base. Fink calls this work "Trinity" and describes it as a representation of the Lima Community (M. Huffman, personal communication, September 21, 1986).

On May 31, 1985, at mid-day, students enrolled in Mike Huffman's Art II class at Lima Senior High School walked a seven-foot papier-maché milkshake, a three-foot hamburger, and several six-foot french fries through the streets of mid-city Lima to the town square where "Trinity" will be installed. The monumental fast food that they carried was marked with the logo of the Kewpee restaurant chain. The students and their teacher stayed several hours in the town square. During this time they discussed with interested passersby the Lima Art Association Sculpture Competition, "Trinity," and the students' alternative to the choice funded by the Association. These discussions were videotaped for later reference. A local art critic covered the event for the city's newspaper, and a subsequent article was published.

This public demonstration by Mike Huffman and his students was motivated by their dissatisfaction with the process and results of the sculpture competition. According to Huffman (personal communication, January 2, 1986), he and his students felt that it was ludicrous for the sculpture competition committee to commission a public sculpture, purportedly reflective of the Lima community, from an artist who would visit the city on only one or two occasions. One student spoke for all when he said, "Who does this guy think he is? He comes here for one day and tells us who we are, what we like, and what we are about!" Writing about the students' alternative, Huffman states, "Our 'Kewpee Piece' was a direct image from the community. Unlike the artist in question, we had a long-standing relationship with Lima. That relationship allowed us to focus on a single aspect common to almost everyone at every social and economic level in the community. We merely repeated expressively a beloved image as subject and theme for our public sculpture."

The action taken by Huffman and his students ended as it began. They walked their sculpture back to the high school. The readily apparent results of their action were not dramatic, although Huffman believes the temporary installation of his students' sculpture "spurred the Lima Art Association sponsors to attempt to include collaboration and participation in their public piece called 'Trinity.' The base will include concrete work, flat slabs of drawings by area school children" (personal communication, March 19, 1986).

The impact and importance of this instance of public action, however, should not be considered in terms of immediate results, but through the example and implications of its challenge to the Lima community. These Lima High School students and their teacher exemplify the means by which young people can be prepared to be competent members of a democratic community. The public debate that they initiated with the Lima Art Association and the citizenry on the square experientially reaffirms for them the importance of free public dialogue. These individuals exercised their rights as citizens to voice their concerns with public policy in an aesthetic-expressive manner, free of intimidation by the educational backgrounds, economic status, or social standing of those with whom they were in conflict. These activists trusted their ability to make their points known to the community and accepted the fact that this same community would pass judgment on the merits of their argument.

A Challenge to Specialization

The conduct of Mike Huffman and his collaborators is commendable for the challenge that it presents to all of the citizens of Lima. Despite the fact that the history of democratic ideas supports public debate, social critics are currently suggesting that this principle is severely threatened or has been eliminated by economic, educational, cultural, sexual, and political prejudices (Gans, 1977; Mann, 1977; Truitt, 1977). It appears that John Stuart Mill's warning on the fallibility of the singular opinions of men and women is no longer being heeded. Fortunately, there are some individuals, like those from the Lima Senior High School, who repudiate this current situation by periodically reaffirming that public dialogue does exist as a responsibility of the ordinary citizen. This reaffirmation of public debate reacts to the current trend in which decision making by citizens is discouraged and replaced by decision making by specialists in narrow fields of endeavor. In the case of the Lima sculpture competition, decisions were made by art specialists schooled in a fine-art or high-art tradition as interpreted and reinforced by Art Association bureaucrats. On this situation in Lima, Mike Huffman states that

> the open question of what is public art is what we wrestled with and continue to discuss. Of course, what always seemed to amaze my students and nearly incites to riot individual groups was the fact that there are those art managerial types in the community who not only know exactly what public art is, but what it looks like and where it shall go. (Personal communication, January 7, 1986)

Wendell Berry (1977) describes specialization of the type evidenced in the Lima sculpture competition as the "disease of the modern character" (p. 19). Symptomatic of this disease is the willingness of ordinary citizens to relinquish their personal responsibility to govern, understand law, maintain health, engineer, educate, and define a personal aesthetic. Citizens have relinquished these rights to specialists who are trained in very specialized fields and who make decisions for others based upon a narrow perspective.

The extent to which citizens have done this is so great that the National Art Education Association (NAEA) can go on record as stating that the purpose of education is not to prepare citizens to make geopolitical decisions, record history, or make important artistic decisions. The NAEA sees such decision making as being in the realm of the "professional." These endeavors, once open to public debate, are now recognized as the tasks of specialists. The NAEA uses this rationale to support an approach to art education that negates students' ability to make and respond to art in favor of students' accepting, understanding, and modeling their responses to conform to the methodologies and judgments of aestheticians, critics, and art educators (NAEA, 1986). The NAEA approach to art education implies that aesthetic discourse is now the specialization of the art expert. Consequently, the ordinary citizen can no longer recognize art without the expert's assistance. Ultimately art is validated by these art specialists or their appointees.

The consequences of this state of specialization are dire. Berry (1977) recognizes the citizenry of America as fragmented by their singular competencies and multiple incompetencies. Citizens are confined to narrow realms of influence and have virtually no voice or ability to make known their opinions in the vast majority of decisions that affect their lives. This incompetence includes the selection of objects chosen for their aesthetic contemplation, as in the Lima example. The Lima Art Association assumed that the citizens of Lima were largely willing to accept that they could not perceive, contemplate, and appreciate the aesthetic in objects or in their day-to-day activities. Berry (1983) does not recognize democracy in this state, but sees totalitarianism in its singularity and fragmentation. It is because of circumstances like those witnessed in Lima, that Habermas (cited in Bottomore, 1984) can decry the influence of technical experts and call for the readdressing of social policy in public debate.

Educational systems contribute to cultural alienation and fragmentation. It is primarily school systems that are responsible for the perpetualization of specialization, through their curricula. A recent study of American life entitled *Habits of the Heart* (Bellah, Madsen, Sullivan, Swidler, & Tipton, 1985) reveals that educators are failing to teach individuals to recognize and actualize a place for themselves in the community. This same study found, however, that educators are succeeding at communicating specialized information and technical skills. An erosion of personal meaning and coherence typifies the findings.

The problem of social fragmentation, described by Berry (1977) and corroborated by Bellah et al. (1985), has been gestating in America since its discovery by white men bringing an industrial economy from the western fringes of Europe (Berry, 1977). Walt Whitman, in the latter part of the nineteenth century, recognized social fragmentation in his own time and optimistically proposed that societal cohesiveness could be regained through art. In his view the artist is the one person who can process and create images that transcend the individual and speak to all (cited in Hyde, 1983).

Art is not the panacea for social fragmentation. Habermas (1983) argues persuasively that singular approaches are terroristic. Consequently, in order for art to achieve Whitman's purposes it must be paired with social purpose and connectedness. This is what Huffman and his students achieved in Lima. The way in which they did this is worthy of investigation.

A Space for Public Dialogue

Evidence suggests that public debate like that initiated by Huffman and the art students in Lima is becoming increasingly rare as specialization continues to dominate the public decision-making process. Consequently, the success of Huffman and his students in their role of social activists is curious. The reasons for their success are worthy of investigation and illumination.

Boyte and Evans (1986) identify the source of democratic change as volunteerism that is not tied to, or motivated by, transitory governmental goals and objectives. They see volunteerism exemplified in egalitarian and participatory collectives connected to churches, labor unions, PTAs, and cooperatives. It is the opinion of Boyte and Evans that these voluntary associations are intimately linked to a person's life in the community by creating and reinforcing the opportunity for extended relationships beyond family and friends. These voluntary associations exist in a space between private life and larger societal institutions. This space is called a free space.

Dissident viewpoints that make for social change are sheltered in free spaces. Boyte and Evans (1986) speculate that several factors contribute to this. First, free spaces offer an independent reality and existence which are distinct from the personal and the larger impersonal realities and existences. Second, they provide a forum for public debate, conflict, opinion airing, and problem solving. Third, free spaces prepare the ordinary citizen for making social change and appreciating democratic values.

Public school systems and the individual school units within them are typically not the sites for free spaces. Their size, compulsory attendance policies, dependence on a fickle constituency for funding, and consequential administrative fear of raising the public wrath contribute to nonfreedom. However, it does seem possible that very small units within a school system can operate periodically as free spaces if given modest administrative support through active encouragement or through passive or active administrative ignorance of classroom activities.

In my opinion Huffman and his collaborators were able to create a free space within a public high school by confronting an aesthetic intrusion that was having direct, visible, and public ramifications on the Lima community. Because both he and many of his students were residents of the inner city in which the sculpture was to be placed, their investment in thwarting this intrusion by the Art Association was significant. The art classroom became a forum for the airing of personal feelings of indignation and outrage.

My conversations with Mike Huffman prior to the spring public demonstration indicate that the free space that materialized in the art classroom was created from a spontaneous, unanimous, and synchronous reaction that he and his students had to his presentation of the Town Square Sculpture Competition. The initial presentation was made as a part of a general ongoing discussion of current events related to art and aesthetics. The art curriculum used by the Lima city schools, and to which Huffman reluctantly and guardedly referred, did not approach art as a vehicle for social action or democratic participation. Lima High School's art curriculum treated the visual arts as a discipline for which there was a discrete and specialized body of knowledge to be learned. Studio technique was emphasized. Art history referred to the history of the so-called fine arts and was primarily used to support studio activity. Aesthetics and art criticism played a similar role.

The intensity of the students' reaction to the sculpture competition, however, succeeded in superseding this discipline-based approach to art and replaced it with a public forum for the treatment of a social issue affecting the common good. Within the resulting free space, Huffman and his students began to see public institutions and government as not representing final solutions, but as servants of public interests. In the case of the sculpture competition, government and public institutions were viewed by the students as failing to represent those interests in a way appropriate to a democracy.

Inquiry for Public Debate and Social Action

The dissident opinions of Huffman and his students were sheltered within the free space spontaneously created within a public high school art class. Within this sheltered environment their viewpoints could ripen, action plans could be developed, and solutions realized. An aesthetic-expressive approach to the problem was taken, and the monumental fast food erected by the students in the Lima town square reflected this choice. However, it is clear that cognitive and moral-practical approaches were also initiated as the students analyzed the sculpture competition in terms of its incongruency with democratic values and the potential effect of this aesthetic intrusion on the common good.

It is readily apparent that Huffman and his students based their public dialogue with the Lima Art Association on their personal inquiry into the workings of the sculpture competition. They conducted their research as ordinary citizens and developed a plan of action without the assistance of specialists in social activism. Although they worked in isolation, they used their intuition to develop a method of inquiry appropriate to their know-how and needs. Their chosen methodology was also philosophically congruent with the outcomes they desired.

Habermas (1972) proposes three forms of inquiry. Two of these forms are associated with technical and practical knowledge obtained through empirical-analytic and historical-hermeneutic methodologies. The third form is associated with a critical-emancipatory orientation. Habermas argues that it is through this third critical form of inquiry that people can discover ideologies that have become reified and are in need of transformation. Davis (1980) equates Habermas's interpretation of reification with unanalyzed power relationships of dependence and oppression. Habermas (1972) proposes self-reflection as the methodological framework through which the transformation of these relationships becomes possible. His choice of a methodological model is Freudian psychoanalysis because of its encouragement of autonomy and responsibility.

Writing elsewhere, Habermas (1983) establishes a relationship between aesthetic-expressive approaches and discourse on the common good for the purpose of social transformation. The making and contemplation of art are, among other possibilities, self-reflective activities. The joining of art making, contemplation, and psychoanalysis in the therapeutic milieu is evidence of the ability of art to act as a tool for self-reflection. Habermas implies that there is a close relationship among art, self-reflection, and aesthetic-expressive discourse in his citation of poet-playwright Peter Weiss's work with workers attending an evening high school in 1937 in Germany. Weiss's efforts were directed toward aiding his students in reappropriating European art in a way that was considerate of their own culture. Habermas argues that these workers were able to subvert the culture of the art specialist and celebrate the viewpoints of the "everyday expert." For Habermas, the ordinary citizen approaches art in a way that includes the history and problems of everyday life. The aesthetic is linked to personal opinions about goodness and truth as exemplified in personal actions that are autonomous and responsible.

Huffman, like Weiss, helped his students to reach a new understanding of their community and the personal and collective power that they could wield within it. In making this process public, they also took on the responsibility of informing other Lima citizens of the results of their inquiry into the Town Square Sculpture Competition.

The results of this particular inquiry were significant. Huffman's students discovered the effects of specialization on art and the ramifications of that specialization on a community. They worked for the transformation of this system by bringing it to the attention of the Lima community and creating a public forum for its debate in their classroom and in the town square. In doing this, they also directed attention to the power relationships existing within the community and presented a view of government and public institutions that challenged their omnipotence by reminding the community of these institutions' public service role. Huffman, like Weiss, facilitated a reappropriation of art by the ordinary citizen. The antidemocratic specialization of art as promoted by the Lima Art Association was temporarily subverted and suspended by a public demonstration that linked the aesthetic with personal and collective opinions regarding what is good and what represents truth. Ultimately, democratic values were reaffirmed in a way that prepared these students for participating in public debate and working for social change within the community.

Conclusion

Decision making by specialists on behalf of the common good is antidemocratic. Specialization is failing in virtually all arenas. The natural environment is in a ruinous or near-ruinous condition. Political specialists have brought the earth to the brink of a nuclear holocaust and the extinction of humankind. Specialists in economics have placed nearly all of the wealth of the United States and many other countries in the control of a very small percentage of the population. If there is a solution to this current state of affairs, it is in the reaffirmation of decision making by ordinary citizens engaged in public discourse and committed to passing that tradition on to others who are younger and less experienced.

Discourse that is aesthetic-expressive in approach and has a critical-emancipatory orientation does contribute to public dialogue in a democracy. As such, children and youth must be prepared to be competent users of aesthetic-expressive approaches and critical-emancipatory modes of inquiry. This preparation is crucial because it is tantamount to the perpetuation of the democratic tradition. Huffman's teaching is an example of one way in which this preparation can take place within a public school setting.

References

Bellah, R. N., Madsen, R., Sullivan, W. M., Swidler, A., & Tipton, S. M. (1985). *Habits of the heart.* Berkeley, CA: University of California Press.

Berry, W. (1977). *The unsettling of America: Culture and agriculture.* San Francisco: Sierra Club Books.

Berry, W. (1983). *Standing by words.* San Francisco, CA: North Point Press.

Bottomore, T. (1984). *The Frankfurt school.* Chichester, England: Ellis Horwood Limited.

Boyte, H. C., & Evans, S. M. (1986). The sources of democratic change. *Tikkun, 1*(1), 49–55.

Coles, R. (1986). *The political life of children.* Boston, MA: The Atlantic Monthly Press.

Davis, C. (1980). *Theology and political society.* London: Cambridge University Press.

Feyerabend, P. (1978). *Science in a free society.* London: Verso.

Gans, H. J. (1977). Democracy and the arts: Adversary or ally? In D. A. Mann (Ed.), *The arts in a democratic society* (pp. 98–117). Bowling Green, OH: Popular Press.

Habermas, J. (1972). *Knowledge and human interest.* (Jeremy J. Shapiro, Trans.). Boston, MA: Beacon Press.

Habermas, J. (1983). Modernity: An incomplete project. (S. Ben-Habib, Trans.). In H. Foster (Ed.), *The anti-aesthetic: Essays on postmodern culture* (pp. 3–15). Port Townsend, WA: Bay Press.

Hyde, L. (1983). *The gift.* New York: Vintage Books.

Macy, J. R. (1983). *Despair and personal power in the nuclear age.* Philadelphia, PA: New Society Publishers.

Mann, D. A. (1977). Introduction: The arts in a democratic society. In D. A. Mann (Ed.), *The arts in a democratic society* (pp. 3–17). Bowling Green, OH: Popular Press.

McCarthy, T. (1981). *The critical theory of Jurgen Habermas.* Cambridge, MA: MIT Press.

Mill, J. S. (1966). On liberty. In J. M. Robson (Ed.), *John Stuart Mill: A selection of his works.* Toronto: Macmillan of Canada. (Original work published 1859)

National Art Education Association. (1986). *Quality art education: Goals for schools.* Reston, VA: The National Art Education Association.

Truitt, W. H. (1977). Art for the people. In D. A. Mann (Ed.), *The arts in a democratic society* (pp. 58–69). Bowling Green, OH: Popular Press.

Chapter 5

Historical Participation: Toward an Understanding of the Historian in Art Education

Paul E. Bolin

The health of a democracy is measured by the degree of participation demonstrated by its citizenry. This axiom presents art educators with some interesting questions. Is historical research in art education flourishing, or is this avenue of inquiry seldom traveled? What does a lack of participation in historical research reveal about art educators' understanding of and concern for history, historical inquiry, and art education? This chapter will examine issues related to these questions and investigate various procedures undertaken by art educators who engage in historical research.

Understanding the Limits of History

I believe many art educators regard history as an incomplete jigsaw puzzle of incidents from the past. In this approach to historical analysis the historian's task is to locate missing pieces and help complete the puzzle and picture of earlier times. This notion that the entirety of the past can be pieced together demonstrates an unsound view of history and historical research. The past is comprised of innumerable complex and subtle relationships. It is impossible to understand and communicate the relative

58

importance of even a few thoughts and actions. For these reasons, historians must acknowledge that a definitive perception of the past is unobtainable. They then will be able to address directly their purpose—that of bringing meaning to selected material, drawn from a vast pool of past phenomena. Discussing the idea of using selected and limited knowledge about the past, noted historian Louis Gottschalk (1965) writes,

> And only a part of what was observed in the past was remembered by those who observed it; only a part of what was remembered was recorded; only a part of what was recorded has survived; only a part of what has survived has come to the historians' attention; only a part of what has come to their attention is credible; only a part of what is credible has been grasped; and only a part of what has been grasped can be expounded or narrated by the historian. (p. 45)

Thus, contextual limitations render it impossible for historians to reform a complete picture of the past. Recognizing the ambiguity of available information from the past constitutes an important and necessary part of historical investigation. Given this view of history and historical research, what is the role of historians in art education? What constitutes the purpose and methodology of their inquiry? The following section discusses some primary characteristics and features of historians in art education. The importance of democratic participation in historical investigation is examined in the concluding section of this chapter.

The Historian in Art Education

Anyone can be a "historian." This label, I believe, should apply not only to individuals who investigate some prominent theme from the past, but to those who derive meaning and value from any incident or artifact of the past. Historians engage in a twofold research process in which description *and* interpretation of prior phenomena are necessary functions. They are not limited to reporting accounts of names, dates, figures, and incidents from the past but are involved in interpretive inquiry into the significance of these necessary facts. According to Carr (1961), historians have "the dual task of discovering the few significant facts and turning them into facts of history, and of discarding the many insignificant facts as unhistorical" (p. 14). The individual interpretive nature of historical inquiry is borne out in the selectivity of significant historical facts. What is "discarded" by one historian as "insignificant" or "unhistorical" may be rightly regarded by another as central to his or her historical study.

Furthermore, facts dismissed as unimportant by a particular historian during one investigation may be the primary basis for a later historical analysis undertaken by the same researcher. The value found in information from the past is produced through the effort of individual historians who pursue answers to specific questions.

Interpretive historical research focuses on the examination of questions generated in the present and answered in light of the past. This interaction between the past and present allows for a more thorough understanding of important issues in both eras. Interpretation is the key ingredient in seeking to understand why an event happened and what significance it holds for the past and present. Historical interpretation is based on assembled facts; therefore, the availability and selectivity of pertinent facts affects an individual's interpretation of an event.

Historical events are so numerous and complex that they cannot all be recorded. For this reason it is the function of historians to select particular facts that address the issues they have identified as crucial to their chosen historical study. The selection of historical facts is described by Hamblen (1985), who uses Carr's insightful analogy of trolling for facts in a "vast and sometimes inaccessible ocean" (1961, p. 26). Carr compares historians to people fishing who, depending on chance, the casting location, and gear employed, usually hook the facts they set out to catch.

Moreover, when considering the selection of historical facts, it is fundamental to recognize that prior personal experiences, cultural background, and intended purpose for writing history also play a significant role in determining what events from the past are selected to be included or omitted by the historian. Munro (1963) describes various conditions that influence historians: Their task "is to select important events and trains of events. In this [they] must rely on standards of importance which are partly subjective, determined by the culture-pattern in which [they] live] and by [their] own personal attitudes" (p .9). Historians do not blindly choose to record events from the past. Cognizant of the numerous factors that influence which facts are selected for historical analysis, historians possess individual characteristics and purposes that affect their interpretation of history.

I believe art educators often view history as the professional march of events through time. Carr (1961) discusses this analogy quite succinctly and states that such a notion of history is acceptable as long as the historian is not perceived as "an eagle surveying the scene from a lonely crag or as a V.I.P. at the saluting base. . . . The historian is just another dim figure trudging along in another part of the procession" (p. 42). Historians should not be regarded as standing outside history, recording events from a location that is distinct and separate from the past; they are members of the historical parade, engaged in a mutual exchange with others in various parts of the procession. Not holding a commanding position over the cavalcade, historians view the proceedings from sites that allow select points of view. Carr addresses the unique perspective held by each historian: "The point in the procession at which [they find themselves] determines [their] angle of vision over the past" (p. 43). For this reason it is necessary to acknowledge the selective nature of historical research and the individuality of historical interpretation.

Historians are both elements of history and products of the past. Recognizing this, we do not undertake historical investigation in an attempt to identify and escape previous circumstances but to help individuals understand how prior occurrences in art education have led to its present condition. It is difficult to accept the notion that the purpose of historical research is to study "what is not now" or "to search out the lost" (Korzenik, 1986, p. 39). This point of view seems to promote the idea that historians reside outside history and undertake research that magnifies the distance between the past and present. It can be an interesting exercise to examine ways in which the past differs from the present, but such action does little to help art educators comprehend how earlier circumstances and events directly influence current conditions in art education. We must not lose sight of the fact that the present is directly predicated on the past.

As historians investigate the past, they should establish their specific interpretive positions. This does not mean that they pursue the past with myopic tunnel vision, desiring to "prove" a particular historical premise; rather, each must establish and maintain a stance that directs a course of interpretive thought. Unfortunately, this approach appears infrequently in the historiography of art education. Historians in art education too often assume they are impartially documenting the past. They perceive themselves as objective recorders and do not recognize the participatory interpretation of their historical analyses. These historians present information about the past; however, the material frequently lacks straightforward historical significance, which is produced by examining specific issues of importance to the present. Once these contemporary concerns are identified, historians can investigate the past for information that may help clarify these concerns, thus becoming the link between past and present, strengthening the relationship and bringing meaning and significance to each time period. History, then, is not seen as a regressive examination of an antiquated time period but instead is viewed as a vital investigation of the past which provides insight into present-day issues.

As historians use information from the past to answer questions and clarify contemporary issues, they are led to other historical questions. At no point in this circular exchange are historians detached recorders. Bowers (1974) writes to the heart of this issue: "Interpretation is *always* made from a frame of reference that reflects both the social and personal dimension of one's biography of experiences" (p. 29).

Democracy and Historians in Art Education

The lack of interest and inquiry in history exhibited by many art educators may be symptomatic of deeper ills in art education. The seemingly indifferent attitude of many art educators toward solid historical research demonstrates an unhealthy nonchalance concerning an in-depth understanding of the events that have shaped present circumstances in art education. Furthermore, I believe a naïve blindness is displayed by art educators when a limited number of individuals are permitted to interpret the field's past and establish the foundation and direction for the future of art education. With apparently little hesitation, the few historical accounts in art education are accepted as providing "the" record of past circumstances in this field. Failure to participate in historical inquiry does not emancipate art education but rather leaves us with little critical basis for future growth and development.

Those individual art educators who are investigating the past in order to understand current directions in their field are developing and democratizing art education. This action is doubly profitable: First, contemporary conditions are illuminated by the past and, second, art education is examined from various viewpoints, thus affording the opportunity for a broad perspective on past and current circumstances in art education and allowing a multidimensional examination of historical and contemporary issues. Relying on a few individuals to record "the" history of art education perpetuates the constricted belief that art education possesses a single history and that the historian's primary purpose is to uncover, sort, and piece together "the" picture of the past.

To avoid some of the problems brought about by this perceived historical deficiency, it is necessary for art educators to take on the responsibility of democratic participation in studying history. Art education would be benefited if present circumstances in the field were used as catalysts for generating and forming questions for historical study. It is also important that individuals not let prior beliefs concerning the past go unchallenged and not accept earlier research as presenting the full historical perceptive on any issue. Various examinations of a single topic help develop a more extensive historical view of the subject. Subsequent investigations may lend support for an earlier historical interpretation, or they may give additional directions for thought. Interaction stimulates further inquiry and generates other possible analyses. This interpretive approach to historical research produces a dynamic outlook on art education history. Individual interpretive participation by historians in art education is essential for the growth and vitality of historical study and for the healthy democratic development of art education.

References

Bowers, C. A. (1974). *Cultural literacy for freedom*. Eugene, OR: Elan.

Carr, E. H. (1961). *What is history?* New York: Random House.

Gottschalk, L. (1965). *Understanding history: A primer of historical method*. New York: Knopf.

Hamblen, K. A. (1985). An art education chronology: A process of selection and interpretation. *Studies in Art Education, 26*(2), 111–120.

Korzenik, D. (1986). Lost past: Historical research and a question of purpose. *Art Education, 39*(2), 37–40.

Munro, T. (1963). *Evolution in the arts and other theories of culture history*. Cleveland, OH: Cleveland Museum of Art.

Chapter 6

Toward Democratic Direction of Technology

___ Beverly J. Jones _____

In 1820, Thomas Jefferson wrote, "I know of no safe repository of the ultimate power of society but the people. And if we think them not enlightened enough, the remedy is not to take the power from them, but to inform them by education" (Ford, 1899, p. 161). Recent philosophical works emphasize the need for critical analysis of the form and content of the knowledge that is selected to comprise education and of how they relate to questions of power. This chapter utilizes Jefferson's outlook and insights of recent philosophy to describe responsibilities of art educators relative to contemporary information-based technology. Assumptions regarding education and art education include:

1. Part of the role of public education is to develop responsive and responsible citizens who understand that both (a) the form and content of information and (b) how it is acquired and maintained are shaped by various aspects of the cultural setting in which it is embedded.
2. Art education shares this role of public education. Although focusing primarily on visual, aesthetic, and artistic aspects of education, art education stimulates the development of knowledge and skills necessary to understand the interaction of these with economic, social, and political factors. Art education assists students in acquiring information necessary to interpret past and present art forms in their own and other cultures and to direct the creation of future forms in accord with consciously chosen values.

64

3. Technology includes not only the physical means of production or process but an underlying conceptual framework. Physical and conceptual components of technology are expressions of culture. That is, they both reflect and act upon the larger cultural context in which they are embedded.

The significance of these assumptions to theory and practice in art education will be explored in terms of information-based technologies as used in general education and in art.

Technology in General Education

As President of the United States, Ronald Reagan has provided impetus to the incorporation of information-based technological innovation in at least one form—computers—in public education. Many states have formed committees for educational excellence which reflect this impetus in their reports. These reports include literature from educational technology, computers in education, and art education and are quite reminiscent of literature from the 1940s to the 1960s advocating the incorporation of television and radio in the public school setting. They also suffer from similar unexamined assumptions:

1. Educational practice can be transferred directly, with no significant alteration, to the new medium of instruction. In the case of television, this resulted in the taped lecture or demonstration. Computers are used as automated page turners or electronic paint brushes. Not only is content duplicated, but process is automated. For example, students are being taught by television rather than learning to understand and control television. Behavioral objectives are being applied to the development of learning packages using television and computers. Consequently, television and computers are used to program students, rather than students designing, programming, or critically analyzing information-based technology. Hidden curricular messages are:
   a. There are simple, correct answers to problems
   b. Knowledge is fragmentary and unrelated to daily life
   c. It is proper that knowledge is both controlled and dispensed by anonymous authority
2. Curriculum content and educational practice will be more effective when a new medium is utilized.
3. Commercial uses of these media are not worthy of study in the school context. Even though students may spend many more hours interacting

with the commercial media than they spend in an institutionalized setting, critical skills for examining the media in either setting are not communicated.

As a result of these three assumptions, the educational impact of electronic media, in the broad sense of cultural transmission, has been ignored. The role of technical innovation as an element of culture change is rarely studied in any area of the curriculum. Concepts related to applications of technology as cultural expression are rarely considered. If effects of technology are studied, it is usually from the stance that innovation occurs and people react to it. The possibility of examining the context in which innovation occurs, especially how and by whom it is initiated, seems to be omitted from educational consideration. Consequently, a process of educating citizens who can consciously choose direction and extent of technological innovation, and who are aware of the aesthetic, economic, social, and political implications of their choices, has not been designed.

Technology in Art

In contrast, contemporary artists, especially those who view art as integral with life or as a force for social change, have performed works or made statements indicating awareness of choices and cultural impacts inherent in applications of information-based technology. Paik is cited by Smagula (1983) as insisting on responsibility of artists to function as communicators, simplifying unwieldy and boring information such as contained in Rand Corporation reports and presenting it visually. Material in the report may affect us all, so it is imperative to have clear access to it. Czuri (1976) describes how computers could be used to retrieve, display, and manipulate statistical data regarding many facets of society. Interacting in real time with a three-dimensional conceptual landscape of statistical data, models of simulated change may be used to examine the results of various sorts of social intervention.

According to Smagula, "In the last few years, Paik's concept of the artist as a pioneering thinker, making new concepts and technology accessible to the general public, has been vindicated. Although he has been experimenting with interactive television for years, only recently has society begun to realize the economic benefits of telecommunications" (1983, p. 248). Paik (videotaped interview, April, 1980) is also interested in the link between art and economics in the postindustrial world. He believes "information has to be recognized as an alternate energy source. Information changes our life style."

Davis's concerns include content of television viewing experience and the technological potential of electronic communication with its built-in biases of immediacy and intimacy. He is especially interested in the artist's ability both to access the technological and to have something to communicate to the public once access has been secured. The importance of the relations between technology and institutions, the alienating private dialectic of television viewing, the social implications of interactive live video, and the populist control of television are key elements in Davis's work (Davis, 1977a, 1977b; Himmelstein, 1981; Ten Eyck, 1986).

Control of Information

Those interested in creating a culture in which power is broadly based, as suggested by Jefferson, are concerned with how individuals and groups within cultures shape the form, content, and transmission of information. This may include simple analyses of specific aspects of content or metalevel analyses of language and other symbol systems such as visual representations and technological forms. For example, at the simple level, educators have studied textbooks to detect biases related to sex, race, and ethnicity. A few studies have examined other educational media such as computer software for similar biases. Sociologists and psychologists have studied popular culture, including television and computer games. However, public school students are rarely taught to analyze information in terms of specific aspects of content. This is especially true regarding analysis of the relation of content to origination, shaping, and distribution of information. Educators, in general, have been slow to consider that it is possible to analyze systems of communication and technological components of those systems at a metalevel. For example, technology may be studied as a cultural expression, to detect what cultural forms are embedded in technology; hence, what aspects of communication may be amplified by technological choices.

There is little doubt that those who politically, economically, and intellectually control the development and implementation of technology have considerable power to maintain or change many facets of society. For example, in regard to information-based communication technologies, Said (1983) states,

A tiny handful of large and powerful oligarchies control about ninety percent of the world's information and communication flows. This domain, staffed by experts and media executives, is as Herbert Schiller and others have shown, affiliated to an even smaller number of governments, at the very same time that the rhetoric of objectivity, balance, realism and freedom covers what is being done. And for the most part, such consumer items as "the news"—a euphemism for ideological images of the world that determine political reality for a vast majority of the world's population—hold forth, untouched by interfering secular and critical minds, who for all sorts of obvious reasons are not hooked into the systems of power. (p. 157)

Others such as Mandler (1978) agree with Said regarding the dubious match of reality with the news. However, Greenfield (1984, p. 54) cites studies done by Scandinavian educators who use the news as a model of "what is really happening."

From my perspective, news is accepted as political reality at least in part because of how information is divided and communicated in educational settings. Fragmentation of knowledge and concomitant belief in the opinions of experts who know no field but their own lay the way for abuse of information-based technologies.

The creation and distribution of information in the form of print, television transmission, video tapes and disks, and commercial computer software are the most commonly analyzed. However, if information-based technology is viewed in the broadest sense, there are many other forms to consider. For example, what information is used to program machinery that produces the artifacts of everyday life? Manipulation of genetic information via technological means now allows the alteration of biological forms. In whose hands should the power of decision lie regarding these choices?

If one takes the Jeffersonian stance, design of educational experiences must be reconsidered. These should make it possible for citizens to formulate cogent choices. This introduces the possibility that multiple points of view from a nonhomogeneous and diverse citizenry may be considered when making decisions regarding technical innovation. In two earlier papers, I describe interdisciplinary learning experiences that raise these considerations regarding manufacture of artifacts (Jones, 1982, 1986). I raise similar questions about information-based technology and communications in the following section.

Educational Design for Directing Technology

What can be done if how information is divided and communicated in educational settings (1) is an important factor in the failure to study cultural effects of information-based technology critically and (2) results, at least partially, from the fragmentation of knowledge and the concomitant belief in opinions of experts who know no field but their own? These are particularly difficult problems, since the education of educators suffers from them. The structure of secondary- and college-level education is based upon the disciplinary division of knowledge and the belief in narrow expertise. Therefore, a two-phase plan is proposed. The first phase is designed to impact the education of future educators, and the second is designed for implementation by educators in their educational settings. Although the specific plan described in this chapter uses public education as an example, with minor adaptations for various sites and audiences, this two-phase plan could be used in other educational settings such as public media, museums, cultural centers, and so forth.

Phase One: Education for Educators

The first phase would consist of a self-selected group of teachers from a common educational site coming together to participate in a program providing (1) technical information about information-based technology, especially television and computers; (2) opportunities to put this information into the context of their own disciplines; (3) a critical contextual view of information acquired in the first and second portions; and (4) opportunities for planning to use all of the preceding to formulate an interdisciplinary learning plan for a particular educational site.

The third section, acquiring a critical contextual view, is most frequently ignored. Areas should include historical development of discipline-based knowledge structures, examinations of postmodern culture in which cross-disciplinary concerns are the rule rather than the exception, sociology of knowledge perspectives, recent philosophical works stressing construction and deconstruction of cultural forms, and, finally, critical examination of previous attempts to incorporate interdisciplinary studies in educational settings.

The studies suggested provide a broad base from which to question many aspects of education. There are numerous questions and learning experiences that could be generated from this base by an art educator in an interdisciplinary educational context focused on electronic communication and information.

Phase Two: Interdisciplinary Learning Example

The example developed in this section is intended to illustrate how an art educator working in a secondary school or a small college could implement some of the concepts acquired in the first phase. With variations based on particular educational sites and audiences, many such examples could be derived.

An initial activity could be the critical examination of the writing and visual products of contemporary video and computer artists, especially those who focus on art as integral to life and art as an agent for social change. Papers by theorists who discuss information and communication technologies may also be studied. McHale (1979), for example, states that "they not only amplify our capacities to process and communicate information and experience but by their function as 'screen' actually reshape the cultural content and perception of society itself" (p. 62). He also speaks more broadly about art as a social model: "The future of art, therefore, seems not to lie so much with the creation of enduring masterworks but, in part, with the exploration and definition of alternative social and cultural directions. It is not the isolated work which may be important but the overall context, or lifestyle and attitude, within which it is produced" (p. 62).

Following this, students would study, design, and create examples of video and computer art in order to raise awareness of the technical and artistic potentials and limitations of these media. Art historical studies of various communication forms, hand lettering, typography, and print media would allow comparison and contrast with preindustrial/handcrafted, industrial/mechanical reproduction, and postindustrial electronic forms. Concepts of both art and technology as cultural expressions could be communicated in concrete examples. For instance, the form of Roman capitals was influenced by the technology of stone carving and also by official attitudes and historical precedents. Variations of these forms are used later in typography and electronic letter forms when an attitude of respect for an official statement is desired. Examine announcements of a presidential inauguration and other official documents for visual confirmation. These activities would provide a series of questions from which to analyze both contemporary art worlds and commercial uses of video and computer graphics. Commercial uses include advertising, entertainment, education, and news. Aesthetic and artistic factors observed during the activities—including their relation to other cultural factors such as technology, economics, and social and political forces—would be the topic of final discussion. These final discussions would be conducted in a setting with instructors from other subject areas and would utilize information derived from simultaneous studies in those areas.

Studies in the other arts and sciences, computer science, electronics, mathematics, social sciences, and language arts would also focus on critical examination, creation, and distribution of scientific, artistic, and commercial information via electronic means. In the social sciences this would include historical and political studies of creation, categorization, control, and distribution of information of various types not limited to electronic information.

Final interdisciplinary discussions would provide students with insights into such questions as, Can informational technology be used to create changes in cultural forms such as education, government, the art world, and mass communication? If new cultural forms are possible, what forms should these take and from what points of view would each of these forms be desirable or objectionable? Should as many points of view as possible, from a nonhomogeneous and diverse citizenry, be considered when making these choices? If so, to what extent is this practical? If not, who should make these choices? What characteristics of previous technological forms are being imitated by electronic technology in each of these areas? What are the reasons for this imitation? What are some benefits or problems related to this imitation? Can informational technology be used by one group of people to influence others? Under what, if any, circumstances is this desirable?

Each of these questions can be addressed from a concern for artistic quality and aesthetic valuing patterns, as well as from social, political, economic, and technological viewpoints. In both teacher education and student learning activities, questions regarding control of technological innovation relative to cultural values and human choice are raised. It becomes meaningful in this learning context to suggest that generated cultural goals may precede and direct technological innovation. The fear that "technology creates an elite class of technocrats and so disenfranchises the masses" (Florman, 1975, p. 56) may be allayed. An aim is creation of an educated citizenry with sufficient knowledge of technology in a cultural context to make choices in accord with consciously chosen goals.

I believe students of this interdisciplinary program would agree with Florman (1975) that

> sober thought reveals that technology is not an independent force much less a thing, but merely one of the types of activities in which people engage. Further it is an activity in which people engage because they choose to do so. The choice may sometimes be foolish or unconsidered. The choice may be forced upon some members of society by others. But this is very different from the concept of technology itself misleading or enslaving the population. (p. 57)

Involved educators may deepen their understanding of the cultural context in which technology is designed, implemented, and controlled. Thus they may begin to ask questions, such as, To what extent are historically based assumptions regarding the nature of knowledge (its form, categorization, legitimation, and distribution) being embedded in the form of new technology? How does this cultural aspect of technology tend to accentuate or promote some uses of the technology over others? How might this affect educational form and practice? If educators believe in the legitimacy of the different values (including aesthetic ones) of various cultural, occupational, and regional groups, how would this affect their view of technological control of information in mass media and educational materials?

Conclusion

In this chapter, technology is regarded as an expression of culture. It is assumed citizens who are technically and culturally knowledgeable can direct development and implementation of technology in accord with generated cultural goals. Art educators are charged with responsibility for preparing citizens who are knowledgeable in artistic and aesthetic values. Art educators and their students are also charged with responsibility for understanding the relations of these values to other aspects of culture, including the technological.

References

Czuri, C. (1976). Statistics as an interactive art object. In R. Leavitt (Ed.), *Artist and computer* (pp. 85–87). New York: Harmony Books.

Davis, D. (1977a). *Art culture*. New York: Harper & Row.

Davis, D. (1977b). *The new television*. Cambridge, MA: MIT Press.

Florman, S. C. (1975). In praise of technology. *Harpers* 251(1506), 53–72.

Ford, P. L. (Ed.). (1899). *Writings of Thomas Jefferson, Vol. 10: 1816–1826*. New York: G. P. Putman Sons.

Greenfield, P. M. (1984). *Mind and media: The effects of television, video games, and computers*. Cambridge, MA: Harvard University Press.

Himmelstein, H. (1981). *On the small screen*. New York: Praeger.

Jones, B. (1982). Microcomputer controlled generation of artifacts as an interdisciplinary teaching aid. *The Computing Teacher, 9*(9), 42–45.

Jones, B. (1986). Significance of technology in art education. *Journal of the Institute of Art Education, 10*(2), 40–49.

Mandler, J. (1978). *Four arguments for the elimination of television*. New York: Morrow Quill Paperbacks.

McHale, J. (1979). The future of art and mass culture. *Leonardo, 12*(1), 59–64.

Said, E. (1983). Opponents, audiences, constituencies and community. In H. Foster (Ed.), *The anti-aesthetic* (pp. 135–159). Port Townsend, WA: Bay Press.

Smagula, H. (1983). *Currents: Contemporary directions in the visual arts.* Englewood Cliffs, NJ: Prentice-Hall.

Ten Eyck, C. (1986). Unpublished research. University of Oregon, Eugene, Oregon.

PART III

The Citizens' Responsibility
to Individual and Group Problems

RULE BY THE MAJORITY WILL CAUSE PROBLEMS when its power limits the expression of differing views by individuals and minority groups. Fortunately, beliefs inherent in the democratic system require the expression and advocacy of minority views as a way of validating the integrity of a country and sometimes changing its prevailing directions. This process, when it functions effectively, is the system of democratic justice.

A society that does not educate its citizens to respect the processes and cultural communication of all its citizens and cultural groups does not function as a democracy. Art is one system of cultural communication that conveys, differentiates, and potentially integrates unique cultural views. It is necessary for art teachers and others who make choices and direct the flow of information about art to be sensitive to the expression of all citizens' values. This premise suggests that art settings should reflect varying art forms having aesthetic potential for different groups of people. For example, children often respond to objects that adults do not appreciate; Oregon buckaroos do not necessarily derive aesthetic pleasure from a Motherwell painting; Soho artists may not appreciate the cornhusk doll made in Iowa; and Ukrainian egg decorating probably will not communicate as strongly to the Irish as it does to the Ukrainian.

Encouraging the appreciation of varying art objects is only one way for those of us who work with and promote the visual arts to contribute to the development of a responsible citizenry. We also educate the public to become sensitive to varying styles of art criticism. There are many "right" ways to talk about art, depending on the context. Artists and appreciators of folk, popular, computer, and tourist arts all have language systems to describe what is valued. The tattoo artist, the van painter, and the cook all have ways of expressing pleasure within their own groups, just as the New York critic does. Art educators and their students should recognize that one system of verbal expression about art can only be enhanced by learning from another system of art criticism. As pointed out in an earlier chapter, Wendell Berry (1977; see Selected Bibliography) has called "specialization" the disease of contemporary people. While specialists have a specific expertise to exercise, it should not be their position to exclude the input, experiences, or interests of others, especially from those activities that involve all humankind on a regular basis. Art educators spread this disease when they teach students that their way of talking about art is less meaningful than the mode of communication of the art specialist.

Economic support for varying systems of aesthetic expression can help the public expand its sensitivity to individual and group values. Arts councils should include on their panels people of color, people living in poverty, and people who are differently abled. These organizations should also allow for varying ways of developing a proposal and evaluating a project. Not all artists and arts groups structure their ideas in the academic manner that an arts council proposal form demands.

A democracy that is truly concerned with the responses and involvement of all its citizens will not choose one system of art criticism, arts organization, art education, art production, aesthetic response, or art history as more valuable in every context. Democracy requires flexibility in determining the appropriateness of these processes and the participation of all citizens. The following chapters will make suggestions toward attaining democratic flexibility and participation in the artworld while focusing on citizen responsibility to individual and group values, thus helping to create a socially relevant approach to understanding and appreciating art.

Chapter 7

Why Art Education Is Neither Socially Relevant nor Culturally Democratic: A Contextual Analysis

___ Robert Bersson _____

The individual-centered and discipline-centered schools of art education share very little in common. They are defined more by their differences than similarities. Yet they do join hands in one area: a common disregard for art's social dimension. Both overlook or undervalue art's social roots and its power as a pervasive force that shapes our most basic attitudes, beliefs, values, and behavior.

The individual-centered approach to art education emphasizes goals ranging from self-realization and psychological integration to artistic individualism and personal aesthetic response. Growing from Lowenfeld's child-centered approach (Lowenfeld & Brittain, 1982), but without the latter's commitment to social responsibility in a democratic society, such self-centered programs almost automatically deemphasize or preclude "extra-individual" sociocultural concerns. Programs dealing with art therapy, education of the whole person through art, and creative experimentation with media would fall within this broad, self-oriented category.

Discipline-centered programs, as conceived by university-based thinkers (Eisner, 1972; Smith, 1982), lack social relevance for different reasons. Built largely upon the formalist view of the Western fine-arts

78

tradition, the discipline-centered approach is grounded in an aesthetic perspective and cultural tradition that is somewhat at odds with the cultural experiences of the multiethnic, multiclass public we art educators serve (Nadaner, 1982). This is not to say that formalism and the Western fine-arts tradition lack significance for widely different publics, but rather that other perspectives and art forms are of equal or greater importance to the lives of our multicultural populace, including our white middle-class mainstream (Rosenblum, 1981). If indeed art education is to be perceived as more than a curricular extra or program of cultural enrichment, it must focus on the "basic stuff" of people's lives, as well as on our exceptional artistic and aesthetic possibilities.

This chapter seeks to understand why much of contemporary art education is lacking in social relevance. To this end, the sociocultural foundations of the individual- and discipline-centered schools of art education must be explored. Individual-centered art education is strongly rooted in subjectivist psychology (Efland, 1979), especially in its most recent humanistic form as embodied in the theories of Abraham Maslow and Carl Rogers. The reasons for humanistic psychology's lack of social relevance are to be found in its narrow focus on the individual self, its ahistorical/asocial world view (i.e., individual development as largely free and independent of social context), and its noninvolvement with and even avoidance of the larger world of social and political activity. For a thorough analysis of these socially limiting facets of humanistic psychology, the reader is referred to Russel Jacoby's *Social Amnesia: A Critique of Conformist Psychology from Adler to Laing* (1975) and Allan Buss's "Humanistic Psychology as Liberal Ideology: The Socio-Historical Roots of Maslow's Theory of Self-Actualization" (1979). To its credit, the Association of Humanistic Psychology (1979) is beginning to recognize the social shortcomings of its approach and may yet learn to integrate its theory and practice with social analysis and activity. But, for the time being, humanistic psychology and its individual-centered relative in art education remain too self-centered, culturally disconnected, and politically isolated to be of very much social significance (Giffhorn, 1978).

Discipline-centered art education, which employs the artist, critic, aesthetician, and historian as its models, most often takes its cultural lead from the established artworld (Hobbs, 1981). Based on the theories, beliefs, and judgments of artworld specialists and connoisseurs (Eisner, 1972), discipline-centered art education looks to the artworld establishment for definition and direction. Returning to the question of social relevance, we must ask why most artists, critics, aestheticians, and art historians concern themselves so little with art's social dimension. Why do they tend to devalue or exclude concerns that are extra-individual or extra-aesthetic in nature? To answer these questions, we must press on further to an examination of the belief system of the artworld and an investigation of the place of origin of its ideology—American society.

Contextual Understanding and Cultural Literacy

That our present conceptions of art and art education are largely determined by our particular American social context is not difficult to discern. Had we been born peasants, nobles, or clergy in twelfth-century France, the French medieval social context would have culturally conditioned us to a far different system of beliefs about art education. The political economy of capitalism and democracy, as opposed to medieval serfdom and clerical/aristocratic oligarchy, forms the foundation of our own societal edifice. Technocracy, as an organizational mode and mentality born from the wedding of science, technology, and bureaucracy, supplies a good deal of the political-economic cement (Bowers, 1980). Upon this foundation, which powerfully influences the shape of the rest of the structure, have evolved the concepts, habits, skills, arts, instruments, and institutions (i.e., culture) of our society. Our psychology, art, art institutions, professional values, and personal lifestyles are molecular parts of this massive, complex organism we call culture. What we think about, how we think, our beliefs, and our behavior are largely determined by our sociocultural birthplace and residence.

Critical examination of our sociocultural context enables us to comprehend the dominant features of our conditioning. This conditioning or acculturation, as social scientists call it, is often so successful as to render us unaware of the very fact that we have been conditioned. Most Western persons, especially Americans, think of their beliefs and actions as freely and independently determined. It is only when strongly divergent cultures, such as those of the American Indians and other traditional societies, contradict our own world view that we become aware that we are products of a peculiarly Western cultural tradition, one shaped substantially by capitalism, democracy, and technocracy (Means, 1980).

Only with contextual understanding and attendant cultural literacy can we art educators sufficiently emancipate ourselves from acculturation in order to discover or envision alternatives—more socially humanistic ones, by my preference—to the prevailing cultural conceptions of art and education. Art educators must pursue far more radical analyses if the profession is to uncover its sociocultural roots and understand its present development. Going far beyond the surface or superficial outer layer, radical analysis demands, as the formal definition of *radical* suggests, our "going to the root or roots, center, foundation, or source" (*Webster's New World Dictionary*, 1966).

Capitalism

Our economic system has had a decisive influence on our culture. Its deepest values and inevitable socioeconomic class divisions have powerfully affected our art and education. Capitalism's encompassing values of private profit, private property, individual freedom, and competition promote privatized forms of individualism, personal striving and achieving, a subjectivist view of reality, and a social fabric which, in its more atomized form, has been characterized as "the me-generation," "the culture of narcissism" (Lasch, 1978), and "the pursuit of loneliness" (Slater, 1970). Dynamic profit-making production of ever-changing, new, and unique products also characterizes the system, harmonizing with the modern value of progress while reinforcing the consumer/owner's individualism, self-esteem, and socioeconomic status (Lasch, 1978).

In our own world of art and art education, self-realization, artistic individualism, and personal aesthetic fulfillment are ever at the height of our concerns, while social concerns and goals are barely in the ball park. This is going on at a time when the very survival of the species and the planet is in urgent doubt. What is clearly needed is a balance or integration of individual and social goals. It comes as no surprise that contemporary fine art is most highly esteemed and financially valued when most self-centered, new, and unique. That privacy and subjectivity command a near monopoly on our paradigms of artistic creativity and aesthetic experience is likewise understandable. Aesthetic and artistic individualism, the myth of the artist as solitary hero and lonely poetic seer, the movement from social concerns to purely subjective ones, and the resultant "separation of art from life" are all established and even cherished values of the bourgeois culture that has come to dominance within the context of industrial capitalism (Hauser, 1951).

In addition to its cultivation of extreme forms of individualism, especially in the arts, capitalism creates inevitable socioeconomic class divisions through an unequal distribution of wealth and power. Specific upper-class groups, because of their wealth and power, gain the capability of financing, influencing, and advancing culture according to their values. In the hierarchy of bourgeois culture, fine or "high" art is the preferred form of the leading classes (Hauser, 1951). Contemporary art education, especially its discipline-centered school, customarily follows these class-based high-art values, which find their socioeconomic place of residence in the artworld with its interlocking network of galleries, museums, pub-lishing houses, and art schools and departments. Wealthy, powerful museum trustees and boards of directors, gallery owners and collectors, art book and magazine publishers, and their cultural counterparts among generally middle-class artists, critics, historians, curators, and educators all participate in harmonious relationships in the sustenance and pro-motion of the artworld system and its values (Feldman, 1978).

College art departments, where many artists, some critics, and most art historians earn their livings, pass on the most cherished values of the Western fine-arts tradition to their students. Art educators at the univer-sity level most often share their art department colleagues' devotion to established artworld values. Because art education students receive part or all of their training in university art departments, they naturally receive a thorough education in the traditions, beliefs, and values of the artworld (Hobbs, 1981). It should therefore come as no surprise that most art educators in schools, museums, and other settings adhere to the ideology and follow the trends of the world of high art. In terms of social position, art educators come to serve as intermediaries between the world of high art and "the people." Certain art educators of elitist orientation have even thought of themselves as educators of the culturally deprived, those per-sons or groups with little involvement in or access to high culture. Without denying the profound significance of Western fine art, we have all too rarely considered the importance of popular, ethnic, neighborhood, or class-based culture in the lives of the people we serve. In capitalist society, with its inevitable socioeconomic class divisions, resultant cultural hier-archies will always be a source of conflict for art educators. Because of our primary location in public settings, we will always find ourselves caught in the dialectical middle between the high culture of the artworld and the multicultural life-worlds of the populations we serve. In this respect, a balance or integration of these different artworlds in our teach-ing is essential.

That the fine-arts tradition dominates the thinking of some of our most distinguished art educators can be seen in Eisner's seminal discipline-centered text, *Educating Artistic Vision* (1972). When the Eisner text is compared to the texts of socially oriented art educators like Feldman (1970), McFee and Degge (1977), and Chapman (1978), the exclusiveness of the focus of discipline-centered art education becomes especially clear. Where the books of the socially oriented art educators encourage critical contextualist thinking and encompass the full range of visual culture—popular, folk, ethnic, applied, mass media, and fine art—the writings of discipline-centered theorists like Eisner (1972) and Smith (1981) focus entirely on the appreciation of acknowledged masterworks of fine art. Such art, according to Smith, is proudly and admittedly "elite art," "the best" art, the "more difficult, aesthetically more rewarding" art, the art whose "artistic merit has been certified." It is also a nonutilitarian, non-instrumental art whose more pronounced formal qualities are best suited to providing aesthetic experience and "educating our artistic vision." In keeping with these formalist aesthetic goals, worthy though limited, Eisner (1972) advocates an art-for-art's-sake "essentialist" position relative to the teaching of art production, criticism, and history. Such art education naturally opposes the balancing or integration of discipline-centered goals with socially relevant contextualist concerns.

Whether advocated by museum board presidents (Rockefeller, 1969), Reagan Administration arts policy makers (Adler, Hager, & Shabad, 1981), art critics (Greenberg, 1961), or discipline-centered art educators (Eisner, 1972), the formalist aesthetic perspective devalues or avoids such "extra-aesthetic" dimensions of art experience as the psychological, cultural, socioeconomic, utilitarian, and political. Seeking "significant form" (Bell, 1979) in its purest and therefore highest fine-art state, formalists also devalue or avoid the broad range of visual culture that strongly affects and/or grows from the lives of the multiethnic, multiclass public we art educators serve. Exclusive in its content, narrow in its perspective, formalism has succeeded in rendering discipline-centered art education socially irrelevant.

Democracy

Although our political and economic systems are tightly interwoven, and even though our current political system is as much oligarchy as democracy, democratic principles might well represent the potential corrective to the cultural inequity brought about in our society through a disproportionate distribution of wealth and power. In its declared tolerance of and respect for individual and group differences, in its promise of equality of opportunity and popular governance "of, by, and for [all] the people," the principles of democracy merit application in the cultural sphere as well as in the political and economic spheres of activity.

Taking a twentieth-century liberal position, discipline-centered art educators (Smith, 1981) argue for the democratization of high culture, that is, the opportunity for all citizens to be educated in "the best" art, which, in the hierarchy of bourgeois culture, is naturally titled "fine" or "high" art. Such cultural policy, laudatory but restrictive, translates to democracy by the few for the many. As such, it bears little resemblance to the policy of "cultural democracy" which calls for art(s) education of, by, and for all the people. Cultural democracy stands for cultural participation as a human right. It opposes the condition of cultural domination by those who, at any given time, possess the wealth, power, and erudition to decide which art and art education is best and which is not, or which is worthy of public and private support and which is not (Adams & Goldbard, 1981).

True cultural democracy, in its generosity and tolerance, can embrace fine and popular art, formalist and contextualist perspectives, individual and social goals. Democracy by the few, whether in its liberal or conservative forms, cannot. Both the liberal Smith (1981) and the conservative Heritage Foundation (Martin, 1981) argue for an art education policy focused on high culture and the pursuit of formal aesthetic goals. Clearly, discipline-centered liberals and conservative government policy makers of the 1980s are in full agreement with respect to the correct content and aesthetic perspective for art education. Where they part company is on the issue of cultural participation; that is, which persons or groups shall receive the benefits of experiences in the arts and which shall not. In opposition to the liberal desire of discipline-centered art educators to educate all persons in fine art, conservative cultural policy, such as that of the Reagan Administration, possesses no generosity or altruism. Rather, it is harshly exclusionary, favoring those who already possess the most wealth, power, and formal education. Conservative arts policy strongly favors the large, established fine-arts institutions, their largely affluent urban audiences, and the most traditional kinds of arts production and educational programming (Martin, 1981). The needs and preferences of the majority of the population are hardly taken into account. Cultural conservatism has meant severe cutbacks in the National Endowment for the Arts "Expansion Arts Program" and virtual elimination of the Comprehensive Employment Act (CETA), which financed work-study for aspiring workers in the arts. It has brought about a sharp reduction in government and corporate support for forms of art that are nontraditional, community-based, or socially or politically oriented (Adams & Goldbard, 1981).

Cultural democracy, as viewed by political conservatives, is a misguided and even frightening proposal, and with good reason. As thinkers like Gramsci (1973) and Hauser (1951) have pointed out, cultural empowerment of the larger population might well result in artistic, critical and socio-historical challenges to the dominant world view by which the power elite justifies and maintains its leading position.

Technocracy

Technocracy, the increasingly technical, bureaucratic, and "rational" way in which nearly every aspect of our work and even leisure time is organized, is most often experienced as anti-individualistic and, at its extreme, dehumanizing and alienating. In the context of a technocratically organized advanced capitalist society, art experience, creative and appreciative, becomes an island of meaningful individuated activity in an increasingly impersonal, mechanical, and standardized life-world. In the flight from technocracy and the abusive aspects of capitalism, artistic and aesthetic experience can fulfill a much-needed vitalizing or transcendent function, irregardless, some believe, of one's class or ethnic background (Marcuse, 1977).

Viewed in sociopolitical terms, however, the effects of individually meaningful art experiences are not necessarily progressive. Recall that high-ranking Nazis like Goebbels and Speer, and many brutal autocrats of the past, have been great patrons or connoisseurs. The editor of the *Journal of Aesthetic Education* (Smith, 1982, p. 18) has gone so far as to assert that "there may even be a covert relationship between aesthetic sensitivity and human callousness." Without going so far as accusing our contemporary museums, galleries, art departments, school art programs, and publishing houses of human callousness, I would assert that these art education institutions structure art experiences so that they have little to say about the human condition, either in its individual or social form. Deemphasizing or avoiding the social roots and effects of art, such experiences might provide personal meaning for some, but at the cost of severing art experiences from the mainstream of our lives. Oscar Wilde's (1891/1948, p. 102) pronouncement that "art shields us from the sordid perils of actual existence" describes well the comforting "art as separate from life" ethos and educational approach of most fine-arts institutions.

The metaphorical meanings communicated by our great metropolitan museums of art—appropriately described as temples or palaces of culture—capture all too well the intentionally escapist or transcendent nature of art experience in technocratic capitalist society. The visitor leaves the disorder of the street and ascends a grand flight of steps. High above the crowds, far from onrushing traffic, she or he passes under classical columns of superhuman proportion and through magnificent portals. Within, all is serene, ordered, hallowed. Art experiences in this gloriously isolated context are conceived and perceived to be separate from and superior to the life of the street. Aspiring to loftier, universal, and timeless realms, art experiences so conceived and taught sever the connection between art and its origins in the problematic, unscrubbed, and unwanted "real world" outside (Duncan & Wallach, 1978). Because the established artworld has been pedagogically successful in separating art from its social origins, art experiences are perceived to be inapplicable to the world of social analysis and action. With the pedagogical exit of art from the world, art experiences, by default, become socially conservative. Having little or no effect on the mainstream of social life, they serve merely to reinforce the status quo. Even the modernist avant-garde, aggressive challengers of the bourgeois order, has been tamed and reinterpreted for formal aesthetic enjoyment. Clearly, the social meanings of art, past and present, are being explained away by the present art establishment's "way of seeing" (Berger, 1972).

What, then, are the most common forms of art experience for the modern viewer? For those who seek that heightened form of experience known as the aesthetic, art can provide experiences that are sensuously and spiritually vitalizing. For those who are specialists in history or criticism, stimulating and demanding intellectual challenges abound. But, for the majority of viewers, art experiences are valued for the more general, down-to-earth pleasure they can provide. Enjoyment, pleasure, diversion— what some have referred to as the hedonic—are primary functions of modern art experience. In the tumult and discomfort of the twentieth century, such pleasure-giving experiences automatically become restorative, rejuvenating, therapeutic. Matisse (Chipp, 1975, p. 135) realized this and hoped that his art "might be for every worker, [whether businessperson] or writer, like an appeasing influence, like a mental soother, something like a good armchair in which to rest from physical fatigue." Nelson Rockefeller (1969, p. 9), longtime board member of the Museum of Modern Art and eminent collector, affirmed that looking closely at art is: "a good game, sharpening one's wits and warming one's heart. It is the greatest recreation ever devised by the ingenious mind of [humankind]. It gives us relief from the pressures, frustrations, and compromises of everyday life."

If the hedonic, therapeutic experience described by Matisse and Rockefeller is the one common to most viewers, as my own exploratory research (Bersson, 1981) seems to show, then the descriptions of viewer experiences as "holidays of the mind," "psychic messages," or "vacations from reality" (Hobbs, 1977; Jagodzinski, 1981) are not at all inaccurate. Customarily considered to be an enlightening activity, modern art experience can easily become the opposite—an experience that intentionally explains away and encourages us to avoid contact with the problematic social reality outside. As with so much of experience in our self-oriented society, social awareness and responsibility are readily jettisoned for personal pleasure, diversion, and escape. Over 60 years ago, the Dadaist

Richard Huelsenbeck (Rubin, 1967, p. 15) wrote, "The Dadaist considers it necessary to come out against art, because he has seen through its fraud as a moral safety valve," an escape hatch from reality and social responsibility.

Yet it would seem that modern art experiences, creative and responsive, could be more than pleasure, therapy, and escape. Understanding art experience in relation to its social context, and pursuing it with a socially humanistic conscience, could lead to experiences that might be individually meaningful and, at the same time, socially progressive. The critical theorist Herbert Marcuse (1977) provides us with a possible model. He writes that "the aesthetic dimension" can function as a last bastion for humanizing, individuated experience in a technocratic life-world where people and nature are being manipulated in increasingly mechanical, impersonal ways. Given contextual understanding and attendant cultural literacy, the life-affirming "beautiful moment" of the aesthetic experience can reveal in jarring contrast the depth and breadth of human alienation in technocratic capitalist society. The American Indian activist Russell Means (1980) has asserted with anger and alarm that the Western "materialist" mentality is succeeding in its quest to rationalize all people and living things for the sake of maximum production and/or profit. Any remnants of the deeply life-affirming "I-Thou" relationship between human beings and between people and nature are being eroded by the technocratic "I-It" imperative. People and nature are rapidly transformed into bloodless abstractions (e.g., input-output charts, cost-benefit equations, kill ratios) to be manipulated for commercial, ideological, or technical ends. The technocratic mentality, on the one hand, has brought us mass production and material and scientific advances. On the other hand, it has played its part in the dehumanization or destruction of individuals, whole peoples, and the environment. Aesthetic experience and aesthetic literacy, understood contextually and pursued with social conscience, can help liberate us from the cultural domination of technocratic capitalism and can help us to envision and act on socially humanistic alternatives to the present society. In this role, aesthetic education provides much more than a holiday of the mind, a frill, an extra, or enrichment.

Conclusion

Our social context, complex and massive in its influence, has caused much of our art and art education to be self-centered, self-referential, or elitist oriented to the point of social irrelevance. Critical contextual analysis makes us aware, in spite of pervasive cultural conditioning to the contrary, that art education can be far more socially relevant and culturally democratic than it currently is.

Although an elite variety of discipline-centered art education appears to be in the ascendancy in the conservative 1980s—supported, not surprisingly, by corporate America in the form of The J. Paul Getty Trust (1985)—the last two decades have seen substantial development in the areas of social relevance and cultural democracy. I believe that a more socially progressive direction is being charted, as embodied in such art education texts as Feldman's *Becoming Human Through Art* (1970); McFee and Degge's *Art, Culture, and Environment: A Catalyst for Teaching* (1977); Grigsby's *Art and Ethnics: Background for Teaching Youth in a Pluralistic Society* (1977); Chapman's *Approaches to Art in Education* (1978); and Lanier's *The Visual Arts and the Elementary Child* (1983). I note also the comparable development at the college level, where socially relevant art appreciation texts by art educators are in wide use. Prominent among them are Feldman's *Varieties of Visual Experience* (1972), Hobbs's *Art in Context* (1975), and Lanier's *The Arts We See* (1982). Witness the development through the 1970s and 1980s of such National Art Education Association affiliates as the Women's Caucus, Committee on Minority Concerns, United States Society for Education through Art, and the Caucus on Social Theory and Art Education, and one can be certain that the current power elite will be seriously challenged to make social relevance and cultural democracy essential components of the art education of the 1990s and the twenty-first century.

References

Adams, D., & Goldbard, A. (1981). A year to remember. *Cultural Democracy, 17,* 1–2.

Adler, J., Hager, M., & Shabad, S. (1981, March 16). The arts under Reagan's ax. *Newsweek,* pp. 28, 31.

Association of Humanistic Psychology Executive Board. (1979). Nuclear power and social transformation. *Journal of Humanistic Psychology, 19*(4), 4–5.

Bell, C. (1979). Significant form. In M. Radar (Ed.), *A modern book of aesthetics* (5th ed.) (pp. 287–297). New York: Holt, Rinehart and Winston.

Berger, J. (1972). *Ways of seeing.* New York: Penguin Books.

Bersson, R. (1981, April). *The modern art museum: Institution of ideology.* Paper presented at the National Art Education Association Convention, Chicago.

Bowers, C. (1980). Ideological continuities in technicism, liberalism, and education. *Teachers College Record, 81*(3), 293–321.

Buss, A. R. (1979). Humanistic psychology as liberal ideology: The socio-historical roots of Maslow's theory of self-actualization. *Journal of Humanistic Psychology, 19*(3), 43–55.

Chapman, L. (1978). *Approaches to art in education*. New York: Harcourt, Brace, Jovanovich.

Chipp, H. B. (1975). *Theories of modern art*. Berkeley: University of California Press.

Duncan, C., & Wallach, A. (1978). The museum of modern art as late capitalist ritual: An iconographic analysis. *Marxist Perspectives, 1*(3), 28–51.

Efland, A. D. (1979). Conceptions of teaching in art education. *Art Education, 32*(4), 21–33.

Eisner, E. W. (1972). *Educating artistic vision*. New York: Macmillan.

Feldman, E. B. (1970). *Becoming human through art*. Englewood Cliffs, NJ: Prentice-Hall.

Feldman, E. B. (1972). *Varieties of visual experience*. Englewood Cliffs, NJ: Prentice-Hall.

Feldman, E. B. (1978). A socialist critique of art history in the U.S.A. *Leonardo, 2*, 23–28.

Giffhorn, H. (1978). Ideologies of art education. *Studies in Art Education, 19*(2), 50–60.

Gramsci, A. (1973). *Letters from prison*. New York: Harper & Row.

Greenberg, C. (1961). *Art and culture*. Boston: Beacon Press.

Grigsby, J. E. (1977). *Art and ethnics: Background for teaching youth in a pluralistic society*. Dubuque, IA: Wm. C. Brown.

Hauser, A. (1951). *The social history of art* (Vol. 4). New York: Vintage Books.

Hobbs, J. A. (1975). *Art in context*. New York: Harcourt, Brace, Jovanovich.

Hobbs, J. A. (1977). Is aesthetic education possible? *Art Education, 30*(1), 30–32.

Hobbs, J. A. (1981). Established ways of thinking. *Bulletin of the Caucus on Social Theory and Art Education, 1*, 3–11.

J. Paul Getty Trust. (1985). *Beyond creating: The place of art in America's schools*. Los Angeles: The Getty Center for Education in the Arts.

Jacoby, R. (1975). *Social amnesia: A critique of conformist psychology from Adler to Laing*. Boston: Beacon Press.

Jagodzinski, J. (1981). Aesthetic education reconsidered, or please don't have an aesthetic experience. *Art Education, 34*(3), 26–29.

Lanier, V. (1982). *The arts we see*. New York: Teachers College Press.

Lanier, V. (1983). *The visual arts and the elementary child*. New York: Teachers College Press.

Lasch, C. (1978). *The culture of narcissism*. New York: Norton.

Lowenfeld, V., & Brittain, W. L. (1982). *Creative and mental growth* (7th ed.). New York: Macmillan.

Marcuse, H. (1977). *The aesthetic dimension*. Boston: Beacon Press.

Martin, J. (1981, February). Money for high art. *In These Times*, p. 24.

McFee, J. K., & Degge, R. M. (1977). *Art, culture, and environment: A catalyst for teaching*. Belmont, CA: Wadsworth.

Means, R. (1980). Fighting words on the future of the earth. *Mother Jones, 5*(10), 22–38.

Nadaner, D. (1982). Recognizing social issues in the art curriculum. *The Bulletin of the Caucus on Social Theory and Art Education, 2*, 72–75.

Rockefeller, N. A. (1969). *Twentieth century art from the Nelson Aldrich Rockefeller collection*. New York: The Museum of Modern Art.

Rosenblum, P. (1981). The popular culture and art education. *Art Education, 34*(1), 8–11.

Rubin, W. S. (1967). *Dada, surrealism, and their heritage.* New York: Museum of Modern Art.

Slater, P. (1970). *The pursuit of loneliness: American culture at the breaking point.* Boston: Beacon Press.

Smith, R. A. (1981). Elitism versus populism: A question of quality. *Art Education, 34*(4), 4–5.

Smith, R. A. (1982). Professor Feldman and the NAEA take aim: An agenda for further discussion. *Art Education, 35*(5), 16–19.

Webster's New World Dictionary. (1966). New York: World.

Wilde, O. (1948). The critic as artist. In R. Aldrington (Ed.), *The portable Oscar Wilde.* New York: Viking. (Original work published 1891).

Chapter 8

Cultural Literacy in Art: Developing Conscious Aesthetic Choices in Art Education

___ Barbara Ann Boyer _____

This chapter describes the significance of promoting "cultural literacy" in art education within a democratic context. The position I am advocating is that the development of students' skills in critical dialoguing and decoding of their own cultural assumptions in art will allow them to take control of and shape conscious aesthetic standards and experiences in their lives as well as develop an appreciation for the diverse viewpoints of others. A framework is provided for teachers in the classroom to develop students' abilities in these areas.

Much that we learn in our own cultures is at a taken-for-granted level. It is this taken-for-granted learning that affects how people will think about and respond to art. What appears to be a simple taken-for-granted concept, such as time, becomes a complex and problematic issue when closely examined. It takes on social relevance for students when within actual competitive settings such as testing in the schools or when comparing workers' attitudes toward punching in and punching out of work. The concept of time is conceived differently in different cultures. For example, in Native American cultures, prior to the influence of white Europeans, time was perceived in relation to cycles found in the environment and/or cultural myths. Such perceptions become acquired through learning and traditional patterns of behavior, which also may be in the process of reformulation or change.

Changes in patterns of behavior occur in larger pluralistic societies through membership in multiple subcultures. A mosaic of values, attitudes, and beliefs is formed by memberships in subcultures associated with variations in geographic location, place and type of work, gender, economic status, ethnic background, and religious orientation. A white male machine shop worker may live in a predominantly middle-class midwestern suburb with an East European ethnic makeup and have been educated in parochial schools. He may belong to various memberships such as the shop union, a bowling club, and a church men's association, which reinforce similar group values and yet maintain diverse and changing values across groups. Congdon (1985) refers to these different memberships that we all belong to as "folk groups": "It is when we begin to see ourselves as well as others as culture bound and culturally changing that our aesthetic preferences begin to be seen in light of the folk groups in which we all belong and to value these 'memberships' " (p. 72).

Although there is increased mobility among people in contemporary society, evidenced most notably in the activities of changing jobs and moving to different geographic locations, transporting beliefs and changing memberships may prove too stressful for some individuals and create feelings of alienation or cultural conflict. An ice cream shop owner in the Midwest related to me that he had moved to the South to get away from the cold and found himself and his family identified as "Yankee outsiders." This family was never able to assimilate into its new cultural environment and eventually moved back to the Midwest. Such feelings of cultural conflict exist in classroom settings where students may have values and attitudes very different from the teacher or a majority of the other students. These culturally diverse students are not able to identify in any way with the values of the school and develop a sense of alienation that eventually may lead to their dropping out of school.

In addition to cultural conflict between groups of people, the continuing advances in technology, mass communication, and transportation have created numerous changes affecting most societies in the world today. One consequence in a modern technological society is the elimination of some skilled labor no longer needed in a highly technocratic setting. Another is the learning of new social structures, with values continually evolving in this social and political environment. These changes create discontinuities in culture that affect the way people will work and their feelings of self-worth and personal expression.

An educational system that allows people to examine, question, and be conscious of how cultural changes affect their own cultural assumptions and feelings provides the basis for individuals and groups to take greater control of their own lives. They can then acquire critical skills and choose to take a more active role in decision making affecting fundamental changes in society. Such a transactional educational system is essential in promoting a citizenry responsible for the continued existence and development of a democratic society. In art education an examination of personal cultural experiences and beliefs and the cultural beliefs of others related to art provides both teachers and students with conscious awareness of their own sense of reality and the active role they can play within democratic processes for making aesthetic decisions.

Democracy

Democracy is defined essentially as government by and for the people, with a belief in social participation and equality for all. More specifically it is "a way of living which (a) stresses individual worth and the integrity of the human personality, (b) has faith in the intelligence and wisdom of [all people] acting together, and (c) is characterized by social relationships that reflect such qualities as mutual respect, cooperation, tolerance, and fair play" (*Dictionary of Education*, 1959, p. 151). It is also said to reflect "the principles of social equality and respect for the individual within a community" (*The American Heritage Dictionary*, 1982, p. 382).

These definitions appear somewhat removed from many of our social working relationships as we know them to exist today in Western society. The use of language and behavior emphasizing beating the competition, getting ahead, the competitive edge, obtaining the advantage, and leaving the competition behind is far more common than patterns of social behavior related to tolerance and cooperation. This priority placed on competitiveness can be traced to an emphasis on changing economic structures that stress strong competitive values; and on world power economics and aggressive corporate strategies where importance is placed on status, material gain, or wealth over human, aesthetic, and environmental qualities of life.

Educators noting the major problems within society have argued for more socially relevant curricula in the schools, which can help in preparing students to become conscious of their responsibility in maintaining democratic principles and help them to gain skills in cooperative individual and group processes. Learning experiences in democratic ways of living help to promote social participation and respect for the rights and equality of all people. Bersson (1986) suggests that the significant role of democracy within school curriculum "might well provide a potential corrective to the cultural inequities brought about in our country" (p. 44).

It is important that democratic processes and thinking carry over into the art classroom. Art represents the feelings, perceptions, and values of people through their visual aesthetic expressions. Students can more clearly appreciate and study the essence of creative expression of different cultures and people as well as the full range of the visual arts in a democratic context. The arts can be observed as dynamic and diverse in a democratic society reflective of rich cultural traditions and changes. Bersson (1986) notes that liberal arts educators, under the guise of democracy, would advocate art education for everyone only within the context of fine-art or formalist approaches. This elitist or ethnocentric view of art education negates an education in a democratic framework representing the full range of art by all types of people and knowledge about their aesthetic perceptions.

Cultural Literacy

The development of cultural literacy, with its implications for developing skills in decoding one's own cultural experiences in art and allowing for greater freedom of choice and responsibility, is essential within the context of art education (Boyer, 1984). The following ideas I have delineated on cultural literacy in art education have been partially derived from Bowers's (1974) philosophy of education, socialization, and existentialism, as well as from concepts and issues in cultural anthropology and art education.

In order to understand the significance of education in developing cultural literacy and particularly the need to do this within a democratic context, it is necessary to recognize the association of freedom with consciousness. Bowers (1974) notes that as long as we have the freedom to make choices and, more important, are conscious of these choices, then we are truly free. Education as one form of socialization has the potential to expand or restrict a person's freedom (consciousness). However, a person cannot exist in a state of total freedom, nor can freedom be described in "either-or" categories. Internal freedom is a dimension of consciousness and exists in a diverse range of possibilities, depending on the conditions determined by the culture and the nature of the socialization process and how it is defined (Bowers, 1974). One might be placed in a restrictive environment and not be free physically to move about but still have the ability and freedom to think, and therefore be consciously free.

An art education in cultural literacy emphasizing democratic principles of freedom and responsibility enables students to develop conscious freedom of thought by being able to interpret and critique their own feelings and cultural assumptions about art. In so doing, they identify and maintain cultural traditions while continuing to modify and expand upon their own conscious aesthetic choices. For example, students can examine various art forms in their culture, such as architecture, film, advertising design, and tape- and record-cover designs, as well as photos, paintings, and other visual forms within their own homes, to understand how individual and group processes and values shape aesthetic principles. More important, students need to have the opportunity to make clear their subjective experiences and feelings at a phenomenological level in order to develop a conscious awareness of the basis behind their personal aesthetic preferences. This conscious aesthetic awareness can become the foundation for understanding differences and similarities in the culture of others. In addition, the parameters of individual preference need to be expanded by speculating about aesthetic possibilities in the future and attempting to solve attendant problems.

The Pervasiveness of Culture

Culture can be defined as the learned shared values, attitudes, and beliefs of a specific group of people, which are continually being reworked and reformulated (Bourguignon, 1979). This sharing and reworking provides a basis for the socialization process and the way in which cultural assumptions about art are transmitted and become internalized. The enculturation process—that is, the transmission of culture from generation to generation, or sharing of mental constructs—provides strategies for dealing with an individual's perceived sense of reality and also determines the ways in which members within society control, embellish, and maintain their quality of life.

Aesthetic experience is a complex and multidimensional phenomenon, influenced at every level by the pervasiveness of culture (Boyer, 1985). A society's particular construct of reality or culture creates parameters or rules for both the artist and the perceiver of a work of art. In addition to cultural conditioning, universal and unique personality factors affect the quality of the aesthetic experience (Boyer, 1985). It appears that aesthetic experiences involving receptivity, selection, and interpretation are modified by the particular references and pervasive qualities determined by the dominance of culture. For example, what is recognized as art, what role the artist is expected to play, the position the perceiver occupies in the aesthetic setting, and the context of the aesthetic occurrence are established by a particular culture and contribute to defining the kind of aesthetic experience possible within that culture.

It should be noted that the culture of a society does not merely provide a set of rules that members consciously act upon and then accept. Rather, the process of socialization teaches members to internalize procedures for being able to interpret and incorporate these rules into experiences at a taken-for-granted level of consciousness. Cook (1976) refers to these as "interpretive procedures" and "taken-for-granted assumptions that enable the member to see the rules in the first place" (p. 350). The school transmits the dominant culture's reality and its preestablished set of references for behavior, and these become internalized. Without opportunities to examine and be knowledgeable about this socialization process, teachers and students are unable to act upon or take part in creating their own cultural assumptions.

Schools have been identified as "arenas of cultural conflict" (Wilcox, 1982) where incorporated skills and concepts often do not include those learned by the students earlier in their lives and currently employed by them. Wilcox states, "Children may have to attempt to function in an alien environment that requires behavior which is in striking contradiction to that which they have been taught to value" (p. 467).

Differences in culture within the classroom create variations in communication modes, both verbal and nonverbal, that act upon and affect differences in aesthetic reception and learning styles (Boyer, 1986). Philips (1983), in a study of American Indian reservation children, found that the children's attention structure and linguistic interaction differed in both selectivity and interpretation from persons of white middle-class backgrounds. For example, the American Indian children's usual mode of communication, their patterns of gaze (not giving the teacher sole eye contact, but looking around at everyone), their use of more physical body movements toward each other, and their not giving responsive physical and verbal cues to speaker statements were interpreted by the Anglo teachers as disruptive or inattentve. The students who acted in a culturally different way by not focusing completely on the teacher were misinterpreted as discipline problems. The students, in turn feeling a sense of alienation, were not able to interpret the teacher's messages.

Wilcox (1982) notes that the school represents the culture of reference, providing the standards for deciding what is, what can be done, and what operational procedures can be used for dealing with people and things. Teachers coming from the culture of reference or dominant culture are less likely to comunicate effectively with students from other cultures, much less be responsive or flexible concerning their needs.

It is necessary to develop an educational program that emphasizes respect and opportunities for students to describe their own experiences in relation to their feelings and cultural assumptions. Such a program in a multicultural classroom would allow teachers and students to work together to examine similarities and differences in their own and other cultures. It would help to sensitize the teacher to the students' culture as well as identify and break down communication barriers between them that may lead to cultural conflict.

A Program for Cultural Literacy in Art Education

The following program for cultural literacy in art education can be developed for use with various age levels. Selected ideas from this program also have been used in developing curriculum experiences for gifted children in an elementary-school art classroom (Plank, 1986).

A program in cultural literacy should begin with studies of art within the students' own cultures, drawing from both dominant and less influential groups. Personal experiences need to be examined to help students understand how their own cultural assumptions influence their aesthetic preferences and attitudes. Themes on cultural issues related to art should be used to provide continuity and focus for more in-depth art learning experiences. These themes or focus areas can center on such concepts as time, space, play, work, roles of men and women, conflict, success, heroes, and the avant-garde. These suggestions only touch upon the many related concepts that artists have dealt with in various periods of history and in different cultures.

Different lenses or screens are used to take the students from a personal introspective view to a more expanding societal perspective and finally to creative imagining and speculations built upon previously acquired knowledge and critical analysis. The particular viewpoints emphasized include (a) personal experiences, (b) personal data, (c) social and historical influences, (d) cross-cultural views, and (e) projective thinking into the future. Five stages are developed in cultural literacy, which center on the preceding perspectives related to art learning.

Stage One: Identifying Personal Experiences

It is significant that in designing curriculum studies in cultural literacy the starting point be the exploration of the students' own experiences, perceptions, and feelings. These should be interfaced with the particular theme or issue in art being studied, such as the concept of time or changing roles of women. This would be what Bowers (1974) refers to as the "phenomenology of the students" (p. 16), where the most important aspect is that the students reveal their state of consciousness and give a descriptive account of their personal experiences. A phenomenological account by students reveals the subjective dimension of a situation, which is essential for constructing what young people actually experience and perceive. A distinction can be made between usual learning experiences (socialization at a taken-for-granted level) and learning in cultural literacy (socialization leading to a personal conscious awareness or phenomenological perception of one's own culture). The taken-for-granted socialization mystifies the human origin of beliefs and creates an objectified, unquestioned reality divorced from the student's own experiences. It is therefore important for the students to develop a connection between their experiences and the art topic under investigation.

The teacher has a primary role in motivating critical dialogue and utilizing and teaching the process of what Bowers (1974) identifies as "culture clarification." Culture clarification can be defined as reflexive dialogue initiated by students or teachers that raises communication to a level of explicit awareness where the cultural origins and assumptions embedded in the communication process are clarified. For example, in introducing a topic such as beauty, the teacher might ask the students to define and describe beauty in their own words. In what areas or places do they find beauty? How does it influence their lives? They would also list words and phrases that they have seen or heard defining beauty. They would then begin to identify aspects of beauty internalized and not questioned in their experience. For example, youthful beauty is often used as a standard in mass advertising of commercial products. This first stage is used to motivate the students into relating to the topic and beginning to identify and question their taken-for-granted assumptions within their own cultural experiences.

Stage Two: Collecting Personal Data

This stage requires gathering data from the students' own perspectives and experiences. The data would be descriptive and much like an ethnography, but a major difference would be that the feelings and moods of the students would be an integral part of the data. The emphasis would be on subjective description (Bowers, 1974).

Cultural literacy in art education requires that the ethnographic type of data be in both verbal and visual formats. Photographs, reproductions, clippings from magazines and newspapers, and drawings could all be types of data collected. A basis for developing material similar to ethnographic research could be started, with the students keeping a personal log of where they found objects or of places that are pleasing to look at or beautiful. These could include locations at home, on the way to school, at school, and in the community. These places could be mapped out and diagrammed, to show possible clusterings or relations. The diagrams could then be compared to other students' mapping and perceptions. Students would also be asked to bring objects from home that they considered beautiful. Objects could include special things from their room at home that they have hung on the wall, a stuffed animal, or a special craft object passed down through their family. It is also significant to observe what students consider unpleasant or ugly to view. This could be an important learning experience for the teacher as well, if an atmosphere of trust and respect were already established in the classroom. Because the students are sharing their perceptions and a part of their life, it is not difficult to stimulate their interest and motivate dialogue.

This stage of examining and making students explicitly aware of objects and materials related to cultural assumptions submerged at the taken-for-granted level is crucial in establishing a foundation for the following stages. Dialogue would focus on how they feel toward objects or places they have identified as aesthetic, why they might feel this way, and how others around them respond toward these objects or places. The teacher's role is particularly important in developing culture clarification because students are most apt to be unaware of or overlook the importance of their own feelings and value judgments.

Stage Three: Social and Historical Influences

It is significant in this stage for the teacher to help students expand upon their personal experiences and connect to the social and historical forces that have influenced their experiences. Descriptive data can be gathered on specific areas in the community that can be identified as particularly aesthetic, such as buildings painted with murals. In what sections of the community are these areas located? Does this place have special significance for the people living there? What social values influence decisions about the appearance of this community place? What colors, symbols, and shapes were chosen? Who makes decisions about developing aesthetic areas in the community? Are decisions made by individuals or by community groups? Do people get the chance to vote on aesthetic decisions affecting them? Are special places created to preserve and exhibit aesthetic objects in the community, such as museums or community centers? Are any of these places related in some way to the community's status or sense of identity? Are the community's place for aesthetics or aesthetic places known throughout the state or even nationally? Are particular individuals or groups associated with these places? Critical dialogue needs to be developed that will lead students to examine their own experiences with aesthetic experiences that relate to the cultural system of the larger community.

Historical studies could be centered around objects identified by students as aesthetic, such as clothing, fashions, posters, and transportation designs. How have different periods in history reflected different aesthetic standards in these areas? What factors have influenced these changes? Compare standards of beauty in particular societies in history, such as the Renaissance or the Flapper Period of the 1920s. Study art forms from these periods. What economic or political forces affected these standards? What are fads in styles or design? How are they developed and for what reasons? What specific groups are associated with fads?

This stage involves investigating hidden assumptions related to historical roots as well as how ideas have evolved and changed over time. It is important that dialogue and questioning in this stage come out of the data gathered from stage two and be related to the students' own experiences.

Stage Four: Cross-Cultural Lenses

The ability to compare and contrast one's culture with other cultural perspectives is essential to acquiring cultural literacy. Comparing aesthetic values and attitudes of others makes it possible to imagine how one's own cultural belief system could be different. For example, personal space is perceived differently in different cultures. People in some European cultures stand closer when conversing with each other and are more animated in their body language. Different cultural perceptions such as the use of space in environment and social interaction are also observed differently in works of art. The representation of space in paintings by Western artists using a traditional Western perspective to orient their view of the individual's relation to the environment differs dramatically from traditional Chinese paintings that stress the significance of nature, use vertical placement, emphasize atmospheric conditions, and have large areas of suggested space with limited details. Cross-cultural studies not only help students to become sensitive to different values and beliefs but help them to understand their own experiences and attitudes from a new perspective. Aspects of the students' culture that were internalized become more consciously apparent and provide a basis for extended in-depth studies.

Students can begin the cross-cultural stage by identifying a particular minority culture within their own area, such as the Amish in Ohio, an Appalachian group, or Native Americans; or any microculture such as coal miners, teachers, farmers, or a community arts group, provided their choices have been extensively researched and documented. Students would investigate some of the basic art concepts in these cultures, such as ideas of time and the use of space; concepts regarding the relation of art to progress, feelings, and the environment; use of symbols and language; and the roles of women, men, and children as revealed in art. Changes over time within the microculture would be discussed. Issues of cultural conflict due to living within a modern Western technological society would be examined. Questions would be raised in relation to the major theme being explored (i.e., beauty and aesthetic preferences). What aesthetic standards have been developed by the group? Who is responsible for developing these standards, and how are they reinforced and established? How are these similar to or different from the students' own aesthetic experiences and feelings? Cross-cultural studies can be expanded to include other technological countries such as Japan or even more diverse cultures such as aboriginal groups in Australia.

It is important to maintain the students' own sociocultural experiences and perceptions as the center for this and all the stages. These various stages in cultural literacy allow students continually to examine and be aware of their own aesthetic values and belief systems. Previous stages can be referred to and recycled in the learning process.

Stage Five: Future Perspectives

This stage promotes expanded thinking, allowing for speculation regarding concepts, projections of new ideas, and the use of imagination related to art. Students need to be able to explore personal concepts and ideas in art and culture to expand their imaginations and express possibilities for the future. There should be critical dialogue regarding changes and their implications, with designed scenarios of how their lives might be affected. The identification of what aspects of the culture related to art could be modified and controlled by individuals and what areas might be beyond their control should be examined. Cultural themes can center around fantasy or fictional types of societies. Literature focusing on the future and projections about society can be used as resource and curriculum material (Naisbett, 1982; Toffler, 1970).

Fine arts, popular arts, mass media, and folk arts centering on fantasy or the future can provide material for examination. Films, documentation, and artifacts from world fairs can be rich sources of data. What future was projected by the people of the 1939 World Fair in New York? What aesthetic objects were highlighted? Which speculations about the future actually came to pass, and which ideas were never realized and even appear naïve and outdated today? What social and political events shaped these projections and dreams for the future? How do political changes and other forces have to be taken into account when designing for the future? Today, for example, transportation and technology in communication leave literally no one isolated or separated from the rest of the world. What might transportation and communication systems be like in the future? How might they take into account human dimensions of design and issues of individual rights and possible invasions of privacy?

Children's literature, science fiction, and animated film can be of major interest and an important part of stimulating students' imaginations and personal ideas about possible societies or what they would like to see happen in the future. Hollywood, for example, has portrayed life on other planets. What kind of beings do they portray and in what types of culture? Do these films suggest a different concept of beauty or aesthetic preference than we might have? Do beings from outer space appear attractive? What aesthetic standards are used? What message do these films communicate about being different? Has there been a change in the motion picture industry's portrayal of outer space; if so, what has influenced this? How do students feel about these films? Can they relate on a personal level to what they see on the screen? What taken-for-granted beliefs or myths in our culture are carried over into the film-making industry? How does the film-maker in animation exaggerate some of these myths?

Students can continue to clarify their own beliefs and cultural assumptions as they create new scenarios in an art form of interest to them. They can be encouraged to work in groups and create a small television production, a mural, a model environmental setting, a dramatization of a model culture of the future with costumes and a stage design, a model community museum of the future (Plank, 1986), or a film or animation of evolutionary concepts demonstrating change over time.

Important questions such as what roles women and men will play in these new cultures will need to be addressed. Will roles of the art historian and art critic be the same? How will aesthetic standards change? Will more people in different cultures be involved in establishing aesthetic standards and at what level of participation? This stage in cultural literacy opens up opportunities for brainstorming and allows for greater imaginative thinking to take creative visual and verbal form.

Major Objectives for Cultural Literacy in Art Education

The development of cultural literacy is essential within the context of a democratic setting and prepares citizens for significant aspects of membership in their community. A cultural literacy program in art education allows for questioning of cultural assumptions, thereby providing for individual freedom and cultivating the responsibility for developing conscious aesthetic choices using individual and group democratic processes. The following are my major objectives in developing a cultural literacy curriculum in art:

1. To develop critical thinking and dialogue in art with skills obtained through using (a) phenomenological approaches, (b) social-historical methods, (c) cross-cultural perspectives, and (d) projections into the future
2. To examine the full range of visual aesthetic forms, including fine arts (historical and contemporary), popular arts, mass media, ethnic arts, and folk arts, beginning with art the student is most familiar with and then expanding outward through all the art forms
3. To develop students' own aesthetic forms, including fine arts (historical and contemporary), popular arts, mass media, ethnic arts, and folk arts, beginning with art the student is most familiar with and then expanding outward through all the art forms
4. To aid in building sensitivity to change and acquiring ideas from diverse orientations and different cultures where ethnocentrism or elitism are not encouraged
5. To respect the individual's background and capabilities as a primary foundation for development of the art curriculum, with the equal rights of all learners supported in a learning environment that allows for expanding on their interests and their own cultural aesthetic traditions

Conclusion

The cultural literacy program in art education outlined in this chapter is not the only approach to developing critical thinking and dialogue in the arts. It could be incorporated with other approaches that the teacher is already using in the classroom. However, a cultural literacy program does delineate an approach that begins with the individual's own feelings and perceptions of reality and builds upon these by progressing through stages that expand on one's way of looking at the world of art. The students are not directed by any absolute standard of aesthetics but are allowed the opportunity to explore, examine, and evaluate their own cultural aesthetics and origins, contrast and compare these with other cultures, and imagine new worlds of thinking. They thus are provided opportunities to take control of their own aesthetic decisions and values.

Cultural literacy in art promotes intellectual development and critical thinking, the essence of education. Cultural literacy is essential at every stage of learning and development. All types of learners need to be included—the exceptional, handicapped, and gifted—and from the early years of schooling to the later periods of life. In order to maintain democracy in an increasingly complex and technological society, people need to take responsibility for decision making and controls that affect their lives. If educational systems promote equality of learning and the belief that students should have the freedom to develop their own critical, conscious choices, then democratic principles will be continued best by those citizens most able to practice individual and group processes in democracy. It is my belief that art education can contribute to the people's quality of life and their sense of social responsibility if it is directed toward expanding their conscious aesthetic choices and promoting respect and understanding for the artistic expression and cultural differences of others.

References

American heritage dictionary (2nd college ed.). (1982). Boston: Houghton Mifflin.

Bersson, R. (1986). Why art education lacks social relevance: A contextual analysis. *Art Education, 39*(4), 41–45.

Bourguignon, E. (1979). *Psychological anthropology: An introduction to human nature and cultural difference.* New York: Holt, Rinehart and Winston.

Bowers, C. A. (1974). *Cultural literacy for freedom.* Eugene, OR: Elan Publishers.

Boyer, B. A. (1984, July). *Cultural literacy for the preparation of art educators in a changing society.* Paper presented at the Twenty-fifth World Congress of the International Society Through Art, Rio de Janeiro, Brazil.

Boyer, B. A. (1985, April). *Culture as a pervasive quality in aesthetic perception.* Paper presented at the National Art Education Association Conference, Dallas, Texas.

Boyer, B. A. (1986). The pervasiveness of culture: Significance for art education. *The Bulletin on Social Theory and Art Education, 6*, 51–58.

Congdon, K. G. (1985). The study of folk art in our school's art classrooms: Some problems and considerations. *Journal of Multi-cultural and Cross-cultural Research in Art Education, 3*(1), 65–75.

Cook, J. A. (1976). Language and cultural learning. In J. Roberts & S. K. Akinsamya (Eds.), *School in the cultural context* (pp. 341–352). New York: David McKay.

Dictionary of education. (1959). C. V. Good (Ed.). New York: McGraw-Hill.

Naisbett, J. (1982). *Megatrends.* New York: Warner Books.

Philips, S. U. (1983). *The invisible culture.* New York: Longman.

Plank, J. (1986). *A method for the development of cultural art activities focused on artistically gifted elementary students.* Unpublished master's thesis, Ohio State University.

Toffler, A. (1970). *Future shock*. New York: Random House.

Wilcox, K. (1982). Ethnography as a methodology and its application to the study of schooling: A review. In G. Spindler (Ed.), *Doing the ethnography of schooling* (pp. 456–488). New York: Holt, Rinehart and Winston.

PART IV

Freedom of Aesthetic Choice
in Work and Play

QUESTIONS REGARDING WHICH ART FORMS are most appropriate for study are not new to art education. Some theorists recommend that we bring the world of the great masterpieces—those works that reside in the great museums of the world—to all students. Others say that we should study other art forms as well, for example, those that have come to be called the popular arts and the folk arts. The question we pose here is, Does the choice of content by those in power in art curricula dictate aesthetic preference to students and the public at large? Is there a widely held belief that only a few people are trained to know what art the general public should appreciate? Does the sole understanding of "masters" by some elite group limit students' education?

The answer to these questions may be that, although the viewing of a Rembrandt or Picasso facilitates an aesthetic response for many people, a public not schooled to appreciate Rembrandt or Picasso is not a public unable to enjoy art. John Berger (1972; see Selected Bibliography), in his writings on art, has reminded us many times that there are forces in society whose interest it is that the majority should value certain things, in this case the "masters." Thus it is likely that there is a public whose aesthetic preferences are simply not recognized by the professional trained by an art school. Those who make choices in curriculum content, museum purchases, and arts organization funding could meaningfully enhance their range of aesthetic choices if they were to understand the world views and training of more diverse groups representative of our pluralistic society. With broadened sensitivity in accepting multidimensional aesthetic values, loggers who carve cowboy scenes, homemakers who make quilts, and the Ozark craftspeople who make fiddles will have something to teach a Rembrandt lover, and vice versa.

Our aesthetic preferences are, to a large degree, learned as part of our lifestyles and are not necessarily the result of a formal education alone. Preferences relate to our economic, religious, regional, occupational, generational, ethnic, and recreational ties. Our aesthetic preferences are connected to our value systems. The imposition on children, youth, and adults of an art curriculum based upon an alien aesthetic has nothing to do with democratic principles and much to do with the notion of a "manifest destiny" applied to art. Economically powerful groups like the Rockefeller Foundation, the J. Paul Getty Foundation, and the Lincoln Center have launched, or intend to launch, projects that are "fine-art" oriented and exclude points of view probably shared by many people. If educators, curators, and arts organizers do not allow and even fight for the freedom of aesthetic choice, then we are working against the concept of cultural pluralism and stifling the aesthetic stimulus that flows from naturally occurring social processes. The following chapters are designed to sensitize the reader to the process of aesthetic choice and its varieties and to suggest how a democratic society can function to insure freedom in this dynamic process, as opposed to choking it off through unnecessary and counterproductive constraints. The focus in this section is placed on the influence of occupations on aesthetic preferences and how the aesthetic impulse functions in organizations and education. The last chapter draws our attention toward an ecological aesthetic and a sensitivity to a "Green frame of mind."

Chapter 9

Occupational Art and Occupational Influences on Aesthetic Preferences: A Democratic Perspective

___Kristin G. Congdon___

Multicultural Art Education:
Democratic in Theory

In the United States and Canada, a culturally pluralistic society is thought to be one where multiple ideas and expressions can come together for the enhancement of a community and a country. Most citizens, theoretically, view the coming together and possible exchange between cultural groups as a positive experience which can enhance the lives of everyone.

To some degree, education has attempted at least in theory to benefit from cultural diversity, as one of its proponents states in this passage:

> Multicultural education rejects the view that schools should seek to melt away cultural differences or the view that schools should merely tolerate cultural pluralism. Instead, multicultural education affirms that schools should be oriented toward the cultural enrichment of all children and youth through programs rooted to the preservation and extension of cultural diversity as a fact of life in the American society, and it affirms that this cultural diversity

110

is a valuable resource that should be preserved and extended. (Lovano-Kerr & Zimmerman, 1977, p. 34)

The founders of democracy in the United States said much the same, and I concur with their foundational beliefs. We believe in and celebrate the freedom of expression and the right to make choices in lifestyles and religion. We believe that no single group should dominate and dictate to others; that everyone has potential and can have successes. And we believe in the right to a free public education that is instrumental in assisting in the preservation of all our democratic goals. These beliefs are our ideals.

To promote a multicultural (and democratic) perspective in education, it has been suggested that multicultural educational approaches be applied to every discipline in order to encourage curriculum-wide consciousness (Rodriguez & Sherman, 1983). This approach is not only for schools with mixed racial populations but for every educational institution. Art educators have just begun to study what a multicultural approach to schooling means and how it can be implemented (Congdon, 1985; Newman, 1970).

The Gap Between Theory and Practice

Unfortunately, there is a vast gap between our theoretical ideals and our everyday practice in education and in daily life. This gap persists because of our fallibility as humans, our inability to know how to expedite theory into practice, and often because of a lack of honest desire to find ways of facilitating our ideals.

Progress in the last few decades has been slow. Multicultural education is often mistakenly identified with ethnic groups alone (Congdon, 1985), whereas we should also be studying the art, criticism, and aesthetics of religious, occupational, regional, generational, and recreational groups, as well as the much-neglected artistic processes of a variety of female populations.

Because it is easier to focus on what we know best, the art curriculum often reflects what we learned as students, viewing reproductions of what appears in the galleries and museums of the world. This, we were told, is the art most deserving of our attention. This approach brings about situations in which some people are the "advantaged" (those who "know" about "good" art) while others are the "disadvantaged" (those who do not "know" about "good" art). As Ianni (1968) contends, "In my experience with the 'disadvantaged,' I have seen very few programs in the arts which do not attempt to take the best of what 'we' have to offer in order to help 'them' fit better in our world" (p. 18). The arts of varying cultural groups, as well as their approaches to appreciating these arts, should be studied without relegating their values in life to a backward, primitive, or simplistic status (Chatterjee, 1980).

The linear approach of Western academic culture has been to categorize certain artistic acts as "more advanced" or "less advanced," according to elitist standards. Time and history in the Western world are linear rather than circular. There is first class and third class; fine art and folk art. Ryan (1981) describes this dilemma in another way:

> We are . . . obliged to agree that all [humans] are created equal—whatever that might mean to us today. . . .
>
> But our lives are saturated with reminders about whose dog is better. In almost all our daily deeds, we silently pledge allegiance to inequity, insisting on the continual labeling of winners and losers, of Phi Beta Kappans and flunk outs, and on an order in which a few get much and the rest get little. . . .
>
> We re-create the ambiguity in the minds of our children as we teach them both sides of the contradiction. "No one is better than anyone else," we warn. "Don't act snotty and superior." At the same time, we teach them that all are obliged to get ahead, to compete, to achieve. Everyone is equal? Yes. Everyone must try to be superior? Again, yes. The question reverberates. (p. 4)

We verbalize that, theoretically, we are all equal; but in practice the linear, one-up/one-down perspective prevails. It has become difficult to observe differences in ways other than hierarchical. Herskovits (1941/ 1970) pointed out long ago that customs are "subjectively compared in terms of better or worse, higher or lower. This means that scholars, drawing comparisons of this nature, have merely reacted to their own conditioning, which has given them a predisposition to bring in verdicts which favor their own customs and to place different cultures on levels that are deemed less advanced" (p. 296). As Lindbloom and Cohen (1979) note, knowledge is political and is based on the values of its proponents.

Those in the established elite artworld view art similarly. Theoretically, perhaps, it is easy to say that many—perhaps all—cultures have superior art; but in reality, the art heralded in New York City is often done by New York artists and other academically trained artists with art-bureaucracy connections. Categorization of art forms by artists themselves also helps establish the idea of the "best art," thus determining which artwork has more or less value. Fine art is, of course, valued as better (Congdon, 1986a); and falling below the "best art" is what is called folk art, tourist art, and popular art. For many, the art of children and the disabled is at the bottom. When we talk about folk artists, mavericks, or native artists (Becker, 1982), we are speaking about how these people stand in relation to the organized artworld. The established artworld—whose views are, of course, subjective—has taken the power to define art categories and thus set up the valued and less valued art strata.[1]

If the art facilitator chooses narrowly from the established elite art forms, aesthetic preferences, art criticism formats, and language systems (Congdon, 1986b) to which students are exposed, a form of cultural invasion takes place. "In cultural invasion, it is essential that those who are invaded come to see their reality with the outlook of the invaders rather than their own" (Freire, 1968, p. 151). The result of the paternalistic, I-know-what's-best-for-you approach to education "can communicate even to very young children so intense a sense of being of no value to the larger society, let alone to parents, that self-esteem and cognition and emotional development are grossly thwarted" (Wallace, 1961, p. 162).

Although as citizens, scholars, artists, and art educators we may believe theoretically in democracy and multicultural education, it does not readily happen. Becker (1982) and Banfield (1984) claim that the government dictates aesthetics economically, and Truitt (1977) and Lippard (1984) link the continuing narrowly focused recognition of "fine art" with the reinforcement of the domination of one class over others. Some have accused our schools, art museums, and other educational institutions of keeping people in their allotted socioeconomic "places." About schools, Ryan (1981) states:

> They are not springboards to social mobility, where individual merit is unerringly identified and nourished. They are, in fact, major social institutions that serve at once to sustain and cement inequality and to prepare a relatively docile work force for various levels in the hierarchy of labor. Its task is not to open the minds of youth to the glories of eternal truth and beauty, but rather to artificially enhance the egos of the children of the well-to-do and brutally assault the egos of the children of workers and poor people. (pp. 136–137)

If cultural invasion and economic, aesthetic, and educational domination do occur in our art educational settings, and I believe they do, we must ask how art facilitators can make changes to insure a more democratic

---

[1]I do not mean to say that categorization of art does not have its positive aspects. Indeed, the title of this chapter is such a categorization. These definitions are done in the spirit of recognizing neglected art forms and giving credence to the enculturation of certain aesthetic preferences.

approach based on the recognition and celebration of multicultural approaches.

Art, Aesthetic Experiences, and Multicultural Perspectives

The assumption behind ideas of cultural pluralism is that there are groups of people with varying ways of living and differing value systems who may respond differently to the various art forms. Speaking of the conjecture that people respond similarly to artistic activities, Bunzel (1938) points out:

> A glance at the varying canons of beauty in different ages and among different people shows the impossibility of assuming the existence of such absolutes. The mutilations of the human body in the name of beauty have always been striking. The Cretans cultivated wasp waists for men and women thousands of years ago, and the ancient Egyptians shaved their heads and wore wigs. The Kwakiutl Indians deform the heads of babies; the Chinese women bind their feet. Australian aborigines cover their bodies with raised scars; certain African tribes file their teeth to points. (pp. 537–538)

Banfield (1984) identifies at least four modes of aesthetic response and maintains that "what we experience aesthetically could not be experienced in the same way by people whose culture—perceptions, thoughts, feelings—vastly differ from our own" (p. 21). D'Azevedo (1958) also writes about the object's aesthetic significance as determined by the values of the members of a sociocultural system.

Aesthetic experiences occur daily as people go about their everyday lives (Dewey, 1934). As Radar and Jessup (1976) point out,

> almost anything, object or activity, private or public, domestic or civic, must please in appearance as well as serve in use to satisfy fully. It would be hard indeed to think of any utilitarian object, big or small, important or trivial, from cooking pots and corkscrews to airlines and office buildings, in which some extrafunctional element of aesthetic appeal is regularly and entirely absent. And this element is one of the familiar sources of the aesthetic in common life. (pp. 105–106)

Certainly occupation influences aesthetic appreciation. Children brought up in a farming family, a steel-working community, or in military life will be influenced by the aesthetic components that become a part of their reality and value system. Since artistic perception takes place within a cultural context, these cultural values become part of an artistic act of creation or a response of appreciation or rejection of a form (Chalmers, 1984).

To return art to the people in a democratic manner, as Truitt (1977), Bersson (1984), and others demand, art education must employ democratic participation in the selection, production, criticism, and modes of aesthetic responses that are employed by art facilitators. In this way, cultural democracy for all people will be promoted. As Bersson (1984, p. 42) states, "Cultural democracy or equalitarianism means pluralism, diversity, variety and difference, and financial and educational support for the full range of visual culture." Art should be studied that is meaningful to the targeted population (Chalmers, 1981; Lanier, 1984), and the art of other cultures must be understood within its appropriate cultural context (Haselberger, 1961; McFee & Degge, 1977). Further, art should be presented as a vital part of people's lives, including their social concerns, moral dilemmas, and human interactions (Beyer, 1984). We must broaden our definition of the term *art* and the way we approach it, value it, and teach others to know it.

Paid Occupations and Artistic and Aesthetic Activities

One step in the direction of broadening our view is to acknowledge and study a most neglected area of artistic expression: those art forms that come about largely from occupational influences and the aesthetic responses of groups of people who have been influenced largely by an occupational lifestyle. By recognizing and incorporating the art and appreciation processes from varying occupational influences into the galleries, museum collections, school curricula, and other community art programs, we can facilitate a more democratic art education.

There are many ways to view occupations and their artistic and aesthetic activities. Jones (1980) suggests that work can often be regarded as an artistic endeavor, that rhythm and skill are involved in work, as is the perfection of form. As an example, he tells about an Astoria, Oregon, woman who, while cleaning tuna, takes special note of her sensory experiences while she handles, manipulates, and changes the materials (Garson, 1975). Jones concludes that present-day researchers rarely treat contemporary workers as artists, whereas the classic cultural studies of Boas (1927/1955) and others did indeed view the physical labors of early industries as art.

The more familiar artists-by-occupation include painters, sculptors, and potters, but there are many others who are also artists by occupation.

Stonecarvers can be identified by their work and placed in certain geographic regions (Gladstone, 1974). Tattooists have skills, designs, and color preferences which are judged aesthetically by the creators, other tattooists, those who are tattooed, and other appreciators (Saint Claire & Govenar, 1981). Other occupational groups such as beauticians, van painters, furniture makers, and window dressers should also be considered.

Less studied areas of occupational art and aesthetics are those employment activities that encourage artistic work in areas generally perceived as being nonartistic. Individuals who work with wood and wood products have a specialized kind of knowledge, and many northwestern loggers have become whittlers and carvers (Oregon Arts Commission, 1980). They learn from other logger/carvers and are encouraged to play with the wood, to test it, and to see what can be done with it. They create wooden chains, fans, and scenes from the old West. Yet, when they are asked about their occupation, they often identify themselves as loggers rather than artists or wood carvers.

Edgar Tolson, a philosopher and sometime-preacher from Kentucky, also carves scenes related to his work experience (Bishop, 1974). His numerous versions of the Adam and Eve theme and his eight-part representation of the "Fall of Man" are among his most recognized works.

Farmers and gardeners still make scarecrows in traditional and unusual dress, as witnessed by the research of Gladstone (1974) and Neal (1978):

> Spring planting with all its hope and cautions stimulated the creative urge and prompted raids on closets, barns, and musty attic trunks for an assortment of old clothes suitable for a scarecrow's attire. Anything from last season's fancy dress outfits down to faded overalls and shredded straw hats was fair game to the scarecrow enthusiast. Then, as now, the purpose was twofold—to frighten away unwelcome predators and to brighten an otherwise unadorned landscape. (Neal, 1978, p. 7)

An organized crop or garden with straight rows is a grower's delight. The careful organization of the plot of land becomes a part of the grower's aesthetic sensitivity and influences the pleasure taken in viewing and arranging other visual aspects of life.

Whalers of the past, using available materials with little commercial value, made scrimshaw, which is widely collected today (Bishop, 1974). Whale bones and the 4- to 10-inch teeth from the whale's lower jaw provided excellent carving materials. Carving served several purposes: "Whaling expeditions frequently lasted up to four years and often proved fatal to the men. The tensions of physical danger, rigorous environment, and many idle hours were relieved by the sailors' pastime of creating scrimshaw objects" (Bishop, 1974, p. 107). When the voyagers returned home safely, the scrimshaw carvings were given to friends and relatives as trophies of the long and perilous trips (Lipman & Winchester, 1974).

The seafaring occupations continue to influence aesthetic preferences. As with other cultural influences, the work that one does, or the work of one's family members, influences personal perception and creative visual observation. As the daughter of a Navy officer, for me the Christmas holidays always included a trip to the navy-base harbor to see the ships decorated with lights. Navy Captain John Bitoff describes some of these displays in detail, ending with the statement, "It was gorgeous!"[2] "Operation Decorama" is usually judged for the best display in each harbor, and Captain Bitoff reports a high level of meaning in this decoration process: It helps alleviate loneliness for the young sailors away from home for the first time during the holidays, and it brings people on the ship together and creates a festive mood. The trips to see the ships were a special time for me, and I know that I appreciate the holiday lights more today because of this childhood experience.

Chuck Haywood, a retired coast guard sailor, ties knots for displays, frame decorations, and commemorative plaques.[3] His aesthetic appreciation of this nautical tradition is connected to his seafaring past and to the stories and folk beliefs associated with the knots, which he learned, in part, from visits with the residents of an "old sailors' home" in Connecticut. The Smithsonian has recognized Haywood's work, calling him "the world's greatest rope artist."

Many cowboys, past and present, decorated their world with carved saddles, riatas, buckles, and spurs (Toelken, 1980). In terms of their visual adornment and folklore, the cowboys, otherwise referred to as buckaroos in northeastern California, northern Nevada, southwestern Idaho, and southeastern Oregon, are an especially rich group (Loomis, 1980). As demonstrated in their clothing and occupational equipment, those who engage in ranching activities have a common love of animals and a respect for the land which create a gentle kind of camaraderie (Taylor & Maar, 1983) and a sense of identity.

The art of industrial workers is now being studied as it relates to the identity and skills of the factory worker. Nickerson (1983) reports that, while many of the handmade products of factory workers are unimaginative, such as knives made from old files, a worker sometimes creates

---

[2]S. Goranson interviewed Captain John W. Bitoff, Virginia Beach, Virginia, on December 11, 1984.

[3]S. Goranson and K. G. Congdon interviewed Charles Haywood, Virginia Beach, Virginia, on May 18, 1984.

something truly inspiring, such as the welder who made a menagerie of 16 animals out of solid titanium. Ohrn (1984) describes the work of Iowa resident Charles Hickson, who, after retiring in 1977 from 30 years of autobody repair, used metal scraps to create an assortment of lawn ornaments, such as a ferris wheel and a Kansas jayhawk. Hickson maintains that everyone who sees the ornaments, all painted black and surrounding his front yard, likes them.

There are many other examples of workers' art from metal sculpting. Orthodontic students at the University of Washington make elaborate sculptures as part of their course requirements. Their professor, Dr. Stanton Hall, gave the following report:

> The introduction of the sculptural approach was an innovation designed to familiarize the orthodontic student with metallurgical properties of orthodontic materials. Instead of asking the student to repeatedly perform wire bending and welding operations in the standard boring manner, the student was instead asked to design and execute a sculpture using routine orthodontic materials. This activity not only accomplished the minimal task of familiarizing the student with the materials, but also exercised their creative and aesthetic appreciation. This exercise is performed during the first quarter of their orthodontic education and culminates in the presentation of awards at the annual Faculty/Student dinner just prior to Christmas vacation. Competition in this activity is keen. (Personal communication, August 5, 1985)

Dr. Hall further explains that awards are given for: (1) the most aesthetically pleasing, (2) the most innovative design, and (3) the highest technical competence. Fourteen to twenty faculty members view and judge the sculptures each year. Several orthodontists in Ohio were aware of these sculptures and spoke to me about them with great enthusiasm and interest.

How one dresses for one's paid work activities also forms one's identity and aesthetic choices. Santino (1986) recounts that the black Americans he studied who had secured jobs as Pullman porters were elated about getting out of denims and into neckties, and Nickerson (1983) reports that a factory worker's job category may be identified by the work clothes that are worn:

> Machinists will wear second-best sports clothes with short-sleeve shirts, frequently topped by an apron, while inspectors, who work in a cleaner environment, may wear long-sleeve shirts and a generally cleaner outfit sans apron. One of the machinists I worked with preferred to wear less expensive sports shirts, bought especially for the purpose, rather than work shirts, because he didn't want to look "like a working slob." (p. 124)

Art as a By-product of Monetarily Unpaid Occupations

Many people spend a great deal of time creating artworks and environmental spaces as a major unpaid activity. Their reasons for creating art may not be economic, nor may they hope to see the works placed in museums or galleries. Academic critics have viewed these activities as being less serious and noteworthy than what has been called "good" or "great" art. However, those who take the time to evaluate critically much of the artistic work done in the mainstream of life, regardless of economic rewards or museum/gallery status, may find some exceptionally exciting creations.

Household arts created before the Industrial Revolution were often made by women, from available materials such as scraps of fabric saved for use in sewing quilts and in hooking, braiding, and weaving rag rugs. Today, the continuation of these types of creative activities and others that are similar in their recycling of materials has been referred to by Lippard (1984) as associated with the act of rehabilitation on both an emotional and practical level:

> Patching, turning collars and cuffs, remaking old clothes, changing buttons, refinishing or recovering old furniture are all the traditional private resorts of the economically deprived woman to give her family public dignity. The syndrome continues today, even though in affluent Western societies cheap clothes fall apart before they can be rehabilitated and inventive patching is more acceptable (to the point where expensive new clothes are made to look rehabilitated and thrift shops are combed by the well-off). (p. 103)

Lippard (1984) suggests that the criteria for excellence in art vary, but good taste should be not standardized by museums alone. Careful evaluation of the judgment of the elite regarding women's occupational art is needed. Many female homemakers bring great sensitivity and creativity to the clothes they make and patch, and to the environmental spaces they create on kitchen counter tops, bathroom sinks, and living room gathering spots. The food they prepare, the tables they set, and even the manner in which they hang wet clothes out to dry often show aesthetic sensitivities. The homemaker's goals differ from the factory worker, the orthodontist, and the farmer. Her experiences and her materials vary. Her perceptions and responsibilities are also different. But she continually creates, makes aesthetic choices, and communicates values.

There are also individuals who spend the majority of their time creating unusual monumental works of art who do not think of themselves as artists. Teressa Prisbrey, in her eighties, built a bottle village in Simi Valley, California, to commemorate her family members (Crease & Mann, 1983). The work consists of a cluster of small shelters and sculptural pieces made mostly of cement and glass. She was motivated by the need to house her collections of pencils, seashells, and dolls, most of which had been tossed away by others.

Some individuals confined in jails and prisons also create art. Female jail inmates may create costumes to identify who they are or who they are striving to become (Congdon, 1984). Other inmates may secretly spend their time making weapons, especially knives, out of any metal they find available (Jackson, 1966). One inmate made an ingenious belt buckle with a secret compartment to hide narcotics and money. As with other materially deprived individuals, incredible creativity can result among prisoners when there is a perceived need, using whatever resources are available.

While those who are paid for work tend to separate their paid jobs from their home life, for homemakers, inmates, and a great many individuals like Teressa Prisbrey, one's occupation is fused to a high degree with one's life.

Conclusion

To democratize the study of art, occupational influences and occupational art should be studied further. It is a good way to recognize and understand cultural diversity, to study art in its context, to democratize the arts, and to achieve aesthetic freedom. It is also a way to gain knowledge about the functions of art in people's lives, knowledge that individuals and groups can use to make rational decisions about cultural change and cultural stability. The result of a broader understanding of how occupations and artistic activities are interrelated should help promote aesthetic freedom.

We understand fairly readily that in all kinds of art *processes* there are individual pieces that can be more highly valued than others. It is also true that not all artistic *forms* can be equally valued by everyone. Thus, as Lanier (1979, p. 105) puts it, "Taste should be the individual's prerogative, as long as—from an educational viewpoint—choices are made on the basis of knowledge rather than a result of ignorance." Aestheticians will continue to study the premises and arguments people use to justify and define activities as being "art," "beautiful," and so forth (Becker, 1982, p. 131). We will not stop wanting to teach children and adults to become aestheticians and art critics, but we will want them to use the widest possible range of criteria for judging so that art from a variety of cultural contexts may be studied and appreciated. To accomplish this, we must begin to understand how people formulate and relate their judgments and artistic processes to their life-worlds, including their occupational contexts.

References

Banfield, E. C. (1984). *The democratic muse: Visual arts and the public interest.* New York: Basic Books.

Becker, H. S. (1982). *Art worlds.* Berkeley: University of California Press.

Bersson, R. (1984). For cultural democracy in art education. *Art Education, 37*(6), 40–43.

Beyer, L. E. (1984). The arts, school practice and cultural transformation. *The Bulletin of the Caucus on Social Theory and Art Education, 4,* 1–13.

Bishop, R. (1974). *American folk sculpture.* New York: E. P. Dutton.

Boas, F. (1955). *Primitive art.* New York: Dover. (Original work published 1927)

Bunzel, R. (1938). Art. In F. Boas (Ed.), *General anthropology.* Boston: D. C. Heath.

Chalmers, F. G. (1981). Art education as ethnology. *Studies in Art Education, 22*(3), 6–14.

Chalmers, F. G. (1984). Artistic perception: The cultural context. *Journal of Art and Design Education, 3*(3), 279–289.

Chatterjee, M. (1980). The arts in cultural diversity. In J. Condous, J. Howlett, & J. Skull (Ed.), *Arts in cultural diversity* (pp. 133–137). Sydney, Australia: Holt, Rinehart & Winston.

Congdon, K. G. (1984). Art education in a jail setting: A personal perspective. *Art Education, 37*(2), 10–11.

Congdon, K. G. (1985). A folk group focus for multicultural education. *Art Education, 37*(1), 13–16.

Congdon, K. G. (1986a). Issues posed by the study of folk art in art education. *The Bulletin on Social Theory and Art Education, 6,* 13–25.

Congdon, K. G. (1986b). The meaning and use of folk speech in art criticism. *Studies in Art Education, 27*(3), 140–148.

Crease, R., & Mann, C. (1983, August). Backyard creators of art that says: "I did it, I'm here." *Smithsonian, 14*(5), 82–91.

d'Azevedo, W. L. (1958). A structural approach to esthetics: Toward a definition of art in anthropology. *American Anthropologist, 60*(4), 702–714.

Dewey, J. (1934). *Art as experience.* New York: G. P. Putnam's Sons.

Freire, P. (1968). *Pedagogy of the oppressed.* New York: Seabury Press.

Garson, B. (1975). *All the livelong day: The meaning and demeaning of routine work.* Garden City, NY: Doubleday.

Gladstone, M. J. (1974). *A carrot for a nose: The form of folk sculpture on America's city streets and country roads.* New York: Scribner's.

Haselberger, H. (1961). Method of studying ethnological art. *Current Anthropology, 2*(4), 341–384.

Herskovits, M. J. (1970). *The myth of the Negro past.* Gloucester, MA: Harper & Row. (Original work published 1941)

Ianni, F. A. J. (1968). The arts as agents for social change: An anthropologist's view. *Art Education, 21*(1), 15–20.

Jackson, B. (1966). Folk ingenuity behind bars. *New York Folklore Quarterly, 22*(4), 243–250.

Jones, M. O. (1980). A feeling for form. In N. Burlakoff & C. Lindal (Eds.), *Folklore on two continents: Essays in honor of Linda Degge* (pp. 260–269). Bloomington, IN: Trickster Press.

Lanier, V. (1979). Enhancing the aesthetic potential. In S. M. Dobbs (Ed.), *Arts education and back to basics* (pp. 96–112). Reston, VA: National Art Education Association.

Lanier, V. (1984). Eight guidelines for selecting art curriculum content. *Studies in Art Education, 25*(4), 232–237.

Lindbloom, C. F., & Cohen, D. (1979). *Usable knowledge: Social science and social problem solving.* New Haven, CT: Yale University Press.

Lipman, J., & Winchester, A. (1974). *The flowering of American folk art, 1776–1876.* New York: Viking Press.

Lippard, L. R. (1984). *Get the message? A decade of art for social change.* New York: E. P. Dutton.

Loomis, O. (1980). Buckaroos. In S. Jones (Ed.), *Webfoots and bunchgrassers: Folk art of the Oregon country* (pp. 86–103). Salem, OR: Oregon Arts Commission.

Lovano-Kerr, J., & Zimmerman, E. (1977). Multicultural teacher education program in the arts. *Art Education, 16,* 34–38.

McFee, J. K., & Degge, R. M. (1977). *Art, culture and environment.* Dubuque, IA: Kendall/Hunt.

Neal, A. (1978). *Scarecrows.* Photographed by A. Parker. Barre, MA: Barre Publishing.

Newman, A. (1970). Promoting intercultural understanding through art. *Art Education, 23*(1), 18–20.

Nickerson, B. E. (1983). Factory folklore. In R. M. Dorson (Ed.), *Handbook of American folklore* (pp. 121–127). Bloomington, IN: Indiana University Press.

Ohrn, S. (Ed.). (1984). *Passing time and traditions: Contemporary Iowa folk artists.* Ames, IA: Iowa State University Press.

Oregon Arts Commission. (1980). [Field notes for the 1980 show "Webfoots and bunchgrassers: Folk arts of the Oregon Country."] Unpublished research project, S. Jones, supervisor. Eugene, OR: Randall V. Mills Archives of Northwest Folklore, University of Oregon.

Radar, M., & Jessup, B. (1976). *Art and human values.* Englewood Cliffs, NJ: Prentice-Hall.

Rodriguez, F., & Sherman, A. (Dirs.). (1983). *Cultural pluralism and the arts.* Lawrence, KS: University of Kansas, School of Education.

Ryan, W. (1981). *Equality.* New York: Pantheon Books.

Saint Claire, L. L., & Govenar, A. B. (1981). *Stoney knows best: Life as a tatoo artist.* Lexington, KY: University Press of Kentucky.

Santino, J. (1986). A servant and a man, a hostess or a woman: A study of expressive culture in two transportation occupations. *Journal of American Folklore, 99*(393), 304–319.

Taylor, L., & Maar, I. (1983). *The American cowboy.* Washington, DC: Library of Congress, American Folklife Center.

Toelken, B. (1980). In the stream of life. In S. Jones (Ed.), *Webfoots and bunchgrassers: Folk art of the Oregon country* (pp. 8–38). Salem, OR: Oregon Arts Commission.

Truitt, W. H. (1977). Art for the people. In D. A. Mann (Ed.), *The arts in a democratic society* (pp. 58–69). Bowling Green, OH: Popular Press.

Wallace, A. F. C. (1961). *Culture and personality.* New York: Random House.

Chapter 10

Making Work Art and Art Work: The Aesthetic Impulse in Organizations and Education

___Michael Owen Jones_____

Increasingly in recent years, newspapers and business magazines are reporting major innovations in job design and the management of organizations, particularly factories. Workers, we learn, are being encouraged to make suggestions about how to improve the way tasks are carried out. In some factories, the assembly line has been replaced by work groups whose members construct a whole subassembly instead of chasing after a conveyor belt in order to do a single, simplistic operation over and over again; or at least the belt stops in front of the worker, who can spend extra time on the task and pull the green handle to send the assembly down the line only when completely satisfied the job is done properly. One novel idea is that every person is an inspector who is responsible for her or his own work, making sure no defect is passed along. Another unusual practice is to permit people to take part in making decisions about company matters affecting their activities and lives.

American companies adopting the notion of nonsynchronous assembly, work teams, quality circles, and consensus decision making or participative management are lauded for "rethinking the concepts of mass production," making significant "advances in manufacturing technique," developing "innovative solutions" to problems of factory design and the use of human labor, undergoing a "cultural revolution" in management theory and practice, and providing "a valuable lesson for all of American industry" (e.g., Jameson, 1984; Main, 1981; Potts, 1983; Weinstein, 1986).

124

What has just been discovered by American business and industry is that people want to control the raw materials and processes of production out of which they fashion objects, and are perfectly capable of doing so. Workers possess skills, insights, and imagination. They maintain standards of excellence. They want to be productive and to produce something of which they can be proud. What these new approaches boil down to is treating workers like artists and aesthetes in whom there is an urge to create and a need to have pleasant social and sensory experiences. At the same time that this trend is welcomed, one wonders why it seems that management is so surprised by a discovery that must have seemed self-evident to most workers.

Concepts of Art and Work: Paradigms and Paradoxes

Judging from much of art education and management philosophy, the answer to the question as to whether or not workers are artists must be a resounding "no!" Art and work have long been considered separate domains. There is art on the one hand and technology on the other. Never mind that the Latin and Greek roots *ars* and *techne* once denoted much the same thing that *craft* now connotes: a useful skill; or that in the Middle Ages an artist was called an artisan, an architect was called a master mason, and a musician was called a minstrel. What is important is that by the Renaissance many of the painters, sculptors, and architects were educated, having been trained in academies of design to practice "the most beautiful arts" rather than in guilds to engage in servile or mechanical pursuits. Design, or art, became that which is elegant, nonutile, and elevating. The close of the eighteenth century saw increasingly widespread use of the term *the fine arts* (a translation into English of the French *les beaux arts*, an expression familiar since the reign of Louis XIV a century earlier). Completing the changing conception of art as works or activities whose principal justification for being is beauty was the successful struggle at the end of the nineteenth century to free the artist from the restraints of academy and salon. "Art for art's sake" was the result (Munro, 1967).

It was also at the end of the nineteenth century that Frederick W. Taylor began to lecture, present papers, and publish essays on the nature of work in what were then modern industrial settings. He was familiar with the craft tradition, having rebelled against his father's plans for him to study law at Harvard, and instead had become an apprentice pattern-maker and machinist. Within a few years he had been promoted to management status, whereupon he set about finding ways to segment the process of labor. He dissociated the process of work from the skills of workers, separated conception of the product from its execution, and concentrated a monopoly of knowledge in management. While Taylor did not invent piece-rate payments, specialization, and standardization, he did articulate a philosophy and give it a name: *scientific management* (Braverman, 1974; Drucker, 1954; Whyte, 1961).

To summarize, "art" has come to be considered a specialized pursuit in which only a few gifted people engage. The products of art are elegant, refined, and nonutile. The process of making art is constrained only by the imagination and capabilities of the artist, who is in control of the tools, materials, techniques, and design of the object. By contrast, "work" in factories, offices, and other organizations can be scientifically structured and managed for greater efficiency. An industrial engineer conceptualizes the operation, the laborer is instructed in it, and someone else supervises the job to insure that it is done in the prescribed way and that variations are not introduced. Managerial control and discipline require placing jobs within a structure of authority, hence the hierarchical form of organization, the chain of command, and one-way communication. The model of organization is that of a mechanical system; the structure is sacrosanct, and people have to be fitted into it. Once in, they have to be told what to do and how, motivated by pay or other tangible inducements to perform, and closely supervised to assure quality and productivity. The realms of art and work, for most people today, are worlds apart.

Learning About Art, Work, and Organizations

How are these concepts communicated? Art educators inform the public of what art is or is not. The process begins at a very young age. Cathy Brooks, in "The Getting of Taste: A Child's Apprenticeship" (1981), writes about how her concepts of art and attitudes of taste developed as a youth in the 1950s and early 1960s.

> The objects and images teachers chose for art projects derived from popular and commercial art. Models of tasteful imagery usually consisted in romanticized portrayal of ideal situations, e.g., a picturesque landscape, a realistic likeness of attractive people with easily recognizable expressions. Subject matter often favored sentimental appeal or related a story with a moral. Words used to describe preferred qualities included, "pretty," "cute," "nice," and "adorable." (p. 8)

In other words, art was treated as a separate endeavor, with the focus on graphic depiction and the production of things intended to have an aesthetic function only (see also Brooks, 1980).

Similarly, notions about organizational life are communicated early through educational experiences. In "The Organization Child: Experience

Management in a Nursery School," Kanter (1972) reports her observations in the mid-1960s of the activities, philosophy, and values of personnel in a nursery school whose popularized neo–Freudian notions produced "children whose world orientations are adjusted and attuned to bureaucratic life" (p. 187). The key concepts were "rationality" and "rational control"—exactly the orientation underlying scientific management and preventing the appreciation of the aesthetic and symbolic ("irrational") aspect of organizational life. Activities in the nursery school were highly routinized, with "work" and "play" compartmentalized in time and space. Even in play, illusion and reality were constantly distinguished and differentiated. Role relationships were clearly delineated; there was no team work or consensual decision making between teachers and children, for the teachers were always socially distinguished from children by their bearing, control of certain resources and activities, and difference in tone of voice when speaking to a child. Games that teachers introduced had rules and procedures, not fantasy or illusion. The world depicted to children was one of rationality, logic, and pragmatism; it was not a world of "fantasy, fairy stories, and miraculous occurrences" (p. 199). Potentially unpleasant tasks (e.g., holding the door for others or carrying a wastebasket) were designated "honors," everyone's artistic output (i.e., painting or sculpture) was "wonderful," and there were no differential rewards for individual achievement.

Kanter (1972) concludes that the nursery school "was an organizational experience" requiring adaptation to its rational, routinized character and orienting the child, "like a bureaucrat, to the reliable performance of structured roles rather than to imagination" (pp. 203–204). "In fact, even though the expressed goal of the school involved promoting the growth of the children, the teachers spent more time managing the smooth running of the organization, just as in a bureaucracy, than they did dealing with the children's individual and psychological needs" (p. 203). Kanter urges the consideration of other ideas emphasizing "the unique and personal in human relations," defining "freedom to mean not the absence of demand and coercion but the absence of routinized structure," and recognizing the legitimacy of emotional expression, where "emotion, feeling, fantasies, and other expressions of non-intellectual personal realities would re-emerge as important parts of the educational process" (p. 209–210).

Art and Work in Everyday Life

At about the same time that many *fin de siècle* aestheticians were insisting that art is primarily the expression of emotion, and Frederick Taylor was counting steps and analyzing motions of industrial laborers in an effort toward increasing efficiency, Franz Boas was recording stories, noting songs, and documenting tools, masks, and the making of totem poles among the Northwest Coast Indians. Eventually he presented a synthesis of his findings and ideas in a book entitled *Primitive Art* (Boas, 1955), first published in 1927. In it, he writes, "All human activities may assume forms that give them esthetic values" (p. 9). While a word or a cry or unrestrained movements and many products of industry like tools and implements seemingly have no immediate aesthetic appeal, he observes, "nevertheless, all of them may assume esthetic values" (pp. 9–10). What is required for an activity to have aesthetic value is that an individual be aware of and manipulate qualities appealing to the senses in a rhythmical and structured way so as to create a form ultimately serving as a standard by which its perfection (or beauty) is measured. Sometimes these forms elevate the mind above the indifferent emotional states of daily life because of meanings conveyed or past experiences associated with them, but they need not do so to be appreciated. Perfection of form is enough to satisfy; if the forms convey meaning, that adds to their enjoyment, but it is not essential.

The last point is especially noteworthy. Search as he might, Boas found little evidence to support prevailing notions of art. Rather than paintings and sculpture among North American Indians, there were baskets, wooden sails, chipped points, rawhide boxes, fringed leggings, and so on. Generating pleasure primarily through formal elements and a high degree of technical skill, these objects did not express emotional states or ideas as "art" was said to do. Hence, the premise of Boas's book (1927/ 1955) is that the essence of art is not communication; artistic effect is based on formal excellence, although various meanings might be assigned to what is created. Throughout his book, Boas speaks of "the perfection of form." He writes that "we cannot reduce this worldwide tendency [to perfect form] to any other cause than to a feeling for form" (p. 58). In other words, people have, as an aspect of being human, the impulse to emphasize the form of objects they make and the activities in which they engage. They also have a compelling need to take pleasure in the achievement of formal excellence (Jones, 1975, 1981, 1982).

Some might object that creating form or perceiving form is not a primary concern or condition, if it is manifested at all, at work and within organizations. Many managers appear to be preoccupied with the "bottom line," enjoying a warm glow when profits exceed expenses and suffering a sinking feeling in the pit of the stomach when the books don't balance. They consider this to be hardnosed economics. A number of supervisors seem to squeeze, mold, and shape budgets, inventories, and people as if all were raw materials to be formed by strong will and dint of personality into some sort of gestalt; they see their role in highly practical terms.

Some administrators say they want their units to run "like a well-oiled machine"; they do not use the metaphor of orchestra or ballet. Common complaints among managers and those supervised are that rarely do they have the resources to do the job as well as they could and often their accomplishments are not recognized or rewarded. Where are the art, the crafting, the aesthetics?

The absence of artistry or its appreciation and of a pleasant ambience in no way negates the need or desire for them. Not everyone dwells on their activities as aesthetic, either; the exigencies of organizational life often preclude rhapsodizing. Most participants would agree, however, that skills and expertise are required in their endeavors and, like sculptors or easel painters, they expect their work to be well received. They would admit that when things go well there are moments of pleasure; memories are later relished, rather as a thespian or musician mentally relives an especially good performance, or a woodworker admires a well-turned piece of furniture.

Making Work Art:
Aesthetics, Management, and the Arts of Organizing

That workers both need and seek aesthetic experiences is suggested by a set of articles in a 1984 issue of *Western Folklore*. Under the general rubric of "Works of Art, Art as Work, and the Arts of Working," the set of four essays and their introduction grow out of a conference on aesthetic expressions held two years before. These articles speak directly to the issue of art at work, with implications for improving organizational life.

In the first essay, "Visual Descriptions of the Work Experience: Insider vs. Outsider Views of Art and Work," Marsha MacDowell (1984) first examines easel painters' views of work, workers, and the workplace. These depictions by Rivera, Evergood, and Sheeler are produced by those who are called "artists" in the contemporary sense. These individuals are noted for their aesthetic and cultural achievements in the form of easel paintings, murals, and sculpture, productions that serve the purpose of contemplation rather than practical use and that elevate the mind above the indifference of daily life. By also examining the insiders' views of work, however, as revealed in the canvases and murals as well as sculpted figures made by factory workers, MacDowell makes us realize that the "common" people also create works of art about work that stimulate the emotions and convey meanings that add to our (and their) enjoyment. The differences between outsider and insider conceptions of work and workers ultimately complement one another. MacDowell reminds us that both orientations serve the student of working life who would more fully understand art and work.

In the second essay, C. Kurt Dewhurst (1984) focuses attention on the artistic output of workers in the workplace, rather than dwelling on the works of so-called fine artists. As he observes in "The Arts of Working: Manipulating the Urban Environment," these worker-artists, usually on their own time, have applied the skills for which they were employed to produce painted and sculpted creations for their own use. They manipulate the raw materials of work in tile factories and auto paint rooms, creating terra cotta lions, frogs, and other figures to be used as door stops, bookends, ashtrays, banks, and garden ornaments, and fashioning earrings, necklaces, and pendants from dried paint. They paint portraits of fellow workers and other subjects on walls, pipes, and columns. They decorate hardhats and tools. They chalk a visual dialogue of verses, jokes, drawings, and commentary on the black rubber conveyor belt of the assembly line.

The third article, "The Joy of Labor" by Yvonne R. Lockwood (1984), develops a theme implicit in Dewhurst's (1984) essay, namely, some workers' propensity to manufacture "homers" or "government jobs." These are objects made with company materials and often on company time but without management's explicit approval or encouragement. Most of the works mentioned by the author as examples of this artistry are paintings, sculpted items, and objects that are ornamental or decorative. She makes the point that folk expression in the factory assumes aesthetic form when the industrial processes become monotonous, boring, or demeaning to the workers. Making homers may be a response to these conditions in that they provide an outlet for both the need to express oneself and the urge to create something. They also offer the worker the knowledge that he or she may get back at the company.

The final offering, "Making Art Work" by Michael J. Bell (1984), offers a different understanding of traditions of work and aesthetic expression. The phrase "making art work" conjures up many images, associations, and meanings. Art is work for those individuals with the occupational designation of artist; working at producing art, they create works of art that, through their imagination and skill, become ennobling and inspiring expressions. As we are coming to realize, however, much of art works: It is practical, utilitarian. Tools and techniques—if they work well—are appreciated for their perfection of form, much as we respond to sculpture and easel painting. We are pleased. We praise the tool and derive greater satisfaction from the good work it enables us to perform. For a concept of art to work, then, it must recognize not only objects as works of art, designated artists as creators, and certain forms as art; it must also see the process of aesthetic expression in everyday life, manifested in a wide range of activities. Bell brings this point home by focusing on a technique developed by an autoworker to help him install a window wiper motor. What the autoworker finds satisfying is not the object itself, in this case a simple and unassuming pad made on company time from the materials available at work, but without assistance of management. Rather, his ability to conceptualize such a tool to lie on, and the process or technique by which he is able to install the motor using this pad, generate the pleasure or satisfaction afforded by greater efficiency, economy, and effectiveness of motion (Bell, 1984).

These essays enlarge our conception of art and work, leading us to a fuller understanding and appreciation of the arts of working. They take us from the pervasive assumption that art is principally objects to the realization that it is a process the outputs of which may be activities or motion rather than strictly tangible products. They make apparent that art is not limited to a particular class of things having an aesthetic function only—painting, sculpture, and ornament—but that it includes utilitarian forms, even tools and work techniques. Finally, they suggest that the urge to create originates in more than a desire to communicate: It may be a response to monotony and boredom, an attempt to restore self-esteem and feelings of self-worth, an outcome of mastery of technique, or a necessary part of accomplishing tasks.

Another set of articles develops these ideas further. Collected under the title *Organizational Ethnography: Fields of Culture and Symbolism in Organizations*, the more than two dozen articles by folklorists, organization behaviorists, and practitioners examine the symbolic, social, and aesthetic aspects of organizational life (Jones, Moore, & Snyder, 1986). Focusing on culture and the symbolic, the authors write about organizations from the inside, as participants or participant observers. They document the art and material culture, present the stories, and describe the rituals by which people reveal their beliefs, values, and concerns. They analyze the customs, language, and joking that help people cope. The writers explain why aesthetics and play are crucial to working, and they describe management practices that provide individuals with recognition, fulfill needs of belonging, and reward excellence. The purpose of the volume is to create fuller understanding of work life from the viewpoint of participants, and to suggest better ways of designing and managing organizations.

One of the five sections of papers treats managing, organizing, and participating in organizations as aesthetic experiences. The thesis is that members of organizations are craftspersons and aesthetes (in addition to whatever else may be said about their interests, intentions, and activities). Workers and managers seek positive sensory and social experiences while avoiding negative ones. They develop skills, which they put to use in doing something or making something worthwhile. They take pleasure in the excellence of forms they create. They develop criteria for measuring the quality of their performance as an aesthetic as well as technical phenomenon. Evidence of this thesis abounds in the observations and analyses of management practices and day-to-day work life in factories and offices considered by the authors.

When we become aware of the ways in which work can be made to recognize and encourage the artistic process and incorporate aesthetic responses, we can see how the results of instituting work teams, quality circles, and participative management practices could be positive. Suspicious at first, workers become enthusiastic when their suggestions are heeded, their ideas rewarded, their accomplishments recognized. No longer monotonous, repetitious, or demeaning, work is seen as challenging. Absenteeism and turnover diminish. Hostility and animosity subside. The quality of product and service dramatically increases.

Given the history of organizational engineering and management theory, the changes in job design and supervisory practices might indeed seem novel, innovative, and even revolutionary. Traditional organization and management theory has been committed to mechanical models, conceptualizing organizations as machines fine-tuned for efficiency and with little attention to the symbolic and aesthetic needs of members (Jones, 1984; Morgan, Frost, & Pondy, 1983; Smircich, 1983). If there is a revolution occurring, then it is the growing awareness that organizations are complex patterns of human activity having social, symbolic, and aesthetic dimensions as well as technical and utilitarian or practical sides, and that for many people work life generates expectations of its being more than "just a job." There are expectations of meaningfulness, fellowship, and personal satisfaction.

Strangely, the emerging conceptions of organizations and work life seem to partake of an art model, recognizing self-motivation, imagination, the capability of conceptualizing form, the desire and ability to perfect form, the need for recognition of accomplishments, and the preoccupation with aesthetic (i.e., positive social and sensory) experiences. But it is a model of art different from what evolved from the Renaissance to the turn of this century. This new model sees art as being integral to human existence, rather than as a world of its own.

Making Art Work:
Managing Experience in Education

I will never forget what a chairmaker in southeastern Kentucky told me 20 years ago when I asked him if he thought chairs and chairmaking were art. Made of black walnut carefully selected so that pieces matched in grain and color, his rocking chairs and dining chairs were much sought after and greatly esteemed for their appearance, structural soundness, and comfort. He reflected on my question while closely inspecting a completed chair, sanding a bit here and filing a little over there where the surface seemed to his delicate touch to be slightly less than perfect. "No," he said, looking up from his work, "chairmaking's not art." He explained in all seriousness and sincerity that he had had an art appreciation course in the local junior college in which he learned what art is: easel painting and sculpture produced by a few highly gifted individuals and intended for contemplation rather than for use. Reluctantly, he allowed as how his work might be "craft" because it was useful, but still, he was nobody special.

The chairmaker had learned through the field of art education what art is, but he had been taught little about himself. This understanding he had acquired through experience, wandering from one northern city to another for several years, working in different factories operating a drill press and making television cabinets and stands. Disillusioned and unhappy, he finally headed back to the hills of Kentucky, where he started doing what many southern mountaineers are infamous for—drinking. Eventually he began to make chairs, discovering an aptitude for this work and deriving a satisfaction from it that he had not enjoyed in his previous work. His self-esteem grew, even though traditional chairmaking in southeastern Kentucky was not one of the activities included in the art appreciation course he had taken.

Educators have always informed the public of their research, beliefs, and theories, and the chairmaker's case is but one example of their often limited approach. In my opinion, the basic question is not *whether* the field of art education should inform the public of the many varieties of artful experience in everyday life and the aesthetic dimension of work and organizing. Rather, the fundamental issue is *how* to do this. I suggest four areas of development:

1. Enlarging conceptual perspectives
2. Conducting ethnographic research
3. Presenting public displays
4. Broadening what is taught as "art"

Enlarging Conceptual Perspectives

To many, "art" is a special class of objects, especially things like painting and sculpture, lacking utility and hence created only to give pleasure. When pressed, however, many are likely to admit that telling stories, cooking, maintaining a household, tending the garden and flower beds, decorating the home, managing people, waiting on diners, operating a drill press, and so on require skills, involve the mastery of technique, and may result in forms that please because of their perfection.

What is needed is not so much another definition of art but another perspective, orientation, or approach that uncovers the aesthetic impulse fundamental to being human. This perspective would direct attention to all segments of society and a host of endeavors including working, playing, housing, and daily activities. Such an orientation would contrast sharply with the elitist approach that sees art as a separate domain divorced from "ordinary people" and everyday concerns; it would be democratic in the best sense of the word, emphasizing equal representation.

Conducting Ethnographic Research

An enlarged perspective can be achieved and implemented to a great extent through ethnographic research. The use of qualitative methods of observation and in-depth interviewing would be directed toward what people make and do in the course of their daily lives requiring skill and resulting in forms that they and others find satisfying. Attention should be directed not only at objects but also at activities, which can be described, photographed, or videotaped.

Questions that might precipitate comments on aesthetic issues include, What skills are necessary to do this task? How do other people do it? Why did you do it this way instead of another way? How do you know when it is well made or well done? What happens or does not happen because of the quality of this activity or object? How do you feel when you do something less well than you might otherwise have done? What gives you a sense of accomplishment and personal satisfaction?

Presenting Public Displays

Increasingly in the last two decades, a variety of art forms from different populations are being displayed in museums and other public forums. Installations are no longer limited to objects but may include extensive photographic documentation of the making and using of the objects, videotapes of the producers, and even living craftspersons demonstrating their skills and answering visitors' questions. The growth of folklife festivals sponsored by state and city agencies has resulted in the presentation of multiethnic music, dance, food, and material culture.

Despite the communication of a greater amount of information, and despite the development of novel techniques of presentation and the enlargement of conceptions of who is "artistic," there are areas that can be more fully developed. Captions regarding objects on display still tend to be preoccupied with who made the object and when, and what "style" it is; photographs seem to dwell on the technological processes of manufacture. Although the objects have been selected because they are aesthetically satisfying to museum personnel, little is communicated regarding the mental process by which the objects are conceptualized by their makers, the standards of taste and perfection governing their forms, the reactions of others, and so on. Festivals tend to be "ethnic display events" that present social and sensory experiences for the audience to participate in, but vicariously, in a staged format that might or might not correspond to their manifestation in more "natural" contexts. In addition, little is presented about how we decorate our homes and personalize our work space; how and why we play, both as a separate activity and as an integral part of working; or what we find pleasant and satisfying in everyday life. In sum, more could be done by way of documenting and then publicly presenting the varied examples of aesthetic expression in daily life vital to our interactions and functioning.

Broadening What Is Taught as "Art"

Two trends in the recent past might be perpetuated or modified. One is the "foxfire phenomenon" associated with Eliot Wigginton (1972). Students are encouraged to document traditions of their family, neighbors, and area. This stimulates the students' desire to learn through the immediacy and relevancy of their own experiences and generates a sense of pride and self-esteem, both in the students and in those whom they interview and whose traditions they record. The second trend is the folk-artists-in-the-schools program in which local craftspersons and performers give programs and workshops in the classroom. Students thus have a unique opportunity to learn about other people's ways of doing things.

As the perspective on aesthetic expression is enlarged, such techniques as these can be modified to include people talking about the satisfying aspects of their work lives, the skills and traditions in which they participate in everyday life, ways in which they and their neighbors maintain their yards or decorate their homes on special occasions, and so on. Moreover, instead of having young students draw pictures of turkeys at Thanksgiving and flags celebrating Independence Day, as still is the custom in some places, they can be encouraged to depict graphically other people's celebrations to which they have been exposed, tell some of their family members' favorite stories, describe food preparation and service in various settings, discuss their preferences in things—all with a view toward helping them appreciate the varieties of artistic endeavors and aesthetic experiences.

Conclusion

To sum up the ideas presented in this chapter as they can be applied to real situations, I would refer to some activities of a trainer in a health maintenance organization in Los Angeles. She conducts workshops and gives seminars on a range of topics to a cross-section of employees, including clerks, nurses, supervisors, and management personnel. She begins one seminar on quality, performance, and care by showing a film of a traditional boatbuilder at work. She feels that personnel need to be informed, or reminded, of the very essence of craft and skill, which too many have lost sight of because they get caught up in the bureaucracy of the system or become jaded by routine.

Another workshop is on innovation and creativity. When they are asked to give examples of each, at first few people can think of any and many feel uncomfortable discussing the subject or consider the topic irrelevant to their work. Because personnel are from different units and therefore are likely to be strangers, she has them break up into smaller groups "to get to know one another." They are instructed to inquire about one another's hobbies, activities they enjoy, the variety of responsibilities they have assumed at work, awards or special recognition they have received at work or in the community, and unusual or novel ways of doing things. Spokespersons from the groups summarize findings. With the trainers' guidance, all people begin to realize the range of their own and others' skills, to appreciate accomplishments, and to learn new techniques for doing things. Their orientation has been reframed; now they are thinking in terms of innovation and imagining better ways of doing things.

It seems reasonable to assume that if people are instructed from childhood that art is not what they do and that the concept of the aesthetic is not relevant to their daily lives and activities, then they will behave accordingly. On the other hand, if their self-concepts and their view of the world directs attention to the aesthetic impulse as a vital element in their humanity, then life might be much more pleasant, not only for them but also for others. Art education has a role to play in this, and, in a democracy, it has the responsibility to do so.

References

Bell, M. J. (1984). Making art work. *Western Folklore, 43*, 211–221.
Boas, F. (1955). *Primitive art.* New York: Dover. (Original work published 1927)
Braverman, H. (1974). *Labor and monopoly capital: The degradation of work in the twentieth century.* New York: Monthly Review Press.

Brooks, C. A. (1980). *The meaning of childhood art experience: A dialectical hermeneutic.* Unpublished doctoral dissertation, Pennsylvania State University, University Park.

Brooks, C. A. (1981, October). *The getting of taste: A child's apprenticeship.* Paper presented at the American Folklore Society meeting.

Dewhurst, C. K. (1984). The arts of working: Manipulating the urban environment. *Western Folklore, 43,* 192–202.

Drucker, P. F. (1954). *The practice of management.* New York: Harper.

Jameson, S. (1984, June 19). U.S. trainees praise Toyota system. *Los Angeles Times,* pp. IV-1, IV-5.

Jones, M. O. (1975). *The hand made object and its maker.* Berkeley and Los Angeles: University of California Press.

Jones, M. O. (1981). A feeling for form . . . as illustrated by people at work. In C. Lindahl & N. Burlakoff (Eds.), *Folklore on two continents: Essays in honor of Linda Degh* (pp. 260–261). Bloomington, IN: Trickster Press.

Jones, M. O. (1982). A strange rocking chair: The need to express, the urge to create. *Folklore and mythology, 2*(1), 4–7.

Jones, M. O. (1984). Introduction: Works of art, art as work, and the arts of working—Implications for improving organizational life. *Western Folklore, 43* (Special section), 172–178.

Jones, M. O., Moore, M. D., & Snyder, R. C. (Eds.). (1986). *Organizational ethnography: Fields of culture and symbolism in organizations.* Unpublished manuscript.

Kanter, R. M. (1972). The organization child: Experience management in a nursery school. *Sociology of Education, 45,* 186–212.

Lockwood, Y. R. (1984). The joy of labor. *Western Folklore, 43,* 202–211.

MacDowell, M. (1984). Visual descriptions of the work experience: Insider vs. outsider views of art and work. *Western Folklore, 43,* 178–192.

Main, J. (1981, June 15). Westinghouse's cultural revolution. *Fortune,* pp. 74, 76, 80, 84, 88, 93.

Morgan, G., Frost, P. J., & Pondy, L. R. (1983). Organizational symbolism. In L. R. Pondy, P. J. Frost, G. Morgan, & T. C. Dandridge (Eds.), *Organizational symbolism* (pp. 3–35). Greenwich, CT: JAI Press.

Munro, T. C. (1967). *The arts and their interrelationships.* Cleveland: The Press of Case Western Reserve University.

Potts, M. (1983, December 27). GE's bet on automation pays off in recaptured jobs, buoyant sales. *Los Angeles Times,* pp. IV-1–IV-2.

Smircich, L. (1983). Concepts of culture and organizational analysis. *Administrative Science Quarterly, 28,* 339–358.

Weinstein, H. (1986, May 24). GM, UAW officials propose Japanese-style operation to keep Van Nuys plant open. *Los Angeles Times,* pp. IV-1–IV-2.

Whyte, W. F. (1961). *Men at work.* Homewood: Dorsey Press.

Wigginton, E. (Ed.). (1972). *The foxfire book.* Garden City, NY: Anchor.

Chapter 11

Toward an Ecological Aesthetic: Notes on a "Green" Frame of Mind

—— jan j. jagodziński ————————————

Within the past decade there has been a growing global awareness throughout all sectors of society that an ecological framework must inform future political and ethical praxes. Philosophers such as Skolimowski (1981) and Bookchin (1971, 1980, 1982) have urged persuasively for a new "Green" vision. Such a frame of mind requires the networking of like-minded people who are striving to transform society in all dimensions of human endeavor, aesthetics being but one of them. As a leaderless network they perceive the entire globe as the new *oikos* (the Greek word for house). Porritt (1984) describes the Green Movement as composed of three main types of Green activists: (1) those whose lifestyle or work includes the practice of Green ethics, for example, organic farmers, alternative medical practitioners, and those who engage in alternate economic and technological practices; (2) those in pressure groups, increasingly the women's movement, the peace movement, animal rights campaigners, and groups opposing nuclear power, the arms trade, and multinational companies; and (3) those who are politically active as elected members of various Green parties throughout Europe.

To make the promise of the title meaningful, it is absolutely crucial to situate this Green frame of mind within the broader flux of our historical consciousness. Without such a perspective, the aesthetic implications of Green politics, like those of any other phenomenon treated in isolation, become groundless and ahistorical. The first part of this chapter attempts to demonstrate that religious patriarchy and the rise of a technological rationality must inform such an understanding. The role of aesthetic thought in a life that is humane is therefore conditioned by these developments. The second part of this chapter outlines the warp and weft of a Green aesthetic.

The Historical Roots of Patriarchy and the Domination of Nature

The Patriarchal Tension in Western Aesthetic Thought

When symbolic representations of nature began to flourish on the capitals of Romanesque cathedrals in the twelfth and thirteenth centuries, St. Bernard of Clairvaux complained in a letter to Abbot William that monks now preferred reading "in marmoribus" to reading "in cordicibus"; that is, rather than "acting with prudence" they preferred examining the pagan sculpture of the capitals and marveling the whole day at the incredible profusion of animals and fabulous beasts, to mediating on God's own text, the Bible (Jauss, 1982). This passage is even more remarkable considering the almost idolatrous devotion of the many medieval monks to scholarship, as described in Umberto's Eco's *The Name of the Rose* (1983). St. Bernard's complaint, written in the twelfth century, came at a time when religious symbolism was accompanied by a discovery of visible nature in the arts. From an authoritarian religious viewpoint, such an aesthetic experience always aroused suspicion of perversion because it produced a tension between things of the world and the suprasensuous world to which they pointed. The pleasure of the present was always in conflict with the pleasure of that which might be.

Such a tension, described by Friedrich Schiller (1954, pp. 64–67) as "the sensuous impulse" versus the "formal impulse," has always existed at the heart of aesthetic experience. Depending on the circumstances of its reception, this tension can be a radical and refractory force or a manipulative power. Schiller's distinction has a long tradition in Western aesthetic thought. Indeed, one cannot possibly comprehend the projection of a Green aesthetic without understanding how the weight of that tradition presses on our backs today.

The tradition has its roots in Greek thought, wherein a distinction was made between theory and practice. This distinction, which at that time was not a dichotomous one, referred to the question of what was the best and most desirable life; what composed the good life, the divine life?

In *Nicomachean Ethics*, Aristotle provides a three-part solution to this question. Pointing to the Assyrian king, Sardanapalus, Aristotle claims that a life based only on pleasure is a "life for cattle," while men of refinement take two kinds of life seriously: the "practical" life of politics, whose representatives identify with the common good; and the theoretical life of the philosopher, who strives for the contemplative and reflective speculation on eternal truths. The hedonistic way of relating to the world is defined as *poiesis*, or "making," an impulsive existence that only the multitude and the most vulgar pursue. In *Eudemian Ethics*, Aristotle talks about the "vulgar arts," pursued by the retailers who buy in markets, hucksters who sell in shops, and those who pursue wage-earning occupations. Only those free of the necessities of life can be full-fledged citizens pursuing the good life. Hence, the political life of the active male citizen (*praxis*) and the contemplative life of the male philosopher (*theoria*) are elevated states of being.

These original distinctions elevated the life of the mind and devalued the body. Aesthetic thought became the contemplation of beauty and form while art was given an inferior status of imitation (*mimesis*). Scattered throughout the writings of Plato and Aristotle is a distinction between the inspired poet or seer who interprets the will of the Muses and the common everyday artist. Tragedy as the highest form of poetry was the imitation of moral action involving the characterological contradictions among Athen's noblest citizens. Further, the Athenian youth of high blood were to listen to and perform only music that amplified the rational character of the soul. They were to avoid the vulgarities of performance that would simply give pleasure to their listeners.

Thus began the long-standing tradition of seeing a separation between high and low arts, between crafts and fine arts. The evidence suggests that this original Greek ranking of the arts may well have taken root during the transitional period during which the pre-Greek matriarchal society, which was under the protection of the mother goddess, was transformed into a patriarchal social order, exemplified by Homer's *Odyssey* and *Iliad*. Fromm (1951) has already examined Freud's misinterpretation of the Oedipus myth in this light and this same insight may be applied to Greek aesthetic thought. Passages scattered throughout Plato's *Ion, The Republic*, and *Phaedrus* indicate a change in gender when it came to dealing with the qualities of art deemed feminine. The feminine Muse of pleasure and pain was not to be engendered at the expense of law and reason in Plato's *Republic*. Both he and his student, Aristotle, spoke disparagingly about the sensuous side of high art, which was said to draw one closer to the body's sensuality and away from the pleasure of mind alone. Aristotle therefore ranked tragedy above comedy, since its form was more capable of depicting "men better than they are." However, the original meaning of the Greek word for tragedy, *trag-odia*, meant the "song of the goat" (Whitmont, 1982, p. 13), suggesting that the original art form referred to a Dionysian ritual, a cathartic reenactment within the domains of desire, joy, aggression, and destruction. In this ritual, the goddess's realm of birth and death, of the ever-dying and reborn power of life, had been symbolized by the sacrificial goat. For the Greek philosophers, such "bodily" displays eventually became barbaric (*barbarikos*). The arts of the household, known as the arts for women and slaves, were the most "bodily" or mechanical of all arts. These craft activities, as we would call them today, received little or no discussion throughout the classics.

Elshtain (1981) further argues that the founding of Western democracy was at the expense of women's voice in the political sphere. The separation of the public sphere from the private sphere, following sexist lines, became entrenched in the Western democratic tradition. The private sphere became the realm of animality, of nature, and of necessity, whereas the public sphere became the realm of freedom, the realm of the polis (city-state), and the agora, the meeting place for free speech and transcendence. Public architecture thereby came to express the unearthly presence. Household crafts, domestic building, and interior design were perceived as minor artistic preoccupations—strictly women's and slaves' work. This Greek model represents one moment of the ever-expanding growth of patriarchy, whereby feminine qualities of humane character development were repressed and replaced by a host of new male gods elevating the character of heroism, male democratic solidarity, physical strength, and a competitive war mentality (Lerner, 1986).

The Greek bifurcation into what Nietzsche (1901/1967) characterizes as the Apollonian (masculine) and Dionysian (feminine) sides of ourselves has resulted in the domination of humanity over Nature and the triumph of patriarchal values. The reparation of this situation means that complementary, holistic thinking must replace the current oppositional logic. The implications of such a position are more far-reaching than at first may be suspected. Christian theology, having come to terms with Greek thought, adopted and sometimes widened the original gulf. From the perspective of radical feminist theologians throughout the world (Daly, 1973; Goldenberg, 1979; Ruether, 1983), all the established major world religions—Confucianism, Hinduism, Buddhism, Judaism, Christianity, and Islam—have succumbed to instating a male transcendent god as a figurehead, thereby celebrating the Apollonian ideal of rationality and reason, the realm of the masculine, at the expense of the earthly and "natural," the realm of the feminine. By treating the more destructive impulses of the sensuous body—anger, hate, aggression, and violence—

in an "officially evil" manner by condemning that part of our nature to be sinful and criminal, we have lost any way of sublimating them creatively. By judging the more joyous, pleasurable, and ecstatic moments of our lives to be merely hedonistic, we have altered our psyche, creating a civilizational schizophrenia.

The power of these assumptions is readily evident in theological thought. Sacred art and the aesthetics that govern it are principally masculine. For most of the 1,700 years of Christian monastic history, monks have been artists or patrons of the arts (Verdon, 1984). Yet, as with their male Greek counterparts, that relationship has always been strained and very much in contradiction to what the New Testament calls the "gratifications of corrupt nature, the gratifications of the eye, the empty pomp of life" (1 John 2:16). The disciplines of the cloister, which demanded obedience and poverty, appeared to be at variance with the exaltation of sensory experience implicit in the visual and performing arts. The dispute between the iconophiles and the iconoclasts (Tatarkiewicz, 1974) provides us with perhaps the most vivid example of the tension that continually persists between an aesthetic stance that tries to do away with a representational image and a position wherein an entirely spiritual god has chosen to express him- or herself to humankind through material creation, ultimately becoming a creature as well. The psychology of the idol hides behind such a tension, for once a spirit is materialized and made concrete, the likelihood that it may be psychologically managed and personified by the layperson is greatly increased, resulting in the usurpation of power from a religious hierarchy. Such pagan, animistic, magical, primitive, proto-religious impulses have been rebuked by the Christian Church. No wonder the artistic image was—and still is—such an important issue for religious patriarchs, for no doubt these archaic religious practices may be traced back to matriarchal roots.

In the patriarchal view, god is perceived as a transcendent being, above and beyond Nature. Under such a view, rules of religious orthodoxy require strict aesthetic canons. The theoretical or contemplative side of the dichotomy is stressed. A male priestly class prescribes the artistic tradition and generates the aesthetic theory, since it has access to the sacred texts. It also oversees the interpretations of the various forms of the deity and dictates the ritualistic reception of the image (Gimpel, 1980/1984).

One can see this state of affairs throughout recorded history. In Egyptian dynastic art, for example, the power, majesty, stability, and timelessness of the pharaoh's rule was translated by artistic canons that demanded gigantism and a maximal frontal view of the body (Panofsky, 1955). In Indian Hinduism, the proper characteristics of images were elucidated in the Sipla Sastras by a series of canons, known as *talamana* or *pramasna*, in which the ideal proportions proper to the various deities were given (Coomaraswamy, 1934/1956).

Indigenous cultures are not exempt from this indictment, either. The Kwakiutl and Bellas Coola Indians of the Northwest Coast adhered to a highly developed system of art conventions in their two-dimensional work, at least in their protohistorical period. For the various transformation masks and totem poles, each artist used the same artistic language, which had been prescribed by the elders and chiefs of the tribes (Holm, 1965). In fact, French's (1985) synthesis of the anthropological literature to date suggests that, throughout the globe, "women are not quite full humans, but semihumans with one foot in man's realm and one foot in another" (p. 109). It is questionable whether any indigenous cultures exist today wherein the sacred art is not rendered by a "professional" craftsman.[1,2] In the Hindu tradition the craftsman had to undergo a whole process of self-purification and worship, of mental visualization and identification, before consciousness with the form could be evoked. Only then could he translate the form into stone or metal. This was also true of Kwakiutl artists. Although apprentices worked in a given sacred tradition, it was constantly kept alive through subtle personal interpretation of the canons. Subtle discriminations to point out individual artists were possible but were kept well within the accepted aesthetic doctrine. The sacred artistic tradition was and for the most part continues to be defined by male hands. Currently, however, within the industrialized world, women artists are attempting to render a new sacred image within the walls of the male Christian tradition (Apostolos-Cappadona, 1984).

A view of god as transcendent has always meant the elevation of contemplative rational thought, provoking Marx's contempt for religion as an opiate of the people. The contemplation of such Platonic ideals presupposed a long and laborious artistic process of self-purification and elevation to reach a vision. Such a vision was said to be a divine madness, the object possessing the artist as much as the artist possessing it. The ideal of such a dialectical mysticism was clearly evident within the context of Byzantine art, which was premised on a thorough understanding of Plotinian aesthetics (Michelis, 1977). Plotinus espoused a variation of the

---

[1]Wherever appropriate, gender-specific words such as *craftsman* have been used to indicate the domination of men over women in that particular social reality.

[2]Caution is needed in making this judgment, since not all the evidence is in. Clearly there have been tribal cultures wherein the woman played a central role in making the sacred art objects, and the present-day Hopi and Yoruba may still accord her that status (Drewal & Drewal, 1983). However, the importance of the female deities needs current reassessment.

contemplative, theoretical life. For him, a life of catharsis which prepared man for the ecstatic union with the Absolute was the highest goal. This meant the experience of illumination, of sublimity. Political life thus became completely degraded. In such a system the movement from the spiritual to the material was clearly considered a descent to a lower realm. Like a pyramidal wedge, the artwork pointed toward the one true spiritual divinity.

The Byzantine Caesaropapacy—that is, the union of secular and spiritual power in the hands of a single autocrat—supports the thesis of the historical prevalence of an aesthetic orthodoxy that masks hidden patriarchal interests. The court was the center of all intellectual and social life, and only artistic commissions for the Church were given by the court. The formalism of ecclesiastical and courtly ritual was represented through the artistic portrayal of Christ as a king and Mary as a queen. They wore royal and costly robes and sat expressionless and forbidding on their thrones. Apostles, saints, and angels approached them with the same awe that mortals were expected to show at Theodora and Justinian's court (Hauser, 1951).

The Roots of Our Ecological Crisis

The Near Eastern development of a transcendental aesthetic as represented by the Byzantine and Islamic empires had elevated the arts to a magnificent display of skill that was eventually surpassed by the Latin West. Islam's quest for the realization of the spiritual ideal through abstraction had produced a whole host of brilliant Islamic mathematicians and opticians (Ibn-al-Haytham in optics and Omar Khayyam in mathematics). Their formulations were expressions of Allah's perfection, an idealistic position consistent with Plato's original belief that numbers could express universal forms. Islamic abstract systems had no other practical utilitarian use. In the late eleventh century there was a massive movement to translate Arabic and Greek thought into Latin (Gilson, 1955). This new knowledge, which expanded in the next 200 years, was read and criticized within the confines of a growing new institution, the university, which had begun to challenge the old cathedral schools. By the twelfth century the Latin West had begun to awaken. The utilization of the newly found knowledge made possible the first technological revolution, based on wind, water, and horsepower.

In this industrialization of the Middle Ages lie the roots of our present-day ecological crisis. Millions of acres of forests were destroyed to increase the area of arable land and to satisfy the great demand for timber in every facet of medieval industry. When wood became too dear, coal was found to be a substitute. By 1285, London became the first city in the world to suffer from atmospheric pollution. Likewise, thousands of villagers throughout Europe were deafened by the din of village forges, while the slaughtering and tanning industries polluted the rivers (Gimpel, 1976). The mill that converted the power of water and wind was used to grind corn, crush olives, shrink and thicken woolen cloth, tan leather, and make paper. Almost all the monasteries made use of waterpower. The efficiency of horsepower in agricultural production was boosted through the introduction of padded collars and horseshoes. Horses were harnessed in such a way as not to interfere with their breathing. Treatises on estate management and farming were written. Three-field crop rotation was introduced. The invention of the heavy-wheeled plow allowed for new plowing techniques that increased grain yield. The result was improved health and a population increase.

Not surprisingly, the mining of stone and then coal became the most important industries in medieval Europe, and the medieval iron industry was fundamental to Europe's prosperity. Every village had an iron smithy which tended to agricultural needs as well as supplying armor to the local knights.

From 1125 to 1275 there was a sustained effort to marry reason with faith. Scholastic thought began to introduce knowledge as coherence. Peter Abelard (ca. 1079–1142), for instance, collected all the contradictory statements he could find on the Scriptures, made by Church Fathers on matters of Christian doctrine. The shift toward the use of reason and rational thought was institutionalized through the rise of the universities. The trivium (rhetoric, grammar, and dialectics), supplemented by the quadrivium (arithmetic, music or harmonics, geometry, and astronomy), formed the seven liberal arts, which reflected the interests of the rising merchant class.

The Despiritualization of Nature

It took the next several centuries to establish the mechanistic world view commonly referred to as the Enlightenment. The move from a theistic theology toward a pantheistic position, wherein god was inside the system, was a challenge offered by the rise of the bourgeoisie during the seventeenth and eighteenth centuries. Nature could be justifiably probed and examined, since it was the work of god (Keller, 1985; Merchant, 1983). Enlightenment signaled the eclipse of god. Eventually the deists—many of whom, like the French philosophers, were the fathers of the revolutionary spirit in England, France, and America—claimed that church and state should be separate spheres. As developers of seventeenth- and eighteenth-century science, they perceived a hidden patriarchal god

(Goldmann, 1964). This naturalization of religion based on reason claimed that the one male god, after creating the world and the laws governing it, refrained from interfering with the operation of those laws. Any kind of supernatural intervention in human affairs was rejected. By the nineteenth century this had led to Nietszche's claim that god was dead and that the new patriarchy had ushered in the era of scientism and the belief in technological progress. The ethics of the will to power were to culminate with the rise of authoritarian father figures like Mussolini, Hitler, and Stalin, embodying the patriarchal god on earth.

It has become painfully clear that the initial thirteenth-century Baconian utopian vision of a science that led to the sovereignty, dominion, conquest, and mastery of man over Nature was a continuation of a patriarchal myth that first emerged during the transitional period known as the Chalcolithic Age (Lerner, 1986; Whitmont, 1982). The mining of minerals (Eliade, 1962) and the smelting of copper, bronze, and then iron were the technological secrets governed by men for the purpose of tooling weapons of war. Male gods replaced and subjugated female gods as patriarchal consciousness spread, redefining what it meant to be human, both for men and women. The Great Mother Goddess of Nature was banished. The animistic gods that encompassed the unitary reality of animals, plants, stones, places, and times were relegated to pagan status, perceived as reasonless, dumb creatures and inanimate, dead matter. From its early beginnings in the second millennium, there have been several historical accounts of the Western tradition that clearly reconstruct how a single male godhead eventually came to be perceived as above Nature; as exemplifying the male characteristics of rationality, reason, clarity, and light, which embodied the true nature of Man, thereby subjugating feminine archetypal characteristics of nurture and intuition (Daly, 1973; French, 1985; Goldenberg, 1979).

The Current Ecological Crisis:
Scientism Versus the Green Perspective

Given the historical backdrop of patriarchy and scientism, ecological thought has received greater and greater prominence as a panacea for what ails us. From the Green perspective, caution is in order. The well-known term *ecology* was first coined over a century ago by Ernst Haeckel (Mason, 1962), a biologist, to denote the investigation of the interrelationships among animals, plants, and their inorganic environment. The term has since expanded to include an ecology of health, an ecology of the city, and an ecology of the mind as presented by Bateson's (1972) work, *Steps to an Ecology of Mind*. This book forms the foundation for Berman's (1984) endeavor to provide a new, holistic approach to "reenchanting the world." By and large, however, having fallen into the service of patriarchal rationality, the meaning of the word *ecology* has been reduced to little more than a metaphor and in most cases has been identified as a very crude form of natural engineering, an "environmentalism" (Bookchin, 1982). This orientation sees Nature as a passive habitat composed of "objects" that are made more serviceable for human use. Nature is thus reduced to "natural resources" and "raw materials," treating cities as urban resources and the inhabitants as human resources. Under the rubrics of cybernetics, synergistics, and general systems theory, this view represents the most sophisticated form of scientism to date.

The basic premise that environmentalism fails to question is, Should humanity dominate Nature? As a result, the ecological programs sponsored by the major polluting monopolies—such as the cement plants, steelworking plants, paper factories, and refineries—are little more than governmental policies that may improve techniques for diminishing the hazards caused by reckless despoliation of the environment. On the surface this appears civil, but it harbors hidden interests, one of the most obvious being that, since such companies can no longer hide their excrement, it is in their interests to appear as concerned corporate citizens. Ecology under this capitalistic pretense means that even the large multinationals have realized that they must take notice of their own excreta and cover up their odors, rather than flushing them out into the air and rivers where people must unwittingly consume them.

Incorporating ecological constraints under this guise means redistributing the ecological costs by increasing prices and decreasing wages. This kind of rhetoric, like talk of pollution control, is good for the company image. It boosts its benevolence index. A good example of such rhetoric, as Castells (1978) points out, was the Nixon Administration's assurance that technology, freed from its uncontrollable appetite and tamed within an ecological framework, would bring social balance. The rhetoric sold. The machines were to replace "slave labor," but the reverse happened: We became enslaved by the machine, which paced our lives and changed our environments. We came to depend on machines both economically and socially.

This situation is not specific to capitalism per se. Communist and socialist governments play the same game, since, in order to avoid a complete economic collapse, they too must exercise a technological rationality that will provide at least a minimum standard of commodity consumption in relation to the more advanced technological countries. There are nations like Yugoslavia and Hungary which, in their major cities like

Zagreb, Sarajevo, Beograd, and Budapest, can boast a style of living similar to that found in any major capitalist city. Each Soviet-bloc country has its favorite showpiece of prosperity and growth which helps preserve the illusion that, despite being tied into a global economy, the nation is doing relatively well compared to its neighbor. Because of this instrumental rationality of the technocrats, who see future productivity in terms of technological innovation, whether they reside in Washington, DC, Ottawa, Moscow, Tokyo, or now Peking, scientism and patriarchy are preserved.

Another, more radical sense of the ecological movement has emerged, one that undercuts current belief systems such as those of capitalism, communism, and socialism. Its definition is very much in keeping with the search for a Green aesthetic. It fights against the technofascism of a centrally determined preservation of life planned by ecological engineers. Its position is basic: All productive activity depends on borrowing from the finite resources of this planet. Because these resources are not infinite, we must refrain from consuming more and more. Ecology from this perspective is concerned with the external limits that economic activity must respect. This is basically the stance of Green Party members, who now hold parliamentary seats in West Germany, Norway, and Sweden and have organized representatives in most of the industrialized world.

To fulfill the mandate of this premise requires a questioning of how consumption might be reduced by making more rational what is produced, by producing things differently, by eliminating waste, and by refusing to produce those goods that are so expensive that they can never be available to all, or which are so cumbersome or polluting that their costs outweigh their benefits as soon as they become accessible to the majority. As Gorz (1980) puts it, "The only things worthy of each [person] are those which are good for all; the only things worthy of being produced are those which neither privilege nor diminish anyone; it is possible to be happier with less affluence, for in a society without privilege no one will be poor" (p. 15).

For Illich (1973) such a vision requires that new tools of conviviality be invented. One of the first steps in the transition toward a stable state industrial economy would be the development of a labor-intensive economy rather than a capital-intensive one. We currently operate in the latter mode, which reflects the current economic belief. The iron law of capitalism is that one either must grow or perish. This means that a certain portion of the profit must be reinvested to increase productivity. A technological rationality requires that the money be rolled into more efficient machinery, thereby devaluing the skills of the labor force and reducing the human to a pair of hands or eyes to watch meter levels.

The labor-intensive economic view is a social-democratic one. It suggests that a highly disciplined and growing subsector of production could give people jobs. It would be decentralized and controlled at the level of neighborhood or community. This view sees an increased economic autonomy for local and regional groups.

The issues of aesthetics are integrally related to both of these perspectives, since currently the design process supports and favors the bureaucratic, centralized model of consumerism. Since the whole system depends upon keeping the rate of profit from decreasing, there is always the need to increase the goods sold or raise the price of the goods by elaborating upon them. Through advertising techniques, product differentiation, and cosmetic redesigning, the consumables are pushed onto the public. As many sociologists have already pointed out (Packard, 1977; Toffler, 1965), we live in a throw-away society where garbological studies indicate that the quantity of wine consumed by middle- and upper-class families does not differ, only the labels do. Status differentiation rests in a product's name. The rich wear designer jeans, drink designer water (Perrier, for example), and live in designer houses such as Michael Graves, one of the Whites, or the New York Five would build. The poor drink the local water; if it is contaminated or polluted, there is always Coke. They buy regular jeans at any department store and live in basic, cubical apartments or houses.

The issue thus becomes one of poverty, but not the poverty related to being hungry and destitute; it is the poverty of rising expectations. Poverty becomes an abstraction created through the fetishism to the commodity. To be poor means to be excluded from what the social order promulgates to be "good," which is available only to the top 20% of the population. To be poor in the 1920s meant that one did not own an automobile; to be poor in the 1930s meant that one never owned a radio; to be poor in the 1960s meant that one never owned a television set; to be poor in the 1970s meant no color television. Today it means not having a video tape recorder and stereo system. Tomorrow it will mean not having a home computer or a laser disc playback machine.

These products are generated and then presented as basic necessities by the culture industries. If we do not have them, we feel we are missing something. As Baudrillard (1975) maintains, it is the maintenance of this inequality that propels economic growth. The perpetuation of false needs—the production of desire—sustains the inequalities between the sexes, between majorities and minorities, between the managerial and working populations, and so on. Goods may have little or no use value but are nonetheless embued with, in Barthes's (1972) terms, a second-order semiological chain of attributes that suggest desirable values such as power, status, freedom, and loyalty—a hidden ideology of meaning. What is one to say, for example, about the rationality of changing beer bottles from the short to the long neck? A Freudian might say that the male consumer society has been sufficiently conditioned by the breastlike short-necked bottle, such that men will always drink beer. But what of the other 52% of the consumers—the women? Perhaps the new phalluslike bottle will increase sales? And so it goes on.

It seems ludicrous to think we can teach principles of design without these hidden psychoanalytic considerations. In our schools, however, the ethics and politics of aesthetics have been cleanly separated in the name of value-free knowledge, a position as old as Greek humanistic thought. There is much valuable information that must be ignored in accomplishing this. Gorz (1980) mentions that the aluminum cans that replaced tin cans require 15 times as much energy to produce, that welded or molded objects assembled without nuts and bolts are impossible to repair, that synthetic materials wear out faster than do natural fibers and leather, and that skyscrapers constructed of glass and aluminum consume as much energy for cooling and ventilation in the summer as for heating in the winter. Production in these terms is meant to sustain high levels of consumption and preserve status differentiation.

Art and Art Education
in Light of the Ecological Crisis

The issue for art education is complex. Too often our discipline has been relegated to the dustbin of leisure, and it will continue to be placed in this position because the whole issue of art suffers from the deep cleavage of fact from value which has characterized Western intellectual thought. The rift between work (production) and leisure (consumption) is the result of the separation between hand and mind, between the thinkers and the doers, between those who design the plans and those who carry them out. If a person has been denied the control over his or her own labor, the realm of freedom becomes confined to so-called nonwork periods—to leisure. Work becomes degraded. Leisure is then differentiated by the choice of consumables and passive communication with television sets.

How can art education, which believes in the dialogue between hand and eye, seeing the individual as a worthy creator, possibly survive in an industrial society? In short, it cannot! As Anyon (1980) pointed out in her study of various status divisions existing in fifth-grade elementary classes throughout the United States, the ultra-elite elementary classes are not engaged in the doing of art but in its criticism, developing future skills for the exploitation of the investment value of art. Children of the working class are more likely to consume the products of popular culture, while middle-class children are given the freedom to draw and paint. Presumably the gallery experience would be in their reach. Each stratum is given a different "cultural capital" (Bourdieu & Passeron, 1977). Many educational critics (Apple, 1979; Bowles & Gintis, 1976; Giroux, 1983) have shown how schooling prepares students for noncreativity, for one-dimensionality. The majority leave schools headed for the mechanized job market, not toward corporate America. We leave decisions up to the experts, to those with specialized objective knowledge.

To a disturbing extent, art education preserves the view that there are only a talented few who "know how to draw," just as the art network continues to present artists as the few who have differentiated themselves above others. This promotes the façade of the superstar in the world of art, as with the latest illusion of the contemporary architectural avant-garde called the New York Five. Thus the artworld bestows privileges on a very select few, either as the consumers of the work (i.e., those who have paid for the labor, such as the corporate elite who commission the current megalithic architecture) or as producers of the work who are now perceived as the new gods. Patriarchy lives!

By and large our design education supports the technocratic rationality just outlined. It supports a formal environmentalist ideology that helps to rationalize the rape of the globe presently carried out by cartels. The historical roots of this development are worth examining. A very fine book by Braverman (1975), *Labor and Monopoly Capitalism*, outlines how, during the growth of monopolistic capitalism at the turn of the century, the skill of the craftsperson, usually an immigrant male from Northern Europe, was appropriated by a managerial elite who took the process and broke it down for assembly-line production. This increased the efficiency of production and reduced the cost per unit. In exchange, the craftsperson was given the status of a shop steward. As many more "hands" were needed during this boom time, immigrants from Eastern Europe were allowed to migrate. Mostly peasants possessing few skills, they replaced the early migrant workers in the factories, who moved up into positions of middle management or became small business owners, police officers, and the like. The separation between those who now possessed the knowledge and the workers who put that knowledge into practice was made visible by the architecture. The physical working plant became separated from the designer's building. The brains were not to soil themselves with the hired hands.

The craft mentality—having a special skill that required a sustained apprenticeship—could not survive in the new emerging modernism. The new social relationships required the separation between the producer and the product. The international craft style referrred to variously as *Art Nouveau, die Style,* and *Style Moderniste* was the last hurrah before the hand and its work were swept up by the machine. What was put in its stead was an abstract formalism that continues to constitute the official fine-arts rhetoric. The concept of pure design was to be pursued by men of genius into greater and greater abstractions. The whole process was of course "aesthetic," that is, gloriously useless and an end in itself.

The key difference between abstraction and abstract formalism is that, with the latter, one can divorce the form from the content, whereas abstraction is simply a cognitive skill. Art thus has become an artificial language removed from the mess of daily life, away from the politics and ethics that would impinge on the art object once it is released from the artist's hands. For Gablik (1976), *Progress in Art* follows Piaget's developmental schema: The more rational an artist is in using the visual elements to make statements, the more progressive and higher ordered is her or his artistic visual thinking. The establishment of abstract formalism, which accepts the same tenets as ecological environmentalism, has been well documented. For the most satirical view, one need only read Wolfe's (1981) *From Bauhaus to Our House* or, to examine its failure, read Hughes's (1981) *The Shock of the New.*

Just as environmentalism has served as a smoke screen for the continued exploitation of the environment, so has abstract formalism served to hide the capitalist interests served by the art it produced. If capital were to begin to talk to itself across national lines, it needed a new language, a language that everyone could understand, regardless of the local traditions. That language turned out to be the philosophy of logical positivism (scientific empiricism), which created a formal artistic language that reduced art to basic fundamentals, a new elementalism free of ideology. Mies's glass boxes were the epitome of this value-free position, since they could house whatever was functionally needed. What was needed of course were all-purpose value-free office spaces. The clean, idealized aesthetic produced the international style in architecture and the *sachlichkeit* aesthetic of the Bauhaus, which, after the second world war, found root in Chicago, as did Joseph Alber's brand of idealistic painting at Black Mountain College in North Carolina.

The failure of this development to provide a solution for living should be a strong reminder of the impending ecofascism today. The members of the Bauhaus were supposed to be committed to a social-democratic ideology. The new architecture was to be created for the worker. The idea was that rational design would produce rational societies. They were to reject all that was bourgeois, which meant nothing since all these architects were, like their social-democratic bureaucrats, bourgeois. The new rationalism was to be dealt with through the machine aesthetic. And so it went. Art and industry mass-produced goods for environmental improvement. Loos (cited in Hughes, 1981) had argued that the disappearance of decoration from the manufacture of products and from architecture would reduce the manufacturing time and hence lead to an increase in workers' wages. That never happened. What did happen was that Mies van der Rohe, Theo van Doesburg, Le Corbusier, Moholy-Nagy, Gropius became the new architects for the growing multinationals. The skyscraper, as the new menhir to modernism, began to dominate the cityscape.

Toward a Green Aesthetic

The preceding historical account is absolutely essential to an understanding of the numerous strands of Green aesthetics that exist today to counter the hegemony of scientism and rationalist aesthetics. It must be remembered that throughout much of the world, the patriarchal cultures validate the work of those artists and architects who continue to embody the original tenets of Enlightenment thinking. These tenets are the elevation of abstract principles at the expense of bodily experiential ones, or what is commonly referred to as the Descartian mind/body or subject/object split. Countering this trend we can see modernist movements such as expressionism, symbolism, Dadaism, surrealism, and postmodernist artforms such as neo-expressionism and performance art, which celebrate the "body" through autobiographical examination and direct audience participation.

It was perhaps Husserl's publication of *The Crisis of European Sciences* in 1936 which exemplified the need to examine the much neglected life-world of humane experience through a phenomenological philosophy. It provided a rationale for the artistic expression of experience as it took place on the level of ordinary intuition—that world of feeling, of human sensitivity, and of understanding. The world of science, which mathematizes nature (Husserl, 1936/1970), eliminates the world of feeling. An either/or tension exists between the two spheres of experience; between the common-sense, intuitive nature of the life-world and the objective-scientific world of exact knowledge. As the realm of purely subjective experience, the life-world is permanently "devalued" in the viewpoint of science. Framed in this way science is unable to make a direct relationship to specific goals formulated in human practice. We have already seen that such a split recapitulates the great rift of Western intellectual thought. With religion (and a patriarchal religion at that) slowly losing its efficacy at the level of ethics and mores, the ethics of pragmatism and utilitarianism have replaced any questions concerning the human good. Ends are not questioned as long as the means are available for their attainment. This either/or logic, this schizophrenic ontological split, allows for the aesthetics of hedonism and consumerism to blossom. The sensual is rendered sexual; the mass media act as the superego, creating normative drives that encourage the libido to desire materialism and reject spiritualism.

In my opinion, a feminist critique would trace the bifurcation of these two natures to the Greco-Roman world, the very source of Enlightened thinking. The denial of the life-world that Husserl (1936/1970) outlined was part and parcel of the patriarchal impulse to control Nature and therefore woman. Since procreation was part of her experience, then birth and death, existential themes *par excellence*, were within her dominion. Being closer to the "earth," man thought woman as never quite cultured. Menstruation, lactation, and menopause were perceived as bodily pollutants, weaknesses to be hidden from view. Bodily functions, excretions, and odors were reprehensible. Furthermore, women provided the bodily necessities of food, water, and clothing. They also socialized or "tamed" their children into their accepted roles as men and women (Ortner, 1974). Given this as woman's lot in life, man perceived her as weak, evil, sinister, and stained.

The Need for a New Myth

Green aesthetics must be seen as emerging strands or "bundles" (Levi-Strauss, 1979) which attempt to recover the feminine, the intuitive; to restore the wounded Earth, which has been ravaged by technological "progress"; to reinstate the goddess Gaia as a new mythic principle (Lauter, 1984; Lovelock, 1979). Myth making informs Green aesthetics. Mythological identification, the living out of a myth toward some teleological end, has been terminated, banished, and relegated to an inferior psychic status through the separation of the human from the divine. Dogmatism has been substituted for conscious myth making. Symbolic imagination has been curtailed by limiting the sacred to nonsensory concepts that cannot be seen or felt but only taught, which therefore must be believed. The realm of faith in its original contextual meaning as *pistis* ("trust in one's own experience") has become blind acceptance, divorced from the subjective world of personal experience. The dimensions of pleasure, joy, and play as manifestations of the spirit, the divine, have been denied.

Books that cultivate Green aesthetics and point toward the new emerging vision include Lauter's *Women as Mythmakers* (1984), Berman's *The Reenchantment of the World* (1984), Whitmont's *Return of the Goddess* (1982), Bookchin's *Ecology of Freedom* (1982), and French's *Beyond Power* (1985). Artists, poets, and architects who are attempting to nurture this vision have turned toward a global consciousness, yet continue to work at the community level.

Feminism and Green Aesthetics

Several notable writers describe the important work of feminist women artists. These authors include Lippard (1983), Lauter (1984), and Munro (1979), who suggests that Nature is to the female artist what the female body is to the male artist. Woman artists are concerned with the reevaluation of Nature, the elevation of women's experiences and therefore biography in general, and the transformation of "culture." Recurring images include the mask, the seed pod, the veil, the shield, the magic box, the shadow, flight, and metamorphosis, among others (Lauter, 1984). In addition, the investigation of humankind's relationship to animal life and the creation of hybrid vegetable, mineral, and animal forms represent another level of symbolism. The appearance of the goddess and the use of archetypal images of a hierarchy of goddess figures in dream analysis and in the creation of art forms has provided a renewed image of woman as a complex of character types (Bolen, 1984). Cosmic imagery is explored here in the forms of stars, planets, galaxies, gaseous tides, clouds, and light itself. Attempts to overcome Hollywood's one-sided image of woman as erotic art object have resulted in women's films that stretch the variety of social relationships among men and women (Kuhn, 1982). New camera techniques have been introduced to represent women's time and space (Kaplan, 1983).

Addressing poetic imagery, Lauter (1984) makes explicit the poetry of Griffin (1978), which again confirms the work done by women to change society, preserve Nature, and transcend the claims of erotic love. Time and space are treated experientially rather than mechanistically. Night, seasons, light, fire, water, stone, and the cycles of nature become celebrated themes. The politicization of feminist art forms through collaboration, networking, dialogue, and the questioning of male social assumptions becomes most acute with performance art, wherein the acting out of ritual becomes a multimedia event.

Lucy Lippard's (1983) book *Overlay* presents many artworks done by both men and women who have taken inspiration from feminist thought and ritual. Many of the artists create architectural sculpture that relates to the human body (and the forms of other living things), is influenced by ancient monuments, and is sensitive to its site in Nature. For example, she describes Alice Aycock's Williams College Project, completed in 1974 at Williamstown, Massachusetts. It is a concrete-block chamber covered over by an earthen mound. Lippard's description is as follows:

> One enters the mound "head first crawling down at an angle, dragging the rest of one's body inside, and ends up lying prone, face down," in a metaphor for the position of a corpse in ancient tombs on which the piece was modeled. Aycock also sees her mound "as an entrance into the mountain," or into the world. Its form echoes that of a mountain visible in the distance behind it, reflecting Vincent Scully's theories about the sacred use of landscape forms in ancient Greece. (p. 198)

This is but one example of the ways some contemporary artwork supports the movement toward understanding and validating life-world experience and the intuitive realm. Because it involves the body, the spectator must become a participant. Space and time once again become magical.

Another activity involves the rekindling of ancient knowledge of female divinity. The association of the mother goddess with childbirth and the giving of life is extended to her function as gatherer and hence provider of food for the band, lineage, or tribe. Women's role in horticulture forms another link to this ecological consciousness, which asks us each to extend our nurturance to the Earth. The themes of birth and death associated with childbirth may also be seen in the birth and death of the cereal crop, as exemplified by the resurrection rituals that were performed using grain during the Neolithic period. Graves and tombs also can be understood as extensions of the need to understand the cycle of life and death. Archaeological digs have revealed evidence of sacrificial burials of crop objects, such as female effigies of the Corn Mother, Rice Mother, Wheat Bride, or Mother Sheaf, as well as blood, flowers, and, as in Çatal Hüyük, actual bodies and body parts of children. Women working with these concepts have played upon the symbolism associated with graves, burial sites, and spring rituals. An example is Faith Wilding's Seed Work, performed in the summer of 1980 in Copenhagen. "Seeds were sent out to women all over the world from an earlier spring equinox ritual where a wax body filled with vegetation was burned to represent an end to oppression, winter, and 'our old selves'; women leaped over flames; the destroyed body was filled with earth and planted with new seeds" (Lippard, 1983, p. 211).

Such "ecological" artists,[3] mostly women, have raised our consciousness

---

[3]*Ecological art* here refers to art "with its emphasis on social concern, low profile, and more sensitive attitudes toward the ecosystem" (Lippard, 1983, p. 224).

concerning the relationship between Nature and women. There is another strand of ecological art that is much more radical in its view, as its vision adds politics to these ethics. One of its central themes is the garden and its symbolism, which takes us to the first chapter of Genesis where Eve and Adam were expelled from the Garden of Eden. In this garden, life has been envisioned as a peaceful world of hunting and gathering, with equality between the sexes. (It should be noted that it takes very little energy to supply a hunting/gathering band with food.) The loss of the garden represents the transition to the realm of agriculture and male patriarchal domination. Woman, as the original gatherer, the primary supplier of life and food, the horticultural goddess and mother goddess, is at one with Nature. The male, by being in conflict with Nature, has condemned himself to a life of labor, to agriculture, where the ox and plow become symbols of toil. Present-day agriculture is more of an exploitation of the land, changing it and taking from it, whereas horticulture works with the land, embellishing it and appreciating it.

Gardens have become romantic or cosmological symbols for an originally pristine nature. The interpretation of what that pristine state might have been like has changed with the vision of the garden presented. The images have ranged from imitations of sacred groves and mountains to erotic enclaves to illustrations in moral texts depicting "sanctuaries from the evil world" (Lippard, 1983, p. 226). Gardens eventually became transitional zones between the world of Nature and the world of culture. They became places for recluses or for erotic pleasure, or, like the Japanese gardens, became interpretations of the ideal paradise.

Another strand or "bundle" of the feminist contribution to Green aesthetics is nurtured by those artists working to combat scientism's frame of mind. These include "reclamation" artists, who attempt to make art from multinational waste. Such art not only avoids commodity status by being placed in isolated sites but avoids the abuse of natural resources by being made from the excrement of the multinational company. Smithson's work with slag heaps, strip-mined wastelands, and polluted rivers is a case in point (Lippard, 1983). Alan Sonfist, in the state of Texas, is planning to build a series of islands over a polluted flood plain, each of which will reflect a different local Texan ecology. He has carried out a number of ecological projects in cities, one of which is a "time landscape" in downtown Manhattan, on an 8,000-square-foot plot of "reforested" land recapitulating the original treed landscape of Manhattan before the current urbanization (Lippard, 1983). There are of course many other artists engaged in greening up the cityscape. A recent anthology on *Environmental Aesthetics* (Sadler & Carlson, 1982) represents the growing number of urban planners who have turned toward an ecological consciousness.

Green Design

Another, more critical, strand, the area of Green design, is represented by a group of designers who are attempting to redesign the plethora of mistakes and needless goods with which multinationals continue to flood the market. Above all, these designers offer a strategy that is in complete opposition to the notion of pure design, to the Bauhausian model still in place. They embody the best that an alternative perspective might provide, since their work deals with the everyday use of things. Their attempt has been to break the public's reliance on prepackaged goods. They have attempted to reinstate "civil society," which has been destroyed through greater and greater centralization of goods as embodied by the cartel capitalist form. By civil society is meant all the relations founded on reciprocity and voluntarism, areas of noncoercion, rather than on law or judicial obligation. Civil society is composed of relationships of cooperation and mutual aid which can arise in communities, neighborhoods, families, and larger domestic communities; relationships among the residents of the same building; relationships within the voluntary associations and cooperatives created by the people themselves in their own common interests. With these kinds of social relationships in mind, the scale becomes reduced to manageable proportions. Such are the ideas of Victor Papanek (1974, 1980), who more than anyone else has attempted to critique current design and offer goods that benefit everyone. His first book, *Design for the Real World* (1974), offers many, many energy-saving and ecologically sound ideas. Here are just a sampling of his and his students' ideas: the reuse of old tires as a pumping device, a low-cost educational TV set to be built by Africans, artificial burrs made of biodegradable plastic which carry seeds for plants that prevent erosion, a radio receiver for Third World countries, and biomorphic analyses to extrapolate secrets from Nature so that there might be harmony rather than opposition between Nature and product. His designs for Third World countries are labor intensive and cheap to reproduce. They exemplify Illich's (1973) notion of "tools for conviviality."

In his second book, *Design for Human Scale* (1980), Papanek continues to stress global concerns at the local level. There are many ideas for cottage industries that would help people take production into their own lives, for example, the manufacturing of chairs by the elderly in retirement homes, and a prepackaged adjustable sink for the handicapped. All such projects hit target groups that are normally avoided by mass-market sales, which are targeted only on the stereotypical consumer.

Papanek (1980) promotes the idea of *co-gestation*, whereby no design is ever carried out without the specific input of the people who will use it, be they children, workers, or secretaries. Their concerns are always listened to. The final design becomes as much their design as the team's design. In toto, Papanek's view supports a move toward a new society where there is "the production of practically indestructible materials, of apparel lasting for years, of simple machines which are easy to repair and are capable of functioning for a century or more, [and] the vast extension of community services and facilities like public transportation, laundromats, clean-burning, energy-saving cars" (cited in Gorz, 1980, p. 8).

Green Architecture

One last strand needs to be mentioned: Green architecture. It stands in opposition to those architects who only build for the rich and managerial elite and who design huge, cost-intensive, energy-deficient megaliths of the current high-technology, postmodernist style. Green architects, like Papanek, recognize the need for a more human scale and the institutionalization of an ecological housing consciousness. Attempts of this nature have been initiated by Malcolm Wells (1981), who documents the possibilities and lists other architects engaged in the same endeavor. Alternative heating sources are discussed. Earth-sheltered housing and underground architecture are proposed. Smaller spaces, neighborliness, and site selection in the style of Frank Lloyd Wright are discussed, but with a difference: Wells's architecture is affordable and not sponsored by a wealthy upper class. In a similar vein, Ronald Wiedenhoeft (1981) makes a parallel effort toward humanizing cities in his book, *Cities for People: Practical Measures for Improving Urban Environments*. Chapters advocate urban repair rather than urban removal, streets for people, and possible alternative modes of movement in the cities.

Conclusion: The Revolt of Nature

The artists, designers, and architects discussed in this chapter are the exceptions to the rule. They have disassociated themselves from the bondage of multinational sponsorship and have refused to be mere appendages to design departments where their labor is confiscated and turned into greater profit. Papanek is a pioneer and a rare example for the new social Green perspective (Bookchin, 1980). It is of course my feeling that art teachers should adopt a more critical stance toward design, perceiving that it will never be a matter of mere value-free problem solving and that it in fact presently embodies social relationships that perpetuate the patriarchal reality. With this understanding, we may help to transform it. Should such a transformation not occur, then the "revolt of nature" (Horkheimer, 1947, p. 109), like a cancer, will continue to grow. Violence and terrorism will continue to increase as instinctual demands are repressed. A Green frame of mind means the recognition that a new collective alternative myth needs to be envisioned. Women and men artists in the ecological movement have been trying to shape this dream. The globe itself must become the new garden, not for rape or profit, but for a new birth. If such a vision is not found, as many feminists have urged, the Earth will meet its end as a result of the male toys of destruction. If we hold on to our present course, the conquest of space will prove to be the new ecofascist technological dream. A small minority will eventually populate the stars, while the rest will remain on a scarred and polluted earth.

References

Anyon, J. (1980, Winter). Social class and the hidden curriculum of work. *Journal of Education, 162,* 67–92.

Apostolos-Cappadona, D. (Ed.). (1984). *Art, creativity, and the sacred: An anthology in religion and art.* New York: Crossroad.

Apple, M. (1979). *Ideology & curriculum.* Boston: Routledge & Kegan Paul.

Bahro, R. (1980). *From red to green.* London: New Left Books.

Barthes, R. (1972). *Mythologies* (A. Lavers, Trans.). New York: Hill and Wang.

Bateson, G. (1972). *Steps to an ecology of mind.* New York: Ballantine.

Baudrillard, J. (1975). *The mirror of production* (M. Poster, Trans.). St. Louis: Telso Press.

Berman, M. (1984). *The reenchantment of the world.* New York: Cornell University Press.

Bolen, S. J. (1984). *Goddesses in everywoman: A new psychology of women.* San Francisco: Harper & Row.

Bookchin, M. (1971). *Post-scarcity anarchism.* Montreal: Black Rose Books.

Bookchin, M. (1980). *Toward an ecological society.* Montreal: Black Rose Books.

Bookchin, M. (1982). *The ecology of freedom.* Palo Alto, CA: Cheshire Books.

Bourdieu, P., & Passeron, J. C. (1977). *Reproduction in education, society and culture.* Beverly Hills, CA: Sage.

Bowles, S., & Gintis, H. (1976). *Schooling in capitalist America.* New York: Basic Books.

Braverman, H. (1975). *Labor and monopoly capital: The degeneration of work in the twentieth century.* New York: Monthly Review Press.

Castells, M. (1978). *City, class, and power.* London: Macmillan.

Coomaraswamy, A. K. (1934). *The transformation of nature in art.* Cambridge, MA: Harvard University Press. (Dover Edition, 1956)

Daly, M. (1973). *Beyond god the father: Toward a philosophy of women's liberation*. Boston: Beacon Press.

Drewal, H. J., & Drewal, M. T. (1983). *Gelede: Art and female power among the Yoruba*. Bloomington: Indiana University Press.

Eco, U. (1983). *The name of the rose* (W. Weaver, Trans.). New York: Harcourt Brace Jovanovich.

Eliade, M. (1962). *The forge and the crucible* (S. Corrin, Trans.). London: Rider.

Elshtain, J. B. (1981). *Public man, private woman*. Princeton, NJ: Princeton University Press.

French, M. (1985). *Beyond power: On men, women, and morals*. New York: Summit Books.

Fromm, E. (1951). *The forgotten language: An introduction to understanding of dreams, fairy tales and myths*. New York: Grove Press.

Gablik, S. (1976). *Progress in art*. New York: Thames & Hudson.

Gilson, E. (1955). *The history of Christian philosophy in the Middle Ages*. New York: Random House.

Gimpel, J. (1976). *The medieval machine*. London: Victor Gollancz.

Gimpel, J. (1984). *The cathedral builders* (T. Waugh, Trans.). New York: Harper & Row. (Original work published 1980)

Giroux, H. (1983). *Theory & resistance in education: A pedagogy for the opposition*. South Hadley, MA: Bergin & Garvey.

Goldenberg, N. (1979). *Changing of the gods: Feminism and the end of traditional religions*. Boston: Beacon Press.

Goldmann, L. (1964). *The hidden god: A study of tragic vision in the penseés of Pascal and the tragedies of Racine* (P. Thody, Trans.). London: Routledge & Kegan Paul.

Gorz, A. (1980). *Ecology as politics* (P. Vigderman & J. Cloud, Trans.). Boston: South End Press.

Griffin, S. (1978). *Woman and nature: The roaring inside her*. New York: Harper & Row.

Hauser, A. (1951). *The social history of art* (Vol. 1). New York: Vintage Books.

Holm, B. (1965). *Northwest Coast Indian art: An analysis of form*. Seattle: University of Washington Press.

Horkheimer, M. (1947). *The eclipse of reason*. New York: Columbia University Press.

Hughes, R. (1981). *The shock of the new: Art and the century of change*. London: British Broadcasting Corporation.

Husserl, E. (1970). *The crisis of European sciences and transcendental phenomenology* (D. Carr, Trans.). Evanston, IL: Northwestern University Press. (Original work published 1936)

Huxley, F. (1974). *The way of the sacred*. Garden City, NY: Doubleday.

Illich, I. (1973). *Tools for conviviality*. New York: Harper & Row.

Jauss, H. R. (1982). *Aesthetic experience and literary hermeneutics*. Minneapolis: University of Minnesota Press.

Kaplan, E. A. (1983). *Women & film: Both sides of the camera*. New York: Methuen.

Keller, F. E. (1985). *Reflections on gender and science*. New Haven, CT: Yale University Press.

Kuhn, A. (1982). *Women's pictures: Feminism and the cinema.* London: Routledge & Kegan Paul.

Lauter, E. (1984). *Women as mythmakers: Poetry and visual art by twentieth-century women.* Bloomington: Indiana University Press.

Leiss, W. (1972). *The domination of nature.* New York: Braziller.

Lerner, G. (1986). *The creation of patriarchy.* New York and Oxford, England: Oxford University Press.

Levi-Strauss, C. (1979). *Myth and meaning.* New York: Schocken Books.

Lippard, L. (1983). *Overlay: Contemporary art and the art of prehistory.* New York: Pantheon Books.

Lovelock, J. E. (1979). *Gaia: A new look at life on earth.* Toronto and Oxford, England: Oxford University Press.

Mason, J. (1962). *A history of the sciences* (rev. ed.). New York: Collier Books.

Merchant, C. (1983). *The death of nature: Women, ecology, and the scientific revolution.* New York: Harper & Row.

McHarg, I. (1971). *Design with nature.* Garden City, NY: Doubleday.

Michelis, A. P. (1977). *Aistetikos: Essays in art, architecture and aesthetics.* Detroit: Wayne State University Press.

Munro, E. (1979). *Originals: American women artists.* New York: Simon & Schuster.

Nietzsche, F. (1967). *The will to power* (W. Kaufmann & R. J. Hollingdale, Trans.). New York: Vintage Books. (Original work published in 1901)

Ortner, S. (1974). Is female to male as nature is to culture? In M. Rosaldo & L. Lamphere (Eds.), *Women, culture, and society.* Stanford, CA: Stanford University Press.

Packard, V. (1977). *The people shapers.* Boston: Little, Brown.

Panofsky, E. (1955). *Meaning in the visual arts.* Garden City, NY: Doubleday.

Papanek, V. (1974). *Design for the real world.* New York: Granada.

Papanek, V. (1980). *Design for human scale.* New York: Van Nostrand Reinhold.

Porritt, J. (1984). *Seeing green.* Oxford, England: Basil Blackwell.

Ruether, R. (1983). *Sexism and god-talk: Toward a feminist theology.* Boston: Beacon Press.

Sadler, B., & Carlson, A. (1982). *Environmental aesthetics: Essays in interpretation.* Victoria, B.C.: University of Victoria Press.

Satin, M. (1978). *New age politics: Healing self & society.* Vancouver: Fairweather Press.

Schiller, F. (1954). *On the aesthetic education of man.* (R. Snell, Trans.). New Haven, CT: Yale University Press.

Skolimowski, H. (1981). *Eco-philosophy: Designing new tactics for living.* Boston & London: Marion Boyars.

Tatarkiewicz, W. (1974). *History of aesthetics: Medieval aesthetics* (Vol. 2) (D. Petsch, Trans. & Ed.). Warsaw: Polish Scientific Publishers.

Toffler, A. (1965). *The culture consumers: Art and affluence in America.* Penguin Books.

Verdon, G. T. (1984). *Monasticism and the arts.* Syracuse, NY: Syracuse University Press.

Walsh, P. (1972). *Man in the landscape.* New York: Anchor Natural History Books.

Wells, M. (1981). *Gentle architecture.* New York: McGraw-Hill.

Whitmont, E. C. (1982). *Return of the goddess*. New York: Crossroad Publishing.
Wiedenhoeft, R. (1981). *Cities for people*. New York: Van Nostrand Reinhold.
Wolfe, T. (1981). *From Bauhaus to our house*. New York: Farrar, Straus & Giroux.

PART V

Responses to
Art in a Democracy

THE CONTRIBUTORS TO THIS ANTHOLOGY, and we as editors, have expressed positions on art, democracy, and education that are didactic, advocate for freedom in making aesthetic decisions, emphasize cultural pluralism, and recognize the tensions that may exist when striving for both individual and collective rights. The many ways in which these concepts are assessed and may be actualized in practice suggest the broadest of possibilities. In this way, the contributors present a mutually reinforcing position on the book's topic.

The following two responses to the preceding chapters depart somewhat from this position. We believe that Mary Ann Stankiewicz and Vincent Lanier are more cautious in their concepts of art and education and are mindful of the traditions and body of knowledge that define the art education profession. Mary Ann Stankiewicz responds to this anthology by linking it to questions about art education practice that arose during the nineteenth century. Comparisons are made to the present time, thereby placing the book within the context of an education debate that has been ongoing in American educational institutions for at least one hundred years.

Vincent Lanier, a witty, outspoken critic and well-respected scholar in the field of art education, takes issue with several of the contributors' points-of-view. Chief among these are the conceptions of freedom of aesthetic choice and cultural literacy. In so doing, he challenges the reader to reassess and question many of the arguments presented here. Vincent Lanier performs a much-needed role in a democracy, that of engaging the participant to reconsider and debate issues.

Chapter 12

Democracy and Art, Then and Now

___ Mary Ann Stankiewicz _____

In their introduction to *Art in a Democracy*, the editors express the hope that their book will raise questions for art educators and others interested in the potential roles of art in a democratic society. A century ago Isaac Edwards Clarke prefaced his monumental report on art education in the United States with a series of papers entitled "The Democracy of Art" (Clarke, 1885). In these, Clarke argued for the appeal and value of art to all Americans, regardless of social or economic class. Clarke's papers reflect the ideology of his day and of the Aesthetic Movement. Roger Stein (in Burke et al., 1986) has argued that the artifacts produced by the Aesthetic Movement of the late nineteenth century can be considered answers to a series of questions asked by men and women in the Anglo-American culture of their time. Clarke's (1885) answers no longer fit our definitions of democracy or art, but the questions, to which the essays in this volume offer answers, continue:

- What should be the goals of art education in a democracy, and who should benefit from realization of those goals?
- Is art the purview of a highly educated, wealthy elite, or can all citizens participate in the arts?
- How should aesthetic policy decisions be made, by a cadre of trained experts or by the public who must live with the results of those decisions?

167

- What does history contribute to understanding art in a democratic society?
- What should be the relationships of art and art education to technology?
- How should ethical responsibilities and aesthetic issues be balanced in a democratic society?

Let us first examine Clarke's perspective on these issues and then compare it with the answers offered in *Art in a Democracy*.

Clarke's Answers

Clarke (1885) had at least three reasons for arguing that art is and should be accessible to all: (1) great art has a universal appeal to those feelings shared by all humanity, (2) the artistic genius is a genius not because he possesses certain unique qualities but because he has more of the universal artistic instincts than do others, and (3) art is a powerful influence on the moral virtue of a community.[1] Like the editors of *Art in a Democracy*, Clarke believed that one cornerstone of democracy should be active involvement by a mature, prepared citizenry. Tracing the great ages of art to ancient Greece and Renaissance Florence, Clarke argued that the best artists arose in democratic societies. When monarchies and other aristocratic forms of government were replaced by republics in which all the people shared the rule and shared responsibility for encouraging the arts, then the democracy of art could be fully realized. In Clarke's scheme of things, all human beings possessed the potential to appreciate art, although only certain individuals exercised the spiritual quality of creative intelligence in making art. The artist put his personality into the work, communicating his feelings to others.

Both the imagination of the artist and technical skills in managing materials and solving problems of representation contributed to the final work of art. Decorative arts—or, as Clarke referred to them, industrial arts—resulted from the application of artistic principles and methods to useful objects. The utility of the resulting artifact had to dominate the artistic expression, but nonetheless the artifact was a work of art, with one exception. Machine made articles could never be art: "It is the personal quality given by the individual artist which distinguishes a work of

---

[1]The male pronoun is used to refer to the artist when the author is paraphrasing or explicating Clarke's ideas. Although such usage is contrary to today's acceptable standards for nonsexist language, it accurately mirrors Clarke's era.

art from every other product of man's labor" (p. ccxv). In spite of this disclaimer, Clarke argued for the parity of fine art and industrial art because the arts in a democratic republic adorned both public and private spaces.

The universality of art was paramount in Clarke's view of democracy. He also believed that a democratic state required universal education and universal literacy. Education was the state's responsibility insofar as it trained citizens to apprehend the truth and to be of value to the community. Preparation for promoting the welfare and prosperity of the nation was the goal of democratic education:

> Training should be such as will conduce to peace and order, as will encourage the largest production of material wealth consistent with the welfare of the producer, and as will enable each one with special gifts to develop them to the utmost, thereby adding to the wealth, power and dignity of the community. (Clarke, 1885, p. cxxiv)

Universal training in those skills basic to industrial drawing could contribute to national welfare and prosperity by preparing workers who could read information contained in plans and working drawings, by balancing the overly literary nature of schooling, by developing children whose creative instincts received early exercise, and by contributing to the discipline of mental faculties as much as any other school subject. Training in drawing would also develop exactness of hand and thought, open a child's eyes to the beauties of the natural world, and lead to richer understanding of the past achievements of human civilization. Although Clarke recognized spiritual as well as material benefits accruing from art education, the economic welfare of the state was foremost in his argument.

Clarke described the United States in the late nineteenth century as the product of changing conditions which made common schools established earlier in the century inadequate to the tasks at hand. Not only had the nation survived a war on its own soil, but other developing nations were reducing markets for raw materials and manufactured goods. Science, invention, and technology had contributed to opening the vast western territories as well as to bringing competing goods from foreign workers to every doorstep.

Clarke used an architectural analogy to describe the altered condition of the country. The past was represented by the frontier log hut; the coming age by the Fifth Avenue mansion of the merchant prince. These new urban palaces and their adornments and furnishings gave "some partial realization of the unlimited wealth of the American people" (p. clxii), a wealth that should be displayed. The coming "era of display" (p. cxlvii) made educational reform imperative. As citizens of the newest great republic, heirs to Athens and Florence, discovered the value of their resources, there would be scenes of luxury and magnificence by which to display the power of the democracy. "As inventions add value to products and create wealth for individuals and communities, so Art, likewise, enhances values and increases wealth" (p. cxxx). The 1876 Centennial Exposition in Philadelphia had shown that British and European workers were already making objects to appeal to the refined tastes of wealthy consumers. The United States was transforming itself from a rural agricultural community into an urban manufacturing power. It was in the interest of the entire republic to educate workers who could compete successfully on the world market because their products possessed artistic virtues.

Therefore, Clarke argued, the public school curriculum should be revised to include industrial art education as a foundation on which to build greater national prosperity. The art curriculum should teach every pupil the elementary principles common to all forms of art. Such shared knowledge would inform both producers and consumers of manufactured goods. The emphasis on universals that can be seen at the core of Clarke's "Democracy of Art" also found expression in his recommendations for art education. His calls for research focused on the need to discover underlying psychological laws of the arts. Moreover, while public schools were to become the primary vehicles for art education, books, magazines, galleries, museums, and store displays could contribute to the dissemination of art knowledge.

The American population was still relatively homogeneous, in spite of increasing immigration. This homogeneity was reinforced by use of English as the common language and by use of models of schooling derived from Great Britain. It seemed natural, therefore, to turn to England as the major influence on the development of art education. There was fortunately an English model for teaching universal principles of art to both workers and consumers, a model that had given rise to the artistic movement that formed the context of Clarke's argument for art education in a democracy.

Clarke's 14 papers on "The Democracy of Art" were grounded in the Aesthetic Movement, a movement that sought to infuse artistic principles into architecture and the production of wallpapers, furniture, metalwork, ceramics, glass, fabrics, and carpets during the 1870s and 1880s (Aslin, 1969; Burke et al., 1986). As it popularized art through consumer goods, the Aesthetic Movement also broke boundaries between fine art and applied art that had been building since the Renaissance. In spite of distrust of the machine revealed by Clarke and some other aesthetes, the objects favored by the movement were both handmade and mass-produced.

Unlike members of the succeeding Arts and Crafts Movement, leaders of the Aesthetic Movement did not want to demolish the growing system of industrial capitalism. Instead, proponents of aestheticism sought to establish a system for the mass-production and broad dissemination of beauty. Hence, they sought and taught rules for correct design, derived from historic exemplars of decorative art but "freely adapted," as one of their favorite phrases put it, for modern conditions of manufacturing. These conditions included not only technological developments in dyes and coloring agents but also new processes of fabrication and image reproduction.

Advances in transportation along with other technological changes made the world seem to shrink. British designers, artisans, and educators emigrated to the United States, bringing Aesthetic ideas with them. Books and magazines showed illustrations of products and Aesthetic interiors from both the United States and England. Design motifs were taken from the Near and Far East, from ancient Greece and medieval Europe. Owen Jones's *The Grammar of Ornament* (1868), one major source of artistic principles for the aesthetes, was illustrated with richly colored chromolithographs of decorative motifs from around the world. Just as Britain claimed a worldwide empire, British and American designers claimed the world as source material. The Aesthetic interior might include wallpapers from England, a Turkish carpet, Chinese porcelain, a chair based on medieval models, fireplace tiles from an American manufacturer, and a Japanese paper fan on the mantle. Much of the production of the Aesthetic Movement was designed for home use; domestic buildings rather than public or religious architecture most clearly displayed the preferred style known as "Queen Anne." Through the Aesthetic Movement, the world's art was brought into America's living room. Is it any wonder that universality was a key concept in Clarke's vision of the democracy of art? America and Britain were establishing cultural hegemony by co-opting the arts of all ages and nations for their own economic growth. Consumption was a virtue. Wealth was a result of hard work and native intelligence; the display of articles of "virtu" [sic] purchased with that wealth became, for Clarke and others, a sign of grace.

Past and Present: A Comparison

Comparing Clarke's "Democracy of Art" with the chapters written for *Art in a Democracy* shows how much our understanding of democratic principles has changed in the past century. Both Clarke and the authors of the present volume raise questions about art education theory and practice in a democratic society. While the contemporary authors are critical of certain aspects of current art education, Clarke was formulating those arguments foundational to art education as we now know and practice it. With Walter Smith (1872) and others, Clarke was establishing the system criticized by several authors of this book. Clarke took social roles for granted: Some men were destined to be wealthy, others to be workers. Woman's place was in the home. Culture was singular, not plural. Its best aspects existed at a distance from most lives, although the Aesthetic Movement sought to bridge that distance through art education and the production and marketing of beautiful goods. While Clarke believed that all human beings could appreciate artistic and natural beauty, he hedged on whether or not the artist was uniquely endowed with creative genius. In contrast, the authors in the present volume regard participation as a human right rather than a special gift. Clarke did, however, assert that everyone could learn basic and universal laws governing the arts. Just as school children were taught the alphabet and grammar of English, so they should be taught an alphabet and grammar of art. Science, the source for understanding the structure of the natural world, offered the promise of, in time, revealing the secrets of art, psychological laws of expression, and those laws governing harmony of form and color. After all, science was showing how political economy worked and how the hierarchies of humanity and nature had evolved.

Nonetheless, parallels can be found between Clarke and the Aesthetic Movement and the authors of these chapters. Aesthetes recognized divergency in art making by embracing both fine art and industrial art; ceramic tiles, stained glass, needlework, wallpapers, and illustration and other book arts were part of the movement. However, all were pressed into service as decor for the middle- and upper-middle-class home. Lower classes striving for upward mobility bought cheaper versions of the artifacts to indicate that they shared the virtue of consumption. The aesthetes embraced the historic arts of all cultures; an art student was expected to learned to recognize Egyptian, Greek, Moorish, Japanese, or medieval styles. When used in aesthetic objects these styles were decontextualized, their symbolism and cultural meaning forgotten. Instead of understanding the unique historical and cultural background of each style, the student designer was taught a universal language of art. It was no accident that formalism as an aesthetic doctrine gained precedence in the wake of the Aesthetic Movement (Burke et al., 1986). The aesthetes also sought a variety of vehicles for the dissemination of art education: instituting public school art programs, founding museums, establishing social organizations to promote art and aesthetic values, publishing books and periodicals devoted to art literature. However, these vehicles, like Clarke's (1885) federal report, shared a common taste that the aesthetes wanted others to adopt.

Clarke was rooted in a vision of virtually limitless natural resources and labor-intensive industries. When he declared that the "art" in a decorative object relied on the human touch, not on mechanical means of production, he was arguing against the kind of mechanization soon to be realized in the mass-production line. Clarke could only envision a world of capitalism, a competitive market for durable and not-so-durable consumer goods. His world was a far cry from ours, which is rapidly shifting to a knowledge-based economy (Carnegie Forum, 1986). In Clarke's world, art was merely another form of capital, an accumulated stock of goods. He expected that whatever benefited upper-class owners would also benefit the lower-class workers. In Clarke's day, one might enhance one's class or change one's social role by native genius, education, and hard work, but most people remained within the class of their birth, in spite of American claims to a classless society.

The Aesthetic Movement paradoxically drew art closer to both work and play. Clarke (1885) and Smith (1872) argued that industrial art education, or vocational training in drawing, was necessary for effective public schooling. Aesthetic values were expected to permeate the workplace, raising standards of skill and the quality of goods produced. At the same time, those goods were oriented toward the segment of the population with increasing leisure—the upper-class woman. Only she had the time and money to shop for the perfect wallpaper for her new shingle-style cottage, for the Persian rug that would harmonize with the blue and rose tones of her imported porcelain.

There is a further irony in the fact that many of the recipients of so-called industrial art education were women. Single women who would never marry, in part because the Civil War and westward expansion had limited their choice of husbands, were offered new opportunities for self-support through training in the arts of design. Wealthy women had the leisure to visit museums and to take community courses in wood carving, ceramics, or art needlework. Only they had sufficient time to invest in hand labor on a carved bed, a painted vase, or an embroidered quilt. As women were removed from active participation in economic production, they often entered the sphere of the arts (Matthaei, 1982). The devaluation of women's work devalued the objects their hands fashioned. Industrial art education, hailed by Clarke for its benefits to male workers, came to fruition in an increasing feminization of that area of art production.

The authors of *Art in a Democracy* argue that the artistic process and aesthetic response are integral to our lives. While Clarke would have agreed with them in principle, he disagreed on specifics. The present volume argues that a systemic view is necessary to art in a democracy, but in Clarke's world the system was presumed. He believed that, by imposing a structure on art and art teaching, one made it accessible to all. Rationality, not mythology, was the key. Today, with the legacy of this aesthetic ideology still influencing art education theory and practice, it is important to continue asking questions about the role of art in a democracy.

References

Aslin, E. (1969). *The aesthetic movement: Prelude to art nouveau.* New York: Excalibur Books.

Burke, D. B., J. Freedman, A. C. Frelinghuysen, D. A. Hanks, M. Johnson, J. D. Kornwolf, C. Lynn, R. B. Stein, J. Toher, C. H. Voorsanger, & C. Rebora. (1986). *In pursuit of beauty: Americans and the aesthetic movement.* New York: Rizzoli and The Metropolitan Museum of Art.

Carnegie Forum on Education and the Economy, Task Force on Teaching as a Profession. (1986). *A nation prepared.* New York: Carnegie Corporation.

Clarke, I. E. (1885). *Art and industry. Education in the industrial and fine arts in the United States. Part I: Drawing in public schools.* Washington, DC: U.S. Government Printing Office.

Jones, O. (1868). *The grammar of ornament.* London: Bernard Quaritch.

Matthaei, J. (1982). *An economic history of women in America.* New York: Schocken Books.

Smith, W. (1872). *Art education, scholastic and industrial.* Boston: James R. Osgood.

Chapter 13

Misdirections and Realignments

___ Vincent Lanier _____

Taken in sum, the chapters in this volume have several fundamental and controversial premises. One is that no work of art, no matter how "fine," is an island unto itself. Every work of art comes into being within a context, at least of era, society, and artist, and one cannot adequately understand it until one is familiar with that context. A second major premise is that in terms of aesthetic potential there is no strict, identifiable demarcation between the fine arts on the one hand and the "unfine" arts (folk, popular, commercial, and so forth) on the other. In fact, some of the authors insist on including many of the experiences of living as capable of generating reactions that can be properly characterized as aesthetic, even beyond art forms. A third premise in many of the chapters is that the element of participation is a paradigm of democratic functioning. Democracy becomes meaningless as a social mechanism unless citizens have some part in decisions that affect them, some share in the flow of social events. Although there are other aspects of the democratic process addressed in this volume, this one appears to be the most clearly and frequently emphasized.

There are two principal areas where the goal of participation might suggest a mandate for the teaching of art. These are, first, the obligation of art education to insure that all students learn how to establish meaningful relationships with all types of works of art and, second, that the visual arts share with other school subjects the exploration of ways in which our society operates and how it can be changed to function in a more humane and equitable manner. The first responsibility is unique to art teaching; the second can involve the entire educational establishment, including art.

Both of these conceptions of relationship between democracy and art education derive their present character from easily identified historical sources. The first inherits a long, and until now uninfluential, tradition first introduced to our thinking in the early 1960s as aesthetic education. Although there are some substantial differences among those who now espouse that ideological position, one common conviction has been that all the arts ought to be accessible to all citizens. So strong is the support for this idea in the literature that it might well serve as the cornerstone of aesthetic education theory. Thus when art education is viewed from the perspective of democracy, it can be said that informed access to works of art is an essential democratic imperative.

The second relationship between democracy and art education owes some part of its recent ideological identity to the writings of Paolo Freire, in particular, his conception of critical consciousness (*conscientizacaão* in the original Portugese) (Freire, 1970). This idea asserts that the purpose of schooling, or of education in its broadest sense, should be to reveal the ways in which the societies we live in function and how they can be altered in more benign directions. Although Freire deals with the teaching of language in his writings, the suggestion that the visual arts can be used as a vehicle for the same process appears reasonable.

Most of the chapters in this volume deal in one way or another with these two points of contact between democracy and art education. In some of these considerations there are problematical issues which should be clarified.

Freedom of Aesthetic Choice

The issue of freedom of aesthetic choice as it is described in this volume is closely related to the idea that the primary purpose of art education is to provide informed access to works of art. So vigorously is this issue raised in some of the chaptes that the following question becomes inescapable: If we teach children about the fine arts, are we contaminating their freedom of aesthetic choice? Some authors seem to be saying that having some objects of aesthetic value, such as the fine arts, made alien to pupils because of their socioeconomic status and then lauded as re-positories of higher aesthetic value is not representative of the democratic condition. That situation says in effect (particularly to the young), "You see how worthless you are, you do not appreciate the finer things in life." In their introduction to Part IV of this volume, Blandy and Congdon address the issue with the statement, "The imposition on children, youth, and adults of an art curriculum based upon an alien aesthetic has nothing to do with democratic principles and much to do with the notion of a 'manifest destiny' applied to art."

In the absence of adequate information, there is no freedom of choice in any context. If we do not know about the unhealthy ingredients in some of our fast foods, nor of the more wholesome alternatives, selecting a fried hamburger for dinner is not an example of freedom of choice. If a teenager has no knowledge of the history or structure of the music of Mozart, selecting country music to listen to is not an example of freedom of aesthetic choice. We can only be said to be free to choose when we know something about the alternatives from which the choice is to be made. Obviously, the act of *imposition*, as suggested by the editors, denies freedom of choice. On the other hand, the failure to provide adequate knowledge also denies freedom of choice. We must accomplish the second without being guilty of the first.

The mechanisim by which to do this is simple enough in theory, though it may be quite another matter in practice: Teachers should deal with knowledge, not preference. Congdon, in Chapter 9, recognizes this point, and Dewey's (1934) distinction between prizing and appraising might clarify it further. Prizing something is to find personal value in it, while appraising something is to discover why it is of value to others. The proper path for art education is to make clear to the learner that prizing is a personal freedom.

The same issue is echoed in another statement in Blandy and Congdon's introduction to Part IV: "Does the sole understanding of 'the masters' in some elite group limit students' education?" It is difficult to imagine how the answer could be anything but an unqualified assent. Informed access to any kind of art—even the preference of some elite cultural group—is always educationally defensible and in keeping with democratic principles. To divide the arts as they are divided now, allotting the vernacular to the larger mass and the fine to the affluent, cannot conceivably be viewed as democratic. However, the fact that the rich enjoy caviar is no reason to spurn it! Hamblen makes this point in Chapter 2 by writing, "Fine art needs to be studied for its aesthetic value and specifically as a cultural expression—and as one expression among many."

Tied in to the concept of freedom of aesthetic choice is a mistrust of the specialist in art, sometimes identified as one who supports an elitist position vis-à-vis both art and art education. In a few of the chapters this concern is exemplified by specific reference to the NAEA statement on goals or the ideological position of the Getty program in art education.[1]

---

[1] Perhaps it is unnecessary, but I will note that I am in no way connected to the Getty program in art education and that I play no role in the NAEA save as a member.

There is some inconsistency in this view. We tend to reject specialists in one area of discourse and accept them unquestioningly in another. I suspect the writers who are most vehement about the harmful allegiance to specialists in art would themselves insist on going to an endodontist instead of their regular dentist for specialized dental care and would not choose to fly in an aircraft designed and built by a panel of laymen.

The antispecialist arguments of some of the authors include an accusation that a small group of experts decides what art is, how it should be thought about, and, ultimately, how it should be taught. There does seem to be just such an art Mafia, of gallery and museum operators, art critics, art historians, and others. Some of the chapters, such as Hamblen's, imply (correctly, in my opinion) that, since art is looked at as a commodity, it must have an exclusive and precious definition in order to keep prices up. But there is, after all, a difference between art and aesthetic experience: The latter may reflect a universal and innate capability; the former is a social institution and requires some body for validation and interpretation. Who should make decisions about art, if not the specialists in art?

One concrete suggestion comes from Chalmers (Chapter 1), who demands that sociologists and anthropologists should help decide, and the idea has merit. On the other hand, it is clear from our own history that those in other disciplines often approach art as a source for data applicable to their own purposes. The educational, cognitive, and behavioral psychologists who used to dominate art education literature sometimes did just that, and at least one of them candidly admitted this difference in concern.[2] This problem of the discipline-restricted use of art is one that Chalmers himself recognizes and alludes to.

The other alternatives seem to be to broaden the base of the criteria specialists use, or to define what art is by popular consensus—in a democracy, the judgment of all of us. To some extent the former does occur, as demonstrated by the changes in the content legitimized by the art museum over the last half century. However, the latter stratagem is a perilous one, until those who formulate the consensus have some clear picture of the range of options, from the Sex Pistols to Sibelius. This point is one part of the justification for insisting that democracy can best be served by making sure that all our pupils have informed access to all the arts, including the fine arts.

One might observe that some of the chapters in this volume replace the specialists they complain about with specialists in the social sciences.

---

[2]Gardner (1973, pp. 23–24) writes the following: "Participation in the arts is so natural and integral a part of human growth that an understanding of this process should provide important clues to many pivotal questions of human development. . . . In a sense, then, I am writing about the arts because they enable me most cogently to express my notions about development."

These latter are in no way immune to the criticisms leveled at specialists in the arts. The argument is reduced, in effect, to insisting that my specialists are right and your specialists are wrong. Moreover, we have already had 40 years or more of experience with self-effacing homage to specialists in psychology, with unfortunate results for the teaching of art. I had hoped we would have learned our lesson. Ultimately, the problem may not be reliance on specialists but correction of the inadequacies of some concepts that some specialists contribute to our discourse.

A similar question can be raised for the notion that art education is too narrowly defined. Blandy and Congdon's Introduction explains the idea with this passage: "There is a strong tendency to draw boundaries around what it is art educators know and do. This is a problem because approaches that confine tend to limit exploration." But what is the alternative? The history of art education is both tragic and comic in the multiplicity of roles we have attempted to play. We have been psychiatrists curing children of their emotional ills; psychologists making youngsters "visually literate," so that they can detect subtleties, cope with ambiguities, and perceive efficiently in every aspect of their lives; we have been English teachers helping them to learn to read; counselors generating enthusiasm for coming to school and staying in school; therapists exercising their right brains in an alien left-brain world; moral leaders making them humane and peace-loving citizens; and, most of all, giants of the classroom who could make them creative in everything they did. Art became the universal panacea with which to cure all of the personal ills that troubled the species. But in all this fantasy of endless bounty, too often little was said about learning what can be learned about art so that the pupil can approach it with insight and confidence. The origins of our discipline—the visual arts in their broadest definition—often seemed to have been mislaid somewhere along the road.

Without becoming enmeshed in psychological speculation, such as alleged distinctions between linear and systemic thinking, it should be asserted that disciplinary boundaries can perform valuable functions. Furthermore, if anything, it may be that the drawing of boundaries in art education has not been tight enough. So eagerly do some of the authors here range into a wide spectrum of other fields that they sometimes ignore what has been done in their own. One example is the idea that the audience or consumers of the arts should be considered in any examination of the social functions of the arts (Introduction). As useful an idea as this is, it was introduced into the literature of art education some time ago (Efland, 1974), though with somewhat different implications.

Another example is the idea that the "unfine" arts are just as worthy as the fine arts of eliciting aesthetic response (and thus, relevant to the curriculum of the art class), which is validated by reference to numbers of documents in the social sciences. The same idea, to varying degrees, is easily available and has been for some years in the writings of Chapman (1978), Feldman (1970), and Lanier (1980), as Bersson indicates (Chapter 7). This is not to suggest that the social sciences emphasized in this book are not valuable sources of concept for us. It is to say that we might start with our own body of thought. There is no reason to reinvent the wheel incessantly.

The concern over disciplinary identification and specialists has one interesting corollary in the mistrust of an entire area of study. Chalmers (Chapter 1) writes, "Most current conceptions of discipline-based art education . . . smack of four narrow specialisms: art criticism, art history, art production, and aesthetics. And within these specialisms there is even more narrowness . . . aesthetics seems to equal 'philosophical aesthetics.'" However, it is quite possible to arrive at the kind of broadening of view of aesthetic experience that Chalmers demands through the proper application of one form of what he calls philosophical aesthetics. The idea that aesthetic response is characteristic of a wide variety of other artworks and life situations in addition to the perceptions of works of fine art is an integral part of the aesthetics of Pragmatism (at least as Dewey described it), as much so as it might be the product of investigations in the social sciences. It is, perhaps, a deductive methodology; that is, the principle is developed first and then applied to given situations; whereas the method of sociology and anthropology is an inductive one, in which the principle is generated out of an examination of specific relevant instances. The conclusion, nevertheless, is the same. It would therefore be more effective to condemn some of the ideas of some philosophical aestheticians than to dismiss all of the discipline.

Cultural Literacy

A major viewpoint vigorously supported in this volume, particularly by Bersson (Chapter 7) and Boyer (Chapter 8), is that the study of the visual arts should be used to promote cultural literacy, which is described as the ability to understand what and how ideas and values are transmitted to us via those arts. This proposal raises two issues: first, that cultural literacy might conflict with other responsibilities of the art teacher and, second, that it may not be an adequate democratic mechanism.

Bersson (Chapter 7) identifies the possible conflict between the so-called essentialist position and the use of art for cultural literacy. In the language of education, the conflict is one among objectives and reflects a rich history in our literature. Over the years, the candidates for the focus of our attention have been numerous and it has been both customary and proper to divide them in some way so that they can be examined more expeditiously. One early division (Lanier, 1964) structured objectives into three categories:

1. Intrinsic value—art is important in the school because it is valuable in itself
2. Cultural value—art can help us understand both the society in which we live and other cultures
3. Developmental value—art can help promote a series of alterations in behavioral disposition

At the time these distinctions were made, there could be little doubt that the third cluster of ideas, the developmental values, were the most highly visible. In fact, it can be documented that creative self-expression was by far the most persuasive conception used as a rationale for art teaching.

Eight years later, ideas of purpose or objective were again divided, this time into two categories: essentialist and contextualist (Eisner, 1972). This rearrangement blunted the force of the earlier distinction by removing attention from questions about those developmental concepts, while it created, instead, a different dichotomy in which all aims that were not clearly intrinsic in their direction became instrumental, by definition. When examined even superficially, it is obvious that an end-in-view such as cultural literacy is significantly different from one which is developmental in that it deals with the accumulation and application of knowledge rather than the alteration of behavioral disposition.

Therefore, in theoretical terms, there is no necessary conflict between an intrinsic view of the obligation of art teaching and the allegedly "instrumental" view of learning about art as a means for developing cultural literacy. In fact, it might be said that one cannot properly understand one's own aesthetic experience unless one is able to analyze how such experience contributes to the ideas and values of our view of the world and ourselves. This is not *using* art for some other purpose, but *understanding* art in a dimension critical to that insight. Indeed, the idea—once we have separated it from the phenomenological jargon in which it is often couched—is a simple and obvious one. Furthermore it has been available within the literature of art education itself for some time (Lanier, 1969). Nevertheless, to the extent that there is a difference between looking at artifacts as evidence for anthropological conclusions and as aesthetic objects, some confusion if not conflict might arise.

A problem does exist when the idea of cultural literacy is carried to its next logical and Freirean step—using art as a means of altering the ideas and values we presently hold. It is a reasonable idea that careful collective analysis with the professional guidance of a teacher can provide youngsters with insight into how their attitude toward the world is manufactured in part by the artifacts of their culture. That this should, indeed, be done in the school is an acceptable proposal, but whether this process by itself furthers democracy is questionable.

The principle that explains this defect of cultural literacy is the axiom of Marx (in Padover, 1978), who claimed that, while philosophers study the world, the point is to change it. Seen through the filter of Freire's (1970) writings, knowing how we are manipulated (or "oppressed", as he put it) by society must be followed by explorations of the ways in which we might change that condition toward what is more compatible with our democratic self-interest. To accomplish the first without the addition of the second can promote frustration rather than participation in the democratic process.

The only chapter in this volume that addresses this question directly is Blandy's. The reader will recall that it describes the incident of Huffman's art class as an instance of participation in the democratic process. Whatever one might think of the specifics of the class's action, it does appear to represent a collective attempt to alter a valuation, in this case an aesthetic one, a piece of public art. Unfortunately, the habit of such participation is not likely to carry over from such an instance to sociomoral contexts. The same group of citizens who make their wishes felt in response to an aesthetic issue can ignore clearly moral problems such as nuclear testing, affirmative action, or pollution. As in the case of creativity, there is likely to be no "transfer."

If we are convinced that we are in fact oppressed, and that such oppression can be removed by democratic participation, then we ought to deal with oppressive ideas and conditions within the moral domain rather than the aesthetic. Polluting the rivers is not a significant wrong because it makes rivers "ugly" but because it is an immoral act, the tainting of what belongs to all for us of the profit of a few. To make matters worse, aesthetic reformation might promote the illusion of significant democratic participation, without there being any substance to it. Those who oppress us would no doubt be delighted to have us expend our energies on peripheral aesthetic issues and ignore by default the important moral issues of our communities.

Among the many implications of the Huffman example, perhaps most important of all to art education is that the social mechanism described has little to do with the fact that the context is a work of art. The same mechanism would operate if there were no aesthetic ramifications to the situation, if the protest involved a sewer or a hospital. To call it art education, as if art had some special virtue in its accomplishment, can be misleading.

A subsidiary problem with cultural literacy is that it can be trivialized, unless close attention is paid to the kinds of content transmitted by the arts that are examined. For example, to discuss the impact of misleading advertising of cosmetic products, while ignoring the effect of the *Rambo*s and *Red Dawn*s in preparing a generation for war, is to contribute little to the enhancement of democracy.

Another aspect of trivializing, which has been more common in education, is to approach significant problems by making them scholarly exercises. The process is similar in its mechanics and its effects to shunting an urgent question to a committee for study; ultimately it can become an "academic" question and its resolution will have been deferred. While we are studying the problem, of course, the damage it produces continues, even though the appearance of amelioration is created. Perhaps no better example of this process can be cited than the frequent "studies" of education. Whatever the findings, and however much we agree or disagree with them, it must be observed that their impact on actual events in the classroom has been minimal. Yet the picture painted is one of intense activity.

This is not a plea for thoughtless action, but it is a corollary of the initial objection to the issue of cultural literacy, namely, that social insight must lead to exploration of how that insight can be used to better the condition being examined.

The chapters in this volume attempt to replace our moribund obsession with psychology and the individual with recognition of the relevance of ideas in the social sciences. Some of this redirection of attention is most welcome. One can applaud the suggestion by Chalmers (Chapter 1) that we have "more politically and culturally aware concepts of art education," and the plea of the editors when they call for the recognition of "the unself-conscious work of the production papermaker, the whittling of a retired carpenter, . . . the self-expression of a Soho neo-expressionist painter, and the traditional basketry of a mother and son of the Ojibwa tribe" (introduction to Part I). Nevertheless, there are some serious misdirections that require reexamination. All of us will agree that there is too much at stake in art education to neglect that task.

References

Chapman, L. (1978). *Approaches to art in education.* New York: Harcourt Brace Jovanovich.

Dewey, J. (1934). *Art as experience.* New York: Putnam.

Efland, A. (1974). Reviews. *Studies in Art Education, 17*(2), 67–69.

Eisner, E. (1972). *Educating artistic vision.* New York: Macmillan.

Feldman, E. (1970). *Becoming human through art.* Englewood Cliffs, NJ: Prentice–Hall.

Friere, P. (1970). *Pedagogy of the oppressed.* New York: Herder & Herder.

Gardner, H. (1973). *The arts and human development.* New York: John Wiley.

Lanier, V. (1964). *Teaching secondary art.* Scranton, PA: International Textbook.

Lanier, V. (1969). The teaching of art as social revolution. *Phi Delta Kappan, 50*(6), 314–319.

Lanier, V. (1980). Six items on the agenda for the eighties. *Art Education, 33*(5), 16–23.

Padover, S. K. (Ed.). (1978). *The essential Marx.* New York: New American Library.

Selected Bibliography

Adams, D., & Goldberg, A. (1981). A year to remember. *Cultural Democracy, 17,* 1–2.

Anderson, T. (1985). Hold the pickles, hold the lettuce, special orders do upset us: The franchise system in American art education. *The Bulletin of the Caucus on Social Theory and Art Education, 5,* 15–26.

Banfield, E. C. (1984). *The democratic muse: Visual arts and the public interest.* New York: Basic Books.

Becker, H. S. (1976). Art worlds and social types. *American Behavioral Scientist, 19*(6), 703–718.

Becker, H. S. (1982). *Art worlds.* Berkeley: University of California Press.

Bellah, R. N., Madsen, R., Sullivan, W. M., Swidler, A., & Tipton, S. M. (1985). *Habits of the heart: Individualism and commitment in American life.* Berkeley: University of California Press.

Berger, J. (1972). *Ways of seeing.* London: British Broadcasting Corporation; and Middlesex, England: Penguin Books.

Berry, W. (1977). *The unsettling of America: Culture and agriculture.* San Francisco, CA: Sierra Club Books.

Bersson, R. (1984). For cultural democracy in art education. *Art Education, 37*(6), 40–43.

Beyer, L. E. (1977). Schools, aesthetic meanings, and social change. *Educational Theory, 4,* 274–282.

Beyer, L. E. (1984). The arts, school practice, and cultural transformation. *The Bulletin of the Caucus on Social Theory and Art Education, 4,* 1–13.

Broude, N., & Garrard, M. D. (Eds.). (1982). *Feminism and art history: Questioning the Litany.* New York: Harper & Row.

Chalmers, F. G. (1981). Art education as ethnology. *Studies in Art Education, 22*(3), 6–14.

Chicago, J. (1977). *Through the flower: My struggle as a woman artist.* Garden City, NY: Anchor Books.

Coles, R. (1986). *The political life of children.* Boston, MA: The Atlantic Monthly Press.

Collins, G., & Sandell, R. (1984). *Women, art and education.* Reston, VA: National Art Education Association.

Condous, J., Howlett, J., & Skull, J. (Eds.). (1980). *Arts in cultural diversity.* Sydney: Holt, Rinehart & Winston.

Congdon, K. G. (1985). A folk group focus for multi-cultural education. *Art Education, 37*(1), 13–16.

Congdon, K. G. (1986). The meaning and use of folk speech in art criticism. *Studies in Art Education, 27*(3), 140–148.

Coover, V., Deacon, E., Esser, C., & Moore, C. (1978). *Resource manual for a living revolution.* Philadelphia, PA: New Society Publishers.

Davis, D. (1977). *Art culture.* New York: Harper & Row.

Devall, B., & Sessions, G. (1985). *Deep ecology.* Salt Lake City: Peregrine Smith Books.

Dewey, J. (1934). *Art as experience.* New York: G. P. Putnam's Sons.

Duncan, C., & Wallach, A. (1978). The museum of modern art as late capitalist ritual: An iconographic analysis. *Marxist Perspectives, 1*(3), 28–51.

Ecker, G. (Ed.). (1985). *Feminist aesthetics.* Boston: Beacon Press.

Evans, S. M., & Boyte, H. C. (1986). *Free spaces: The sources of democratic change in America.* New York: Harper & Row.

Feyerabend, P. (1982). *Against method: Outline of an anarchistic theory of knowledge.* London: Verso.

Freire, P. (1968). *Pedagogy of the oppressed.* New York: Seabury Press.

Gablik, S. (1984). *Has modernism failed?* New York: Thames and Hudson.

Gans, H. J. (1974). *Popular culture and high culture.* New York: Basic Books.

Grigsby, J. E. (1977). *Art and ethics: Background for teaching youth in a pluralistic society.* Dubuque, IA: Wm. C. Brown.

Habermas, J. (1971). *Knowledge and human interests.* Boston: Beacon Press.

Hamblen, K. A. (1984). Artistic perception as a function of learned expectations. *Art Education, 37*(3), 20–25.

Hamblen, K. A. (1986). Exploring contested concepts for aesthetic literacy. *Journal of Aesthetic Education, 29*(2), 67–76.

Haselberger, H. (1961). Method of studying ethnological art. *Current Anthropology, 2*(4), 341–384.

Hein, H. (1976). Aesthetic consciousness: The ground of political experience. *The Journal of Aesthetics and Art Criticism, 35*(2), 143–152.

Hein, H. (1978). Aesthetic rights: Vindication and vilification. *The Journal of Aesthetics and Art Criticism, 37*(2), 169–176.

Hess, T., & Baker, E. C. (1971). *Art and sexual politics.* New York: Macmillian.

Hobbs, J. A. (1984). Popular art versus fine art. *Art Education, 37*(3), 11–14.

Ianni, F. A. J. (1968). The arts as agents for social change: An anthropologist's view. *Art Education, 21*(1), 15–20.

Jones, B. (1982). Microcomputer controlled generation of artifacts as an inter-disciplinary teaching aid. *The Computing Teacher, 9*(9), 42–45.

Jones, M. O. (1975). *The hand made object and its maker.* Berkeley and Los Angeles: University of California Press.

Jones, M. O. (1984). Introduction: Special section: Works of art, art as work and the arts of working—Implications for improving organizational life. *Western Folklore, 43,* 172–178.

Jones, M. O., & Greenfield, V. (1984). Art criticism and aesthetic philosophy. In S. J. Bronner (Ed.), *American folk art: A guide to sources* (pp. 31–50). New York: Garland.

Jopling, C. F. (1971). *Art and aesthetics in primitive societies*. New York: E. P. Dutton.

Kaplan, E. A. (1983). *Women & film: Both sides of the camera*. New York: Methuen.

Kuhn, A. (1982). *Women's pictures: Feminism and the cinema*. London: Routledge & Kegan Paul.

Lanier, V. (1969). The teaching of art as social revolution. *Phi Delta Kappan, 50*(6), 314–319.

Lanier, V. (1980). Six items on the agenda for the eighties. *Art Education, 33*(5), 16–23.

Lauter, E. (1984). *Women as mythmakers: Poetry and visual art by twentieth-century women*. Bloomington, IN: Indiana University Press.

Leff, H. L. (1978). *Experience, environment and human potentials*. New York: Oxford University Press.

Levi, A. W. (1985). The art museum as an agency of culture. *Journal of Aesthetic Education, 19*(2), 23–40.

Lippard, L. R. (1976). *From the center: Feminist essays on women's art*. New York: E. P. Dutton.

Lippard, L. R. (1983). *Overlay: Contemporary art and the art of prehistory*. New York: Pantheon Books.

Lippard, L. R. (1984). *Get the message: A decade of art for social change*. New York: E. P. Dutton.

Loeb, J. (Ed.). (1979). *Feminist collage: Educating women in the visual arts*. New York: Teachers College Press.

Mann, D. A. (Ed.). (1977). *The arts in a democratic society*. Bowling Green, OH: Bowling Green University Popular Press.

Maquet, J. (1986). *The aesthetic experience: An anthropologist looks at the visual arts*. New Haven: Yale University Press.

Marcuse, H. (1977). *The aesthetic dimension*. Boston: Beacon Press.

Matthaei, J. (1982). *An economic history of women in America*. New York: Schocken Books.

Mavigliano, G. J. (1984). The federal art project: Holger Cahill's program of action. *Art Education, 37*(3), 26–30.

McFee, J. K., & Degge, R. M. (1977). *Art, culture and environment*. Dubuque, IA: Kendall/Hunt.

Metcalf, E. W. (1983). Black art, folk art, and social control. *Winterthur Portfolio, 18*(4), 271–289.

Mill, J. S. (1966). On liberty. In J. M. Robinson (Ed.), *John Stuart Mill: A selection of his works*. Toronto: Macmillan of Canada. (Original work published 1859)

Nadaner, D. (1984). Critique and intervention: Implications of social theory for art education. *Studies in Art Education, 26*(1), 20–26.

Nochlin, L. (1971). Why have there been no great women artists? *Art News, 69*(9), 22–39; 67–77.

Okin, S. M. (1979). *Women in western political thought*. Princeton, NJ: Princeton University Press.

Osborne, H. (1985). The end of the museum? *Journal of Aesthetic Education, 19*(2), 41–51.

Otten, C. M. (Ed.). (1971). *Anthropology and art.* Garden City, NY: The Natural History Press.

Postman, N., & Weingartner, C. (1971). *Teaching as a subversive activity.* New York: Dell.

Radar, M., & Jessup, B. (1976). *Art and human values.* Englewood Cliffs, NJ: Prentice-Hall.

Rajchman, J. (1985). The postmodern museum. *Art in America, 73*, 110–117, 171.

Schellin, P. (1973). Is it Wilshire Boulevard which is ugly or is it we? *Art Education, 26*(9), 6–9.

Schroeder, F. E. H. (1977). *Outlaw aesthetics.* Bowling Green, OH: Bowling Green University Popular Press.

Schumacher, E. F. (1973). *Small is beautiful: Economics as if people mattered.* New York: Harper & Row.

Sherman, C. R., & Holcomb, A. M. (Eds.). (1981). *Women as interpreters of the visual arts, 1820–1979.* Westport, CT: Greenwood Press.

Silbermann, A. (1968). A definition of the sociology of art. *International Social Science Journal, 20*(4), 567–588.

Silver, H. R. (1979). Ethnoart. *Annual Review of Anthropology, 8*, 267–307.

Smith, R. A. (1985). A right to the best: Or, once more, elitism versus populism in art education. *Studies in Art Education, 26*(3), 169–175.

Snyder, G. (1980). *The real work: Interviews and talks, 1964–1979.* New York: New Directions Books.

Steiner, E. (1981). *Educology of the free.* New York: Philosophical Library.

Thompson, R. F. (1983). *Flash of the spirit: African and Afro-American art and philosophy.* New York: Random House.

Villemain, F. T. (1966). Democracy, education, and art. In E. W. Eisner & D. W. Ecker (Eds.), *Readings in art education* (pp. 407–419). Waltham, MA: Blaisdell. (Original work published 1964)

Williams, R. (1985). *The sociology of culture.* New York: Schocken Books.

Williamson, J. (1986). *Consuming passions: The dynamics of popular culture.* London: Marion Boyars.

Wolf, J. (1983). *Aesthetics and the sociology of art.* London: George Allen & Unwin.

Wolfensberger, W. (1972). *Normalization: The principle of normalization in human services.* Toronto: National Institute of Mental Retardation.

Wolff, J. (1981). *The social production of art.* London: Merlin Press.

About the Contributors

ROBERT BERSSON is Associate Professor of Art at James Madison University in Harrisonburg, Virginia. He recently published articles in *Art Education* and *Art and Artists* on cultural democracy, social relevance in art education, and aesthetic experience in a technocratic society.

DOUG BLANDY is the Chair of the Division of Art Education/Art Therapy at Bowling Green State University, Bowling Green, Ohio. He recently published the *Directory of Accessible Arts*, co-edited with Jennifer Kinsley, and an article on normalizing approaches to disabled students in *Art Education*. He is active in presenting papers to national and international organizational groups on art education and activism, democracy, and the disabled citizen. In February of 1987 he was a project director with Kristin G. Congdon for the exhibition, "Boats, Bait, and Fishing Paraphernalia: A Local Folk Aesthetic" in the School of Art Gallery, Bowling Green State University.

PAUL E. BOLIN is a recent Ph.D. recipient from the University of Oregon and is currently on faculty there as Assistant Professor of Art Education.

BARBARA ANN BOYER is Assistant Professor in the Department of Art Education at Ohio State University in Columbus. Her latest articles have appeared in *Viewpoints Journal, Bulletin of the Caucus on Social Theory and Art Education,* and *Visual Arts Research.* She has received grants for the development of a computer data base to analyze social-cultural research in aesthetics and to develop an art education Black scholars recruitment and retention program. She edited the *Newsletter for the United States Society for Education Through Art* from 1984 through 1986 and is on the editorial board of *Ohio Art Education Journal, Viewpoints Journal,* and *The Arts Education Review of Books.*

189

F. GRAEME CHALMERS is a Professor in the Visual and Performing Arts in Education Program at the University of British Columbia in Vancouver, Canada. He has published extensively on approaching art from a cultural context in *Studies in Art Education, Art Education, Journal of Aesthetics and Art Criticism, Canadian Review of Art Education Research,* and *Bulletin of the Caucus on Social Theory and Art Education.* His research interests include the social and cultural foundations of art education and the history of art education. He is a member of INSEA and Chief Examiner in Art and Design for the International Baccalaureate.

GEORGIA C. COLLINS is Associate Professor of Art at the University of Kentucky in Lexington. She is co-editor, with Rene Sandell, of *Women, Art and Education* and has published articles in journals such as *Art Education, Journal of Aesthetic Education,* and *Studies in Art Education* and has contributed to the *Handbook for Achieving Sex Equity Through Education.* She has reviewed several books for major journals.

KRISTIN G. CONGDON is Assistant Professor of Art Education/Art Therapy at Bowling Green State University in Bowling Green, Ohio. She has recently published articles in *Journal of Aesthetic Education, Art Education, Studies in Art Education, Journal of Multi-cultural and Cross-cultural Research in Art Education, Visual Arts Research,* and *Bulletin of the Caucus on Social Theory and Art Education.* She has contributed to *Women Art Educators II,* edited by M. A. Stankiewicz and E. Zimmerman; *American Folk Art: A Guide to Sources,* edited by S. J. Bronner; and has done several book reviews for *Journal of American Folklore.* Most recently she produced a videotape on a traditional artist, titled "John Mason: the Furniture Doctor," and is currently working on another video on Bernadine Stetzel, an artist from Fremont, Ohio.

KAREN A. HAMBLEN is Associate Professor and the Area Director of Art Education at Louisiana State University in Baton Rouge. Her recent publications include articles in *Design for Arts Education, International Journal of Contemporary Sociology, Journal of Multi-cultural and Cross-cultural Research in Art Education, Arts and Learning Research, Studies in Art Education, Eastern Anthropologist, Art Education, Journal of Aesthetic Education, Canadian Review of Art Education Research,* and *Bulletin of the Caucus on Social Theory and Art Education.* In 1985 she received the Manuel Barkan Memorial Award from the National Art Education Association, for scholarly merit of published work, and in 1986 she was named California's Outstanding Higher Educator by the California Art Education Association State Council. She is currently an editorial board member of *Studies in Art Education.*

JAN J. JAGODZIŃSKI is on the Faculty of Education at the University of Alberta, Edmonton, Alberta, Canada. He has published widely in the field of art education and is recognized for his honest and intelligent social criticism.

BEVERLY J. JONES is Associate Professor of Art Education at the University of Oregon in Eugene. She has published extensively on the topic of the use of technology in art education and the theory and practice of computer usage in the field of art. In 1982 she won The National Art Education Association Women's Caucus Mary Rouse Award.

MICHAEL OWEN JONES is Professor of History and Folklore and Director of the Center of the Study of Comparative Folklore and Mythology at the University of California–Los Angeles. His recent publications include articles on aesthetics and organizational life in journals such as *Western Folklore* and *Material Culture* and in anthologies such as *Organizational Culture*, edited by P. J. Frost et al.; *American Material Culture and Folklife: A Prologue and Dialogue*, edited by S. J. Bronner; and *American Folk Art: A Guide to Sources*, also edited by S. J. Bronner. He is currently working on a project called "Bringing Out the Best in Us: Positive Management Practices at UCLA," which is based on the assumption that a supportive social environment promotes self-esteem which in turn affects productivity and quality of performance. Another project he is working on documents and analyzes how and why people individualize and personalize their work spaces.

VINCENT LANIER is Professor of Art at the University of Arizona in Tucson. He is the author of *The Arts We See* and *The Visual Arts and the Elementary Child*. An extremely prolific writer, Lanier has recently published articles in *Studies in Art Education*.

JUNE KING MCFEE is Professor Emerita of Art Education from the University of Oregon. She has recently published in *The International Encyclopedia of Education*, *Journal of Multi-cultural and Cross-cultural Research in Art Education*, and the *Foundations of Aesthetics, Art and Art Education*, edited by F. Farley and R. Nepurud. She is the author of two widely used textbooks. The Women's Caucus of the National Education Association grants a June King McFee Award to a worthy researcher every year, in her honor.

RUSS MCKNIGHT is a Visiting Scholar at the Logan Elm Press at the Ohio State University in Columbus. His recent photographs have been shown in the exhibition, "Boats, Bait, and Fishing Paraphernalia: A Local

Folk Aesthetic," in the School of Art Gallery at Bowling Green State University; at Owens Illinois in Toledo, Ohio; and at the Panet Museum in Whitbey, England. In 1985 he had a one-person show at the Center of Creative Studies in Detroit.

MARY ANN STANKIEWICZ is Associate Professor of Art Education at the University of Maine at Orono. She has recently co-edited, with Enid Zimmerman, *Women Art Educators* and *Women Art Educators II*. Her articles appear in *Studies in Art Education, Art Education*, and *Journal of Aesthetic Education*. She is on the editorial board of *Studies in Art Education* and *Visual Arts Research*. She is a contributing editor to *The Arts Education Review of Books* and was the president of the National Art Education Association Women's Caucus from 1985 to 1986.

Index